Modern Philosophy

Modern Philosophy is an exploration of the ideas of six major thinkers from Descartes to Hume. It takes a fresh and engaging look at the common themes that dominate this period, as well as examining the differences in the work of the six philosophers.

Through vivid and witty prose, Richard Francks skilfully presents ideas that have informed the development of philosophy as we know it, and which present a challenge to beliefs and attitudes that most of us now share. In this work we find the source of modern philosophical inquiry – questions such as the existence of God, the Mind and Body problem, the idea of the self and the existence of the world had their birth in these texts – as well as broader questions about political and social philosophy.

Thinkers discussed:

René Descartes

John Locke

Baruch Spinoza

George Berkeley

Gottfried Wilhelm Leibniz

David Hume

This book will be ideal for anybody coming to the ideas of these philosophers for the first time.

Richard Francks is Director of Undergraduate Studies in the School of Philosophy at the University of Leeds.

Fundamentals of Philosophy
Series Editor: John Shand

This series presents an up-to-date set of engrossing, accurate and lively introductions to all the core areas of philosophy. Each volume is written by an enthusiastic and knowledgeable teacher of the area in question. Care has been taken to produce works that while even-handed are not mere bland expositions, and as such are original pieces of philosophy in their own right. The reader should not only be well informed by the series, but also experience the intellectual excitement of being engaged in philosophical debate itself. The volumes serve as an essential basis for the undergraduate courses to which they relate, as well as being accessible and absorbing for the general reader. Together they comprise an indispensable library of living philosophy.

Published:
Richard Francks
Modern Philosophy

Dudley Knowles
Political Philosophy

Piers Benn
Ethics

Alexander Bird
Philosophy of Science

Stephen Burwood, Paul Gilbert and Kathleen Lennon
Philosophy of Mind

Colin Lyas
Aesthetics

Alexander Miller
Philosophy of Language

Forthcoming:
Greg Restall
Logic

Suzanne Stern-Gillet
Ancient Philosophy

Simon Glendinning
Continental Philosophy

Modern Philosophy

The seventeenth and eighteenth centuries

Richard Francks

Routledge
Taylor & Francis Group

LONDON AND NEW YORK

First published 2003 by Routledge
11 New Fetter Lane, London EC4P 4EE

Routledge is an imprint of the Taylor & Francis Group

© 2003 Richard Francks

Typeset in Century Schoolbook and Futura by
RefineCatch Ltd, Bungay, Suffolk
Printed and bound in Great Britain by
TJ International Ltd, Padstow, Cornwall

British Library Cataloguing in Publication Data
A catalogue record for this book is available from the British
Library

ISBN 1–857–28762–2 (hbk)
ISBN 1–857–28565–4 (pbk)

To P.
Sine qua non

Contents

CONTENTS

CONTENTS

CONTENTS

Preface

What this book is for

Travel broadens the mind. By seeing the different ways in which other people live and think we can learn a huge amount – not about them, but about ourselves. When we see the different lives other people lead, we become aware of possibilities we had never thought of. Most importantly, it is often only when we encounter people who do not share them that we become aware of beliefs which we have always held, have never questioned, and have never even been aware of believing – that is the real shock of discovering people whose language has no plurals, whose tradition has no heroes, whose cities have no old buildings, or whatever it may be.

Philosophical beliefs are often of that kind – we have never thought of them, we aren't aware of holding them, and yet the attitudes to ourselves and to the world around us which those beliefs express are constitutive of the people that we are, and of the lives that we lead. Reading the History of Philosophy therefore broadens the mind in the same way as travel does. When we encounter people whose philosophical beliefs and attitudes are importantly different from our own, and we ask ourselves whether and why we want to agree with them, we become conscious of possibilities we had never previously considered, and we become aware of principles which we have always taken for granted, but have never previously acknowledged as our own.

The aim of this book is therefore to do for you what travel does (or at least, what it can). It tries to set out briefly some central

ideas of six people whose world was not ours, and whose philosophical positions are different in various ways from anything that
anyone around us holds.

The intention is not to inform you about the past, but to challenge your present beliefs, and to enable you to ask yourself
whether you are willing to accept what they say, or whether you
can find some good reason to reject it. For that reason I shall make
no attempt to evaluate what they say, or to tell you what I think
about them. I shall try as far as possible (give or take the odd rant
of my own) just to present their ideas as persuasively as I can,
and then let you do the rest. At the end of each chapter there are
questions you might want to use to help you think about what has
been covered.

I hope you have a pleasant journey.

Acknowledgements

However bad this book may be, it would have been a great deal worse without a lot of help from my friends. I am grateful to John Shand, whose idea it was and who was very helpful and patient along the way, and also to the friends who read it in its early stages and made suggestions which have improved it a lot. Specifically I want to thank Carol-Ann Custerson and Peter Frankland for their brave attempts, and especially Roger Woolhouse, for his painstaking and invaluable help in removing some of the errors. I also want to thank an anonymous reader for some very helpful (if rather grudging) suggestions. And I am grateful to colleagues in the School of Philosophy at the University of Leeds, who for several years put up with my spending time on this, when I could have been doing something more useful.

Chapter 1

Introduction

How modern is 'Modern' philosophy?

Six 'Modern' philosophers

Is there such a thing as the Modern Age? And if there is, are we in it?

The six philosophers who are the subject of this book are Descartes, Spinoza, Leibniz, Locke, Berkeley and Hume. They are all standardly referred to as 'modern' philosophers, even though the most recent of them died well over 200 years ago. It is a title they used of themselves, and one that was used about them by their contemporaries, but its use today suggests two things, neither of which is obviously true: that there is something which is common to all six of them, and that they are somehow connected to us, but not to the people who went before them – in other words, it suggests that there is such a thing as Modernity, or The Modern Age, to which both we and they belong.

When you come to look at what they actually wrote, though, that suggestion seems hard to sustain. For one thing, they are very different one from another. Not only were they a diverse group in terms of nationality, language, tradition, religion, politics, social group and personality, but they also lived in very different times and places, and wrote about different subjects. Their lives cover a period of some 180 years, from the birth of Descartes in 1596 to the death of Hume in 1776. One hundred and eighty years is a long time, and a lot happened in the world they knew between those dates. When we come to look at them in detail, we will see that their lives and their ideas overlapped and criss-crossed in a whole variety of different ways. There is no single theory or belief that they all share, and which marks them out as belonging to the same epoch. There is no one clearly stateable question which was the burning issue of that long and eventful period and which they all tried to answer. Instead, we will see theories and questions come and go in their writings, issues sometimes moving into centre stage, and at other times receding into the background. Sometimes they agree on a certain topic, sometimes they disagree; most often they deal with related issues in significantly different ways and with very different emphasis, so that you would be hard pushed to say for certain whether it was the same question they were asking, or a different one.

Not only do they seem to be disparate and diverse, but when you read them they also seem almost impossibly remote from our present lives and concerns. Three of them we read in modern translations, of course, which takes some of the edge off their remoteness, and even with the three who wrote in English we usually have updated typography, spelling and punctuation, which do a lot to make them seem a little less alien. But still their writings seem at best seriously archaic, and sometimes downright bizarre. Their interests, their concerns, their attitudes, their judgements all seem seriously foreign, irrelevant to our lives. What is obvious to them just seems weird to us, and what is obvious to us they have no knowledge of.

For all their diversity and remoteness, though, I think it does still make sense to say that they are all in a significant sense modern thinkers, and that we ourselves are still recognisably of their era. The problem is that, as is often the case with our families and friends, what holds us all together is much less obvious than what divides us. So here is my theory of Modernity, and with it comes a little test for you to apply to yourself, by means of which you can decide whether you yourself are a Modern thinker, or whether you want to say that, as far as you are concerned, Modernity is a thing of the past.

Appearance and Reality, or two kinds of expert

In the seventeenth century people began to think in a new way.[1] The basis of that new way of thinking was a fundamental distinction, which I am going to call the distinction between Appearance and Reality. Here is an example of it in operation.

Imagine you're sitting in the garden, eating an apple. The weather's decent, the light's good. Your eyes, ears, taste buds and other sensory equipment are in normal working order, and you are not currently under the influence of any distorting passions or of any mind-affecting drugs. You are, however, a philosopher, and so half-way through eating your apple you suddenly stop, and start to think about it.

'Here', you think, 'is this apple. It is round and green and shiny and sweet, and I pulled it off my next-door-neighbour's tree not half an hour since (when she wasn't looking). I can see the apple, I can feel it in my hand, I can smell it and taste it, and I can hear the crunching noise it makes when I bite it. I know where it came from, and I know what kind of apple it is. All in all, I think I know this apple pretty well. But I wonder what it's *really* like, deep down, in itself. I wonder what a scientist would say about it.'

Does that little story make sense to you? If it does, then you understand what it is to be Modern. I think the chief distinguishing feature of the Modern era is that distinction between on the one hand our subjective experience of the world – the way it looks, and feels – and on the other its independent, objective reality – the way it really *is*. The six philosophers in this book are all of them involved in some way or other with defending, explaining, clarifying, using, opposing or re-interpreting some distinction of this kind, and I think it is still a central part of the way that our society understands itself and the world around it. But before the seventeenth century it was not standardly made out in anything like the same way.[2]

It is important to realise that the distinction I am talking about here is not simply that between real and illusory, actual and non-actual, true and false. It is very hard to imagine people who could live without being able to make out *that* kind of distinction in some form or other.[3] But that is not at all the same as saying that we have to operate with a systematic distinction between Appearance and Reality, subjective and objective, the world as we know it and the world as it really is. Because not only did people before the seventeenth century not standardly make a distinction like that, but we ourselves manage to get along without it in large parts of our lives.

Think, for example, about tables, physicists, and stamp-collectors.

The table in your kitchen (if you have one) is to all intents and purposes solid, brown, wooden and (except when you move it out of the way to hoover) stationary. But as we all know, it isn't *really* like that. *Really*, the physicist tells us, it is in itself a whole world of microscopic and submicroscopic particles, waves, or fields of matter. Those particles are not themselves wooden, but are made of more elemental stuff, and they are not really brown, but invisible; and they are certainly not stationary – in reality, they are whizzing around at high speed, and the whole thing is *really* no more solid than is a cloud of water droplets, or a swarm of bees.[4]

That is a classic example of the Appearance/Reality distinction in operation: the table as it appears to be, as it features in our daily lives, is quite different from the way it really is, as the physicist knows it. Three points in particular to notice:

(1) The properties which objects really possess are in fact radically different from the ones they seem to possess. (The table looked solid, brown and immobile, but is really none of those things.)

(2) But more than that, not only do things seem to be other than they really are, but in fact many (at least) of the properties that things seem to possess turn out not to be possessed by *anything at all*. It isn't that the table, which seems to be brown, is really yellow, or pink, or a tasteful shade of puce; really, as it is in itself, the table isn't *any* colour. Colour has turned out to be a feature not of the world, but our experience of it, so that

not only is the table not brown, but *nothing* (really, in itself) is brown. And really nothing, in itself, is solid or immobile, either.

(3) And the third point is just an extension of that second one. Not only does the world not really possess a lot of the properties it appears to have, but it turns out to have a lot of properties which nothing in our experience *does* possess. Valency, for example, or non-locality are contemporary examples of properties which we say that things in themselves do possess, but which we have never directly experienced anything as having.

It is important to realise that we make this distinction in some places, but not in others. Think of stamp collecting as an example. The expert philatelist knows massively more about stamps than does an ignorant person like me. I see a funny-looking green stamp with a picture of some mountains on it and a couple of flags; the expert sees a Swiss two-cent commemorative issued in 1887 to celebrate the visit of Crown Prince Helmut of Bavaria and his wife Pauline, or whatever it might be. The expert knows the stamp's history, the way it was made, and which factory it was printed in. She can tell you its place in the history of the Swiss postal service, its current value, how many examples are known to survive and where they all are, and a whole mass of other stuff that I can't even dream up to use in this example. Is that the same as the physicist's expert knowledge of the table?

It seems to me it's quite different, and the reason it is different is that we don't make any kind of appearance/reality distinction in the case of stamp collecting.

Try it. Does the philatelist know what the stamp is *really* like, while I know only how it *appears*?

No. My knowledge of the stamp is superficial, trivial, limited to what you can see in a cursory inspection, while hers is encyclopaedic, broad and deep and informed by a lifetime of devotion to the subject – but my view of the stamp is not *mistaken*, as my view of the table was. The properties I thought the stamp had are still there in the expert's account, though they are incorporated into a very different context. And the new properties which she detects in it and I don't, like the overprinting of the price or the dodgy perforation, are things which I too can come to see, just as she does. In general we can say that my understanding of the stamp is preserved in the expert's account – though greatly enhanced and expanded – whereas in the case of the physicist my account was *replaced* by a very different kind of story.

Stamp collecting is not in any way peculiar in not making the kind of systematic Appearance/Reality distinction we saw in physics: the same is true of large areas of our day-to-day knowledge.[5] The point I am making is that before the seventeenth century the distinction was *not* standardly made in relation to the expert's knowledge of nature, but it has been ever since. And that is what I think makes it true to say that our six philosophers, like us, were living in, and trying to come to terms with, the Modern world.

The shock of the old

The fact that the Appearance/Reality distinction is now so familiar makes it hard for us to realise that in the seventeenth century it was anything but. Yet in the time of Descartes the idea of a distinction of this kind was not only not obvious, it was also politically and socially dangerous, theologically unacceptable and intellectually plainly absurd.

That absurdity is not easy for us to see; but try to imagine how crazy it must have appeared when people first began seriously to claim that the sky is not in fact blue, that there is a world of invisible creatures living and dying in the clearest water, and that the earth itself, the solid centre of our world and of our lives, is in reality racing through the heavens and spinning round at enormous speed. When you think about it, any one of those claims would take a great deal of swallowing to anyone who hasn't been brought up to believe it, and who has not been trained since an early age into the Cartesian, Modern belief that the reality of things is not revealed to the casual observer, but is established by the subtle calculations of the expert.

In its religious aspect the shock of the new metaphysic was no less acute. If Descartes and his kind were right, then most people in the world were guilty of a kind of large-scale and seemingly inevitable misunderstanding of the way things really are, and that seemed to call into question people's views of their relation to the world and to the God who made them. Traditional theology had been made out in terms of traditional metaphysics, and by this time was very strongly Aristotelian in character; if the world was not as it had always been taken to be, then large areas of theological doctrine and biblical interpretation would have to be rethought – a process which was bound to be difficult and dangerous in the context of the ongoing battles over the Reformation.

Politically, too, the new ideas raised problems: traditional learning cannot be questioned without calling into doubt traditional authorities and traditional educational systems. A large-scale error of this kind seemed to make fools of all established authorities, and like the Reformation to invite people to make up their own account of the world, and to recast it anew. Even thinkers like Descartes who were careful not to enter directly into religious or political argument therefore came to be seen for what they were – dangerous radicals with new ideas which if accepted called into question all existing authorities and institutions.

Since that time, of course, we have learned to adjust our political, social and theological opinions in such a way as to preserve the Modern conception of science. Our view of ourselves and of our relations to each other, to nature, to other peoples and to other ages are all of them intimately bound up with the parts played in our lives and in our consciousness by the practice and products of science. And for that reason it is still true to describe us as living in the Modern age which came into being in the seventeenth century. It may well be true (I think myself it is to be hoped) that we are now at the very end of that period, and that the culture we inhabit will soon move into some kind of Post-Modern age; but it hasn't happened yet. And until it does, the attempt to understand and respond to the different carefully worked-out versions of Modernity which were produced by our six thinkers can help us to make sense of the ragbag of disparate Modernist views that we call our contemporary common sense, and which play such a large part in the lives that we lead, and the attitudes and beliefs that we currently inhabit.

So try these six views for size, and see if any of them fits with the kind of life you want to lead, and the kind of views you want to live with. All you will find here is a rough sketch of these philosophers' thoughts, a broad outline of how they saw the world: I hope it will be enough to give you some sort of a feel of what it would be like to see things the way they seem to have done. Some of their ideas I hope you will find ridiculous, some infuriating, some exciting; some I expect you will find dull. However you find them, I hope they will make sense as genuine alternatives to the attitudes and beliefs you started out with, and that through seeing them and learning to distinguish your own views from them you will come to understand some aspects of your own life a little better.

PART 1
René Descartes

Biography

René Descartes was born in 1596, when Francis Bacon was thirty-five years old, William Shakespeare nearly thirty-two, and Kepler only twenty-four. He was fourteen when Galileo published his epoch-making telescopic observations, and a nervous 37-year-old when Galileo was condemned for his advocacy of a heliocentric system. He died in 1650, a year after the execution of Charles I in England, and two years after the end of the Thirty Years' War. His best-known publications are *Discourse on Method* (1637), *Meditations on First Philosophy* (1641) and *Principles of Philosophy* (1644).

Descartes was born in the town of Châtellerault[1] in west-central France, some 70 kilometres south of Tours, into a family of provincial gentry. His mother died when he was a baby. He was brought up by his grandmother, and went away to school at the Jesuit college in La Flèche when he was ten years old. As a young man he spent four years as a gentleman soldier in the Netherlands and Germany, but he gave up plans for a legal career and for the rest of his life lived for the most part on the income he derived from the sale of his share of the family property. Most of his productive life (1628–49) was spent at various addresses in the Netherlands, but at the age of fifty-four he moved to Sweden at the invitation of Queen Christina, only to die of pneumonia within six months. He never married, and his only daughter (her mother was a maid at a house he stayed at in Amsterdam) died at the age of five.

He was persuaded very early on that the traditional learning in which he had been trained was dead, and that truth lay with the new approaches advocated by people like Bacon, Kepler and Galileo. He carried out his own investigations in such fields as optics, meteorology, mechanics and anatomy; but his real achievements were not in his practical inquiries into natural phenomena, but in the theories he produced to accommodate his own and other people's discoveries, and in his literary success as an expositor of and publicist for those views. His written output was huge, from formal Latin treatises dedicated to the learned fathers of the Sorbonne, to more popular French-language pamphlets for the reading public, and countless formal and informal letters to friends and people in power, explaining and defending his views, criticising those of his opponents, and generally doing everything he could to sell his gradually developing revolutionary theory of the nature of the world, of God and of human beings.

His ideas were always controversial, and his works were banned by the Catholic church after his death. This didn't prevent him from being enormously influential in all areas of intellectual inquiry, from physics and biology to politics and art criticism. He came to be seen as the great revolutionary, the great moderniser, the first true champion of the Enlightenment, and his name was invoked with reverence right up to the nineteenth century even by people who knew nothing of what he actually thought and wrote.

Chapter 2

Material Monism or the Great Soup of Being

Descartes' account of the natural world

Overview

I said in the Introduction that what binds our six philosophers together, and to us, is their involvement with and reaction to the distinction between appearance and reality – between the way we subjectively experience the world and the way it objectively is. Descartes is the clearest example of that, and although he is the earliest of the six, and so the most distant from us in time, he is, despite the seeming strangeness of some of his ideas, perhaps the most recognisably modern thinker of them all.

Descartes' whole work is concerned with explaining and defending his idea of science, and with setting up and justifying the distinction between appearance and reality. I shall start by setting out something of what he thought the world is really like when you look beyond the appearance to the reality underneath, looking first at his account of nature (ch. 2), then at the relation of God to that new world (ch. 3), and finally at the place of human beings in it (ch. 4). But among philosophers Descartes is famous as much for the way he seeks to sell his ideas as for the content of them, so we will then look at the way he tries to persuade you that his is the right view to take and the only way we can establish a secure and lasting understanding of the world and our place in it (ch. 5).

Material Monism: Descartes' universal soup of matter

To begin, then: what, according to Descartes, is the world around us really like? Nowadays, of course, we have our own answer: the world of appearance – the familiar, vital world of colours, objects, values, actions and events – is generated by a hidden world of atoms, molecules, subatomic particles and invisible forces. Descartes' answer was essentially just the same, but it differed in some details.

Strange though it sounds on first hearing, Descartes held that in reality there is only one physical object in existence. Everything that we nowadays call a physical object – from the stars in the heavens to the dust on the top of your wardrobe – Descartes says is really just a part or an area of that one thing, differentiated from other so-called separate things by relative motion. In reality, as it is known to the scientist, the whole physical universe is just one giant object – a vast continuum, like a universal soup of matter which fills up the whole material universe. That infinite soup is uniform and homogeneous, but it is full of motion; it contains eddies, currents, seething whirlpools, lapping waves and quiet lagoons – and those areas of differently moving material stuff are what we perceive as objects in space.[2]

It is a surprising picture, and one which at first sight strikes us as quite bizarre. Why should anyone believe such a thing? The answer is that like our own story of a world of invisible particles, it provides an *explanation* of the world around us; Descartes is claiming that looking at the world in this way provides us with a complete explanation for all natural phenomena. Everything we see around us – the movements of the heavenly bodies, the weather, the tides, the lives of animals, the growth of plants and the workings of the brain – can all be explained scientifically, by a single set of simple laws, because all of them alike are at bottom the results of mechanical interactions between parts of matter in motion.

I am not going to attempt here to set out Descartes' whole physical theory; instead I am going to try to give an idea of what it would be like to see the world as he saw it by explaining what I think are three central features, and then considering a couple of examples of it in operation.

Telling things apart: individuation in a plenum

How could it be that everything in nature is just one huge object? Consider an analogy. All the seas and oceans of the earth are quite clearly in reality one undivided expanse of water: there are no walls or barriers dividing the north Atlantic from the south, and even though the Americas separate the Pacific from the Atlantic, the two are actually linked both to the south and (though the water here is frozen) to the north. Yet the undivided nature of the oceans doesn't prevent us from dividing them up, not only into oceans, but also into a whole array of different seas, bays, straits, channels, inlets, passages, gulfs and even the odd bight.

The distinctions between those different areas of the sea are in one sense perfectly clear. There are unambiguous rules governing the use of such names, and unarguable facts about the differences and relations between them. The Gulf of Mexico, for example, is not the Straits of Melaka, or anything like it; and anyone who is in either one of those watery areas is quite certainly and undeniably not in the South China Sea and is also a very long way from either the Bay of Plenty or that Great Australian Bight.

At the same time, though, the divisions are in a sense arbitrary. First, there is no correct answer to the question of just how many of these watery objects there really are. Take the Pacific, for example: is it one ocean, or two? Sailors and map-makers tend to separate the north Pacific and the south Pacific, but no-one talks of the east Pacific and the west Pacific – not because north and south are really separate in some way that east and west are not, but just because they have down the years found it convenient to make the one distinction and not the other (largely, I suppose, because of the significance of the Equator in respect of weather systems and ocean currents). Second, not only is it not at all clear how many seas, oceans etc. there really are, but also the boundaries between any two of them are very vague. If for example you are sailing from the North Sea into the Baltic, it is clear that you will have to pass through the Skagerrak and the Kattegat in order to do so. For each of those areas there will be times when you are unambiguously in the one and not in the other; but there will also be a lengthy period when you are rounding the top of Denmark when there is no clear answer to the question of which you are in. The same is true of any such pair of sea areas – in fact Skagerrak and Kattegat are relatively clearly defined cases; the area of uncertainty between, say, Arabian Sea, Indian Ocean and Southern Ocean is many times larger, so large that in the time of wind-powered ships, when most of these terms were invented, you could travel for days without being able to give any clear answer as to which area you were currently passing through.

The uncertain and ill-defined nature of these maritime distinctions – the uncertainty over how many there really are, and the vagueness of the boundaries between them – reveals only what we knew all along: that the different areas of the oceans are not really separate things, but only conventionally defined areas which we invent for our convenience when talking about sea travel. In Cartesian language, they are none of them different 'substances', but ultimately only different 'modes' or 'modifications' of the one mass of water.[3] The distinction between such things is not a 'real' distinction – a distinction between different things – but only a 'modal' one – a difference in the *way* something is.[4] And Descartes' physical theory consists in saying that the differences we ordinarily make between objects in the world – between my head and my hat, between a fish and a flea, between the sun and the stars and the earth and all the so-called things they contain – are at bottom merely modal distinctions. Just like the seas and the straits and the sounds, they are not really separate things, but only modes, or conventionally individuated areas which we invent for convenience in our daily lives.

Our seafaring analogy in fact breaks down when we realise that sea areas are typically defined by the land masses that surround them. The Cook Straits, for example, separate the two main islands of New Zealand; the Bay of Biscay is the area between Brittany and Spain, etc. With Cartesian matter, by contrast, there is no comparable thing outside the one extended substance which could serve as a reference point for individuating physical objects. A better analogy in this respect would be not the seas but the ocean currents. Currents are stable, enduring things with their own names and distinguishing characteristics, but they are separated from each other and from the waters around them only by the fact of their shared *movement* – that the particles of water that we call part of the current all tend to move together, in a certain direction and with a certain speed, relative to the particles of water around them. Whirlpools and tornadoes are good examples of the same kind. In a whirlpool the water is exactly the same as that in the calmer waters around it; yet the whirlpool can be identified, named, and separated from other whirlpools and from non-whirlpools by the mere fact that the particles of water within it tend to stay together, and to move very rapidly with respect to the water around them. According to Descartes, the common-sense distinctions we make between, say, my table, the air around it and the floor it stands on, and indeed between all the so-called objects in the world, are of exactly the same kind as that between a whirlpool and the water around it.

The idea seems a little less strange when you think about it, and especially if you take it, as Descartes did, to the microscopic level, when the same kind of arbitrariness we saw in the case of the seas becomes apparent.[5] How many objects, after all, is a table? Is it just one, or should we count the top and the four legs as separate? And what if the top is made up of several different planks joined together? And then there are the screws and nails that hold it together . . . and the particles of glue . . . and the varnish, and the coffee stains, and the dust – not to mention all the individual atomic and subatomic particles that go to make it up. And the boundaries between the table and its surroundings, which seem so clear to common sense, are they really any more clear-cut than those between the Bristol Channel and the Irish Sea? Looked at through a suitably powerful microscope, after all, you can see particles of floor attached to the table legs, and bits of the legs rubbed off onto the floor; and the surface of the table has dents and ridges and hollows which are filled with dirt and dust and air and coffee and cat hairs which are engrained with varying degrees of firmness into its pores, as well, of course, as the particles of air, water and who knows what besides which exist within the structure of the wood itself. Is there really a clear line to be drawn between what is the table and what is not? On a day-to-day level, of course, there is – but then in the same way the map-maker can and does draw a neat line between Tokyo Bay and the rest of the Pacific. The difference here seems to be only one of scale: we are aware of the conventionality and even arbitrariness of geographical distinctions, whether on sea or land (how thick is the USA/Canada border?), but not of those between familiar objects, just because of our relative size. But all we have to do is to imagine ourselves transformed into dust mites to begin to see the table/floor distinction as being as gross and arbitrary as our sea areas, when compared to what we would then regard as the clear, sharp boundary between one speck of dust and another. And then, of course, the philosophers of the dust mite world will gleefully point out that a particle of dust is in reality no more separate from another than is a table from a chair; and what their dust mite readers would have to do in order to see that would be to imagine themselves transformed into creatures which stand to dust mites as dust mites stand to people, and then they would see that . . . and so on and so on, without end. Whatever level you go to, all you have to do is to ratchet up the degree of magnification a few more thousand times, and you can raise the same old questions all over again: since space is an infinitely divisible continuum, any boundary you draw must in the end be an arbitrary one.[6]

So perhaps Descartes' story is not as crazy as it looks. Notice also another strength: when we ordinarily make the distinction between table and surroundings we seem to do so, just as Descartes said, on the basis of relative motion. Thus the dust on top of the table we say is not a part of it because you can wipe it off, whereas the varnish we *do* regard as part of the table because it's stuck on – i.e. in Cartesian terms the varnish is at rest relative to the other bits which we regard as part of the table, whereas the dust is sometimes (whenever it's dusted, for example) in motion with respect to them.

At this point an objection may be occurring to you. Perhaps it is true that, at the microscopic level at least, there is no hard and fast boundary to be drawn between the table and the air around it; and perhaps it is even true that the distinction we normally make is one which would more or less coincide with a distinction based on relative motion. But surely it is also true that there is a further distinction between them, and one which also plays a part in how we tell them apart: that the table is made of wood, and the air is made of – well, just air!

Well, yes and no. Air and wood are certainly different, in the sense that they have very different properties, so that we can easily tell them apart – you can sit on the one and not the other, for example, breathe the other and not the one, and so on, and so on. But the question to ask is *why* they have different properties. Is it because the particles of the air are themselves essentially airy, whereas the particles of the wood are very wooden? To give that answer would be to offer no explanation at all for the differences between the two. (In fact, it would be an answer of just the kind that Descartes and his contemporaries were so critical of when offered by then contemporary Aristotelians – (see Box 15.1). Descartes' answer is much more rational, much more scientific, and holds out the possibility of a real explanation for all the differences we observe. According to him, the particles of the wood are only different from those of the air in the sense that they are differently organised. The wood is hard ultimately for the same reason as a very fast-moving whirlpool feels hard to the touch and the water around it doesn't: because at the submicroscopic level the particles which make it up are moving together at the same speed and so are very difficult to separate, whereas those in the air are moving randomly in various directions, and so are easily pushed apart.[7]

I am not trying to persuade you to adopt Descartes' material monism as a true account of what the physical world is like, only to show you what it means, and to suggest that whether or not you want to accept it, it is certainly not the stupid and archaic story it might seem at first sight. (And in fact it is no more ridiculous – though it may be less true – than the scientific pluralism we have been brought up on.) The question of its viability will depend at least in part on whether or not you can accept his denial of the existence of atoms, and also of the possibility of a vacuum.[8] But we can't go into those things here.

Moving things around: the nature of motion in a plenum

In the Cartesian world, then, the difference we make between objects is a conventional one based on relative motion. And the difference between the molecular parts which make them up is of the same kind; and so is that between the parts of the molecules, and the parts of those parts, . . . and so on as far as you may want to go. But if the whole universe is full of this matter in motion, how does it ever manage to move at all? Surely the possibility of motion itself depends on the possibility of an empty space for things to move into? Otherwise the matter of the world would be like snooker balls in a triangle – none of them can move around until you take one out.

Descartes says this is not so. All the motion in the world is what he calls 'circular': i.e. not a simple matter of object A's moving from one place to another, but a very complex exchange of positions by large numbers of distinguishable areas of the continuum. After all, it is not in fact true that the balls in the triangle can't move until you take one out: if only you could push them hard enough without destroying the triangle they *would* move – the balls would break up, and the resulting dust and lumps would push through the gaps between the remaining balls, displacing the air that was there before; and if the snooker triangle were a closed system like the physical universe, the air molecules would themselves move round to fill the space created by the original collapsing ball to complete a 'circle' of relative positional changes.

According to Descartes, that is the kind of process that is going on when a planet moves around the sun – it shoulders its way through the dense crowd of very fine and very mobile particles which lie in its path, which of course instantly shove one another around to fill the space it has vacated – in the way that the particles of water in a river move around behind a fish that swims through it. The same process is occurring when a leaf falls off a tree – you can see it twisting and turning as it navigates its way through the air around it, pushed downwards by the gravitational flow of invisible particles which are streaming out from the earth, and which force any unsupported object such as the leaf down behind them; and in so doing the leaf shoves the air particles around so as to fill the space which it has vacated. According to Descartes, every natural physical process is basically this kind of 'circular' motion. Why does the wind blow? Because the turning earth sets up 'circular' motions in the air. Why do the trees grow? Because particles from the soil are pulled in at their roots and pushed along the channels within the fabric of the tree, causing the matter of the tree to bulge out under mechanical pressure at the weak points in its surface which we call the buds.

How matter moves: the laws of motion and the mathematisation of nature

We are beginning to see how Descartes conceives of all the phenomena of the natural world as in reality nothing but patterns of motions within the universal soup of material substance. The crucial point to grasp about this story – indeed in many ways its whole point – is that those motions are not random, but are all, however complex and involved, very rigidly governed by deterministic physical laws. Every one of the uncountably many complex circles of interaction which go to make up even so simple a thing as stirring a cup of cocoa with a spoon is covered by strict rules. Given the shape of the spoon, the way it is moved and the structure of the sides of the cup, there is only one possible path for each particle of milk, sugar, cocoa and dust, only one possible path to be travelled by each air bubble, micro-organism, trace of washing-up liquid or particle of dandruff in the cup, and only one possible outcome of all the uncountably many collisions which take place between all these things when the cocoa is stirred. And what goes for the cup of cocoa, of course, goes for the whole of creation, which is nothing but a giant cup of cocoa, stirred up at creation and continuing to swirl around in all its beauty and complexity and variety until the coming of the Day of Judgement. It is an astonishing vision; yet according to Descartes the whole process is governed by just three simple mechanical laws.

(1) *Inertia*[9] The first and most basic principle is that even though all the works of nature are the mechanical productions of matter in motion, nevertheless in itself that matter is

19

completely inert and capable of nothing. It will not move, unless it is pushed; and once it is started into motion, it will not stop until something comes along and stops it. 'Every particular thing remains as far as it can in the same state, and never changes except as a result of running into others.'[10] There is therefore no portion of matter in all the universe that has an attractive power over other matter, or a tendency to move in this way or that, or any kind of affinity for being in one place rather than another. All such powers, sympathies, virtues and potentialities beloved of his predecessors are banished from nature by this first and most basic law.

(2) *Rectilinear motion* This powerlessness or inertia of matter means that when once something has started it moving it will move in the simplest, least complicated way possible – in a straight line. It cannot of itself tend either to right or to left, either up or down, and will deviate only if something shoves it in one direction rather than another. Thus any non-rectilinear motion – such as that of the moon around the earth, for example – must be a composite one, the result of two or more impulses driving it in different directions – like a stone whirling round in a sling before release, which is both pushed out in a straight line away from the centre, and simultaneously pulled back by the restraining string.

(3) *Conservation* The final law is a law of collisions: that when objects collide, motion is passed between them; but any gain of motion by one body is exactly matched by a loss of motion in the other(s).[11]

With those three very simple laws, Descartes aims to explain everything that happens in nature, because everything that happens is the result of the mechanical interaction of parts of the continuum; and with those three laws we can in theory, if only we have enough information about the objects in question, work out in advance exactly what they will do. What he is offering us, therefore, is nothing less than a complete science of nature, encompassing everything from medicine to meteorology, astronomy to agronomy, chemistry, physics and biology – an account of the world as it really is, behind the way it appears in our experience of it.

There is one further aspect of the story which it is worthwhile to bring out here, and that is the extent to which Descartes' mechanistic science is also a *mathematical* science. Galileo had said that the book of nature is written in the language of mathematics,[12] and Descartes' mechanism is the ultimate expression of that line of thought.[13] For Descartes, as we have seen, every event is the deterministic outcome of precisely stateable laws, such that if we knew the exact quantities involved we could in theory predict with certainty the outcome of everything that happens. For Descartes that alternative, mathematical description of the event is not simply a useful calculating tool, it is *the only true description* of what is really going on. What the uneducated person who lives in the World of Appearance sees in gross physical terms as the crashing together of two separate lumps of stuff – with often dangerous and unpredictable consequences – consists in reality of a stately transformation of number sequences in accordance with perfect and unchanging laws. That is what every event in nature really consists in, when stripped of the crude physical categories in terms of which it is seen by the material eye of corrupt and fallen man; but as Descartes is going to show us, we are not trapped for ever in that view, and can through the kind of study we now call science escape to a purer, more intellectual understanding of things.

Examples

Descartes doesn't stop at this outline of the theory of mechanism. He is not content merely to work out the theoretical basis of his new view of the world, but in order to show that his mechanical science can work he sets about outlining, often in some detail, the way it will work in fields such as meteorology, anatomy, chemistry, optics, dynamics, astronomy and many more. I am not going to attempt to summarise that work here, but will outline briefly two examples he himself gives in order to illustrate the way the new metaphysic of nature was intended to work.

Example 1: creation of the Earth and the solar system

Descartes was a convinced Copernican,[14] but afraid to admit it. He wrote a naturalised, non-biblical account of how the Earth came into existence, but presented it as a kind of science fiction fantasy: in order to avoid denying that the Earth was actually created by God in six days and set at the centre of the universe, he instead presents us with a fable, which shows how a world *exactly like* our own *could* have come into existence in another way. (Unfortunately when he heard of the condemnation of Galileo he abandoned even this indirect account. His treatise was never finished, but large parts of it were published after his death.)

In what we have of the treatise Descartes conceives of the giant soup of matter as having been stirred up at creation, and thereafter following out its determined course in accordance with the three laws above. At the time of creation, there was Chaos – a vast confused swirling of matter with no settled shapes or patterns discernible in it. Yet behind that seeming confusion the three laws of motion were in operation, and gradually out of their repeated operation in the vast welter of collisions that ensued there came to be an order emerging, and over time the universe as we know it slowly began to develop. The constant bumping and grinding together of parts of matter eventually resulted in three different kinds of particle. They are not different kinds of stuff, of course, since all of them are merely matter; but that universal matter has shaped itself into parts of different sizes – rather in the way that the continued action of water on rock results in boulders, pebbles and sand.

The first kind of matter is large, slow-moving lumps, which are pushed together by the constant jostlings of matter around them to form large aggregations. The second kind is small, rounded particles which tend not to cohere together, and move around easily, and the third kind is extremely small, highly energetic particles which move around very quickly indeed.

Matter of the first kind, which Descartes, using the traditional terminology of his day but redefining it to suit his new theory, calls 'earth', makes up the planet Earth and all the other planets in the sky, and also makes up all the lesser objects which we normally refer to as material objects. Matter of the second kind – called 'air'

– is much less obvious to our senses than the first, but is what in fact fills most of the universe. It fills the air, it makes up what we now call gases of all kinds, and it also comprises the more rarefied airs which fill the spaces between the planets. The third kind of matter – the 'element of fire' – we encounter in the extremely energetic particles which make up flames, and also in electricity and nerve impulses. And streams of such particles also make up what uneducated and superstitious people think of as mysterious and apparently immaterial forces, such as gravity and magnetism.

The solar system, then, is an arrangement of those three kinds of particle that has resulted from the operation of the laws of motion on the original chaos. The sun is a mass of fire particles of immense energy; the air which swirls around it carries the Earth and the other planets around as leaves are carried in a stream; and the intense activity of the sun's fire particles pressing on the interplanetary air is the lines of mechanical pressure which we know as rays of light, pressing down on the Earth, which is an old star which has hardened and cooled over time.

Example 2: the human body

Descartes' account of the human body is included in his fantasy of the alternative world parallel to our own, but also – since he saw it as less controversial – occurs in his published works.[15] He sees the human body (we will see later – ch. 4 – that there is more than this to a human being) as being just like any other physical object – a mechanical system governed by the three laws of motion. The 'life' of a human body, like that of any animal or plant, is not a mysterious principle which animates it, but the purely mechanical consequence of the operation of the 'fire' particles within it. Fire particles are extremely small and extremely energetic. In the course of the process of digestion and the circulation of the blood around the body, these particles are extracted from the blood by a kind of distillation process which takes place in the brain, and from there they travel out along the nerves, filling the muscles and causing the limbs to move by a kind of hydraulic process.

The story sounds quaint and archaic, but is in fact strikingly similar to our own, except that where Descartes talks of fire particles or 'animal spirits', we might talk of 'neural impulses' and the like. When I put my foot too close to a fire, the fast-moving particles in the fire attack the flesh of my foot and start to break down the organisation of its particles (to burn it). That process sends a kind of shock wave along the nerves of the foot, via the spinal cord to the brain, where the pressure opens various channels in the brain which allow the animal spirits to flow with incredible rapidity (as fast, you might say, as an electrical impulse) along the relevant nerves to expand various muscles and contract others in such a way that the foot pulls away from the fire, the head turns to let the pressure waves from the fire fall on the eyes so that I can see what the problem is, and the legs move in such a way as to carry me to safety.

Reading

Descartes' philosophy of nature is set out in his major work, the *Principles of Philosophy* (1644), especially parts 2–4. For a shorter and more accessible presentation, read the incomplete *The World* and *Treatise on Man* – parts of a projected work which Descartes abandoned after the condemnation of Galileo. Both are summarised in very compressed form in Part 5 of *Discourse on Method*.

Questions to ask

(1) In the seventeenth century it was widely held that there could be no 'action at a distance': the moon, for example, could not cause effects on earth – such as tides – unless there were some medium through which it operated. Is that true? If so, what do you take to be the medium in the case of gravity? If not, how is action at a distance possible?

(2) Descartes claims that a vacuum is impossible, because if there were literally nothing between the stars, for example, then they would be touching. Does that argument work? If not, is that because you believe in Absolute Space – you think of it as

an independently existing container, within which objects are arranged?

(3) Descartes thinks the question of whether or not there are atoms and vacuums can be settled a priori, by arguments such as that above. If contemporary science believed in atoms and/or vacuums, would that show he was wrong?

Chapter 3

The possibility of atheism
Descartes and God

God and the world

In the last chapter we sketched out Descartes' new account of
the hidden reality of the natural world. But traditional science
was inseparable from traditional theology. Did he want to throw
out the one as well as the other?

Well, it depends how you read him. Most of the time he plays safe
by avoiding theological issues and concentrating on the science,
leaving it to others to decide how to fit them together, and that
gives rise to the familiar picture which I shall refer to as God the
clock-maker. But later on in life he does suggest a theological reading of his world view which may have been just a sop to the authorities, but which if taken seriously points to a different, stranger,
and more interesting story which I shall call the God of Science.
This chapter will focus on strictly metaphysical issues, on the question of how Descartes thinks of God and of God's relation to creation. In Chapter 5 we will look at the question of whether we have
any good reason to believe there is such a thing as God at all.

God the clock-maker

According to the first picture, the God of Descartes is quite familiar. He is omnipotent, omniscient, eternal, and all-good. He created the universe, and all that is in it: i.e. in Cartesian terms he created the original soup of inert matter, set up the first chaos of disordered motion, and laid down the three laws by means of which that soup would in time – as he of course foresaw – come to develop into the world as we know it. Human beings he creates separately, and individually (see ch. 4), and to them alone he gives the power not only to react to the world around them, but also to understand something of the way it works. He also gives to each individual human being the power of free will.

The important thing to realise about this account of things is that once the world is created, God's involvement in it is fairly limited. He conserves it in being from moment to moment, and he watches over and cares for all the people he has created, but his direct involvement is slight: he allows the laws he has laid down to generate by mechanical means the consequences he has foreseen, and he allows the people to exercise their free will. His direct interventions are relatively minor: he creates human souls, and he communicates directly and indirectly with human beings – hearing our prayers, and inspiring the prophets, for example. On rare occasions he also acts directly in the natural world to produce what we see as a miracle. And of course he sent his son to redeem mankind, and one day will come to judge both the quick and the dead.

That is now a fairly traditional account of God's way with the world: the idea of God as the divine clock-maker, who wound up the mechanism of the world at creation, and leaves it to run its course with only minor interventions, powered, in Descartes' case, by an unending series of pushes and pulls and impacts between the different areas of the continuum, which goes on rattling around until Judgement Day.

There are two aspects to this familiar story of God's relation to the world. From the point of view of *ontology* – of what there is – God is revealed as the first cause and ultimate reason for nature, but he is essentially separate from it, not intimately involved with it on a day-to-day basis. It is his work, as the pot is the work of the potter, and if God were somehow to cease to exist, the world he had created would remain as a pointless and purposeless repetition of mechanical processes. From the point of view of *epistemology* – of our knowledge – again the story is one of separation. A knowledge of God is essential for our salvation and for our moral development, and also for an understanding of the ultimate purpose and ground of the world around us, of its first cause and of the possibility of human knowledge. But there is *no need at all* to refer to God for practical purposes, or for an understanding of the operations of nature. The life of the atheist may, from the Christian point of view, be empty and desperate, but she will be no more likely than is the Christian to walk into buildings or fall under buses, because a knowledge of God is not necessary for our physical survival. The atheist's learning may leave her with no understanding of the point of life, or of the origin of existence, but she will be no better and no worse than the Christian at giving an account of why the rain falls when it is cloudy, why the tides turn, and what keeps the planets moving in their orbits, because a knowledge of God is not necessary for an understanding of nature.

This ontological and epistemological separation of God from our practical and scientific lives is of course historically very significant. If God and the practical world are separate, then there is no reason for the Man of Business to be a man of religion: providing he knows enough of God to know his duties in life, he is free to concentrate on his commercial activities, and can leave the religious dimension to the specialists, and to his Sundays off. And in just the same way the Woman of Science need have no involvement in the world of religion, either. Providing she does not interfere in religious matters, she is free to inquire into the workings of nature, secure in the knowledge that nothing she finds there will contradict the teachings of the church, because, as Galileo said in defence of his freedom to inquire into astronomy without church interference, the Bible teaches us how to go to heaven, but not how the heavens go.[1]

There is a great deal in Descartes to support the idea that this is indeed his position. The whole structure of the physical apparatus we have seen seems to us to lend itself easily to this kind of reading: the natural world is an independent, law-governed system which, once brought into being and started into motion, must rattle on regardless under the influence of the laws of inertia and conservation. This view is supported by Descartes' own scientific works, which contain few references to the nature or existence of God, and seem to show that all that is required for a complete science of nature is an understanding of matter and of the laws which govern it – both of which, of course, were divinely created, but both of which for all practical and scientific purposes can be understood purely naturalistically. Descartes does offer proofs of God's existence (see pp. 54–6) and as we will see he says that any rational person can see simply by thinking about it that God does and indeed must exist. But in fact those proofs themselves tend to strengthen the idea of God as external, and *additional* to the natural system: the mere fact that God's existence has to be proved can itself be taken to suggest that it is something we could live without believing – and the nature of the proofs he offers, which most readers (both today and at the time) find less than persuasive, strengthens the idea that theism is not the only option for someone who accepts Descartes' view of the world. In fact, some people have suggested that Descartes was himself a closet atheist, and that his Christianity is mere lip service to a powerful religious establishment which he did not dare to offend. There is no doubt that he moved to the Dutch Republic and suppressed publication of his works in order to avoid religious persecution for his views, and there is no denying that for fear of church censure he often obscures his real opinion (e.g. the way he presents his account of nature as a description of a new world, not of this one), and some-times says things which on any account of his position he simply does not believe.[2]

The God of science

But there is another way to read this story, which may be nothing more than a smokescreen which Descartes throws up to deflect attention from the radical implications of his work. On this second account Descartes' position is perhaps harder to grasp, because less familiar to us. It is certainly a stranger, more mysterious conception of God; I think it is also a richer, more subtle, and more attractive one.

The key point to grasp here is Descartes' claim that God is the one true substance. What does that mean? We saw earlier that according to Descartes a physical object – a small fish, to take a random example – is in the final analysis not a 'substance' but only a 'mode'; it is not an independently existing object, but only a temporary and conventionally defined aggregation of matter, in the way that the different seas of the world are not really separate things, but only conventionally defined areas of a bigger thing, namely the waters of the Earth. Now we discover that according to Descartes matter itself, the universal soup of physical being, is in its own turn not a real substance either: matter stands to God, he claims, in a way which is somehow analogous to the way the fish stands to matter in general.

If we take this literally, then, Descartes is claiming that just as the fish is only a manifestation, a 'mode' or 'modification' of the underlying matter, so in a similar way matter itself is only a consequence or an expression of God – not a thing in itself, but only a manifestation, a way of being, of something else, i.e. of God. What is real, what, ultimately, there is in existence, is God; and everything else that in any sense exists is not *another* thing, *in addition* to God, but only an *expression* of God, a way in which God manifests himself, or something that God *is doing*.

The insubstantiality of everything except God is an explicit part of Descartes' metaphysics, which is stated quite unambiguously – though how sincerely is open to dispute. God is the only true substance; matter, like a human mind (see ch. 4), can be *called* a substance, but not in the same sense as God is a substance.[3] Matter is substantial in the sense that it is *more* of a substance, closer to being a substance, than any individual material thing; it is not a real thing, but it is more of a thing, more 'thinglike' or 'real' than they are (cf. ch. 2 footnote 4, p. 270). More than that, it is very close to being a substance in the sense that it doesn't depend on anything else other than God for its existence, whereas any individual thing depends also on matter.

Now, if all that makes any sense at all, then it seems to point to an account of God and his relation to the world which is very different from that of the divine clock-maker. On the clock-maker model, the world is a *product* of God, like the potter's pot, or the baker's loaf. But if God is the only true substance, then the relation between God and the world is very much closer and more immediate than that; the world is an *expression* of God, not a product; it is analogous not to the potter's pot, but to her pot-making activity. On the clock-maker model, as we saw, if God could cease to be, the world would remain as pointless and absurd, but as no less real than before. On this account, what becomes of the world if God could cease to exist? The answer is the same as what would happen to my house if suddenly there were no matter; or what would happen to pot-making if suddenly there were no potters: without God, its underlying reality, the world would be like a smile without a face, or a thought without a thinker – it would be nothing at all.

There are other aspects of Descartes' account of God which fit in with this reading. He says that God's activity of conserving the world is identical to his creation of it – i.e. that God doesn't simply make the world, and then let it run, but rather he is *continually* creating it from moment to moment, so that any change in the world – for example, a leaf's falling off a tree – is not simply a matter of the operation of the divine clockwork, but is rather to be understood as God's creating the world anew, replacing the world with the leaf on the tree by a world in which they are separate.[4] It is still of course true that there is a mechanical explanation of the fall of the leaf in terms of the weakening of the stem when the matter which makes it up withdraws into the tree in response to the change of season, but such mechanical explanations are now seen as descriptive not of the nature of matter, but of the activity of God, whose constant recreations of the world around us are not random and unpredictable, but follow simple, intelligible rules.[5]

What we have in these remarks of Descartes', in other words, is not the modern, naturalistic story of the divine clock-maker, but a mechanised, mathematicised version of the traditional notion of creation as a process of 'emanation'. The world, on this view, streams out from God, as light streams out from the sun. God is not identical with that material world, any more than the sun is identical with its light (base, corrupt and corrupting matter can be no part of the divine essence); but he is its source, its basis, its underlying reality; it is his expression, his activity, his appearance. And just as the sun is itself too bright for us to look at, but we perceive it indirectly because everything we see we see by its light, so God himself is beyond our comprehension, but we understand him indirectly, through his creation.

On this reading what Descartes has done is not to replace this older tradition with the God of mechanism, but to provide a mechanical, mathematical interpretation of it. If God is the reality of which nature is the appearance, then a mechanical understanding of nature is a knowledge of God. In particular, as we have seen, an understanding of natural laws is not an understanding of God's *product*, but an understanding of his *behaviour*. Thus each of the three mechanical, naturalistic laws is capable of a religious reading. Descartes' belief in the conservation of motion is his belief that God sustains his creation from moment to moment, and that each state of the world corresponds perfectly to the previous one: nothing is lost in the recreation of the world from one moment to the next. Similarly, the principle of inertia is his belief that nothing God does is done without a reason: anything he does at one moment follows on naturally and rationally from what he had done before. The principle of straight-line motion is an interesting case, where the theological dimension is less obvious but equally real. The world as we know it, of course, contains *no* straight-line motion: any motion we ever observe – the flight of an arrow, the fall of a leaf, the rotation of the planets – is to some degree curved. The reason, of course, is that a motion such as the flight of a cannonball is a *complex* one, made up of the thrust of the powder, the downward weight of the ball, the resistance of the air, and so on. For Descartes this exemplifies the way that the divine perfection – straight-line motion – is unattainable under the circumstances in which we live: but it nevertheless underlies all the motions of earthly objects as their origin and their explanation.[6]

The point here is not simply that the Cartesian laws of motion are capable of being given a theological interpretation, or that there is some kind of analogy between mechanical and divine explanation; the point is that on this account, unlike the clockmaker story, there is *no separation* between Descartes' mechanics and his theology. This is clearer if we bear in mind what we saw at the end of the previous section. I tried to show there that in Descartes' eyes the reality of nature is not a material mass which happens to be fully describable in mathematical terms, but rather the mathematical description is the only true account of nature, and the sensory terms in which we more often think of it are in fact a distortion of it, an appearance of that reality. We can now see that point more clearly. For a Cartesian, the challenge of science, to escape from the world of appearance to the world of reality, to discover the truth behind the outward show of things, can also be represented as a spiritual or religious challenge: to escape from the view which is natural to our physical embodiment, and to see the world as it really is, as God himself sees it, in purely non-sensory, mathematical terms.

I have tried here to sketch two readings of Descartes' account of God. On one, which I have called the clock-maker view, Descartes is a very modern thinker. If he is not himself an atheist, he certainly paves the way for atheism by producing an account of God and his relation to the world which means that the atheist scientist, though she may be damned for all eternity, is not mistaken in the way she sees the world around us. On the second account, the God-as-Substance view, Descartes' position would be much less familiar, because it would combine the fields of science and religion in a way that we find hard even to understand. On this account his invention of the appearance/reality distinction is at once not only a practical inquiry and a scientific research pro-gramme, but also a theological treatise and a programme of moral reform. If this second account is correct, for Descartes the notion of an atheist scientist is in fact an absurdity.

Reading

Descartes was extremely wary of writing on theological issues, and you need to read everything he says on the subject with that in mind. His official position is set out in *Principles* Part 1, but rele-vant comments can be found throughout his work, for example in *The World*, and also in his voluminous correspondence.

Questions to ask

(1) If we are not convinced by proofs of the existence of God, does it follow that we should be atheists? Compare: if we are not convinced we can *dis*prove the existence of God, does it follow that we should be theists? Where does the burden of proof lie, and why?

(2) If we understand God as the underlying reality of everything that is, does that mean he can't not exist? (How can reality be unreal?)

(3) God is usually taken to be outside of time. If that is so, then creation, because it is something that God does, cannot have happened at a time. Does that mean that any theist must regard creation as an ongoing process?

Chapter 4

The limits of mechanism

The place of human beings in Descartes' world

We have now seen an outline of Descartes' account of nature, and of the relation of nature to God. But where do people fit into that story? The short answer is that they are somewhere between the two, mixing the nature of the one with that of the other. Human beings in themselves are miniature versions of God, living out their lives on Earth, temporarily and somewhat uncomfortably united to the material universe. The story is one which is quite familiar and very natural to us, and has clear implications for the way we should live our lives.

The limits of mechanism

We saw earlier that Descartes regards the human body as ultimately just a 'mode' of the material continuum. Our bodies, just like any other material object, have no true individuality or substantiality, but are conventionally defined areas of the one material substance – areas which are constantly changing, as parts are added (growth, digestion, regeneration of cells) and taken away (excretion, decay, abrasion by surrounding bodies). According to Descartes (who was writing before Leeuwenhoek's discovery of spermatozoa), conception is the result of the mixing of two fluids, each of which acts in the manner of a yeast on the other. The growth of the body, like all other natural events, is a mechanical process, in which particles filtered out of the blood are added to the parts of the body. The blood is pumped by the heat of the heart and cooled and condensed by the air in the lungs, and the digestive processes distil food to extract from it what the body needs. All this is a matter of extremely sophisticated, but conceptually very simple, mechanical processes, as are our instinctive reactions, and our sensory perception (see pp. 23–4).

The story strikes us as a rather crude one, but perhaps not as implausible. Yet some things might seem harder to deal with by these means. Is there not more to a living human being than an extremely sophisticated mechanical robot? A simple robot, after all, doesn't actually *do* anything: it may appear to, but in reality it is only carrying out the instructions it is given – its 'actions' are simply the effects of forces operating on it. But some acts by humans and by animals seem not to be of that form. An animal, after all, is *alive* – it is a *source* of activity, not just something which passes on the causes which affect it. Take for example the heart of an animal. If you cut it out of the body (as Descartes did), it continues to beat for some time. It isn't being pushed, or driven, yet somehow from within it there arises some sort of activity. Does that not mean that it contains within it some kind of energy, power, principle, virtue or soul which gives it life?

To his contemporaries the question seemed a very natural one – but Descartes is very clear that it is completely mistaken. *All* the processes of life in the body are for him simple mechanical ones; however striking or unexpected they may seem, they are in reality just speeded up, scaled down and massively more complex versions of familiar mechanical devices like pumps or mills, driven by readily comprehensible mechanical forces in accordance with the three laws of nature. (The beating of the heart, for example, is a consequence of its heat: substances in the blood are rapidly vaporised in it, as a result of which they expand very quickly, forcing the heart to expand, and driving the blood out into the arteries.) Any talk of life forces, animal souls or whatever is he says mere words, the result of our ignorance of the scope and diversity of mechanical processes.

So far, then, Descartes would agree with contemporary common sense: the actions of the body can all be explained by general physical theories (mechanical in his case; electrochemical in ours) without the need to postulate mysterious faculties or life forces. But even for him, there are limits: some things, he says, cannot be explained mechanically, but the division is to be made not between the living and the non-living, but between the human and the animal. Here is my attempt to explain his point of view.

People v. animals: four differences

(1) Take an example. Animals, like human beings, but unlike other things in nature, have plans, goals, aims: a dog can look for something; a cat can try to get out of a washing machine. But do animals make plans for the future? Some animals, of course, do things which will have future consequences, and even do them because of their future consequences. A bird, for example, will build a nest to keep its future chicks warm. But is it true to say that the bird *anticipates* the birth of its chicks, and knows they will need lots of twigs, feathers, bits of moss and old shoelaces in order to keep them warm? Or is its nest-building behaviour purely instinctive – i.e. is it that the mechanisms of the bird's body are such that, when they are triggered by the changing of the seasons, the bird automatically begins nest-building, with no *understanding* of the need for it, but only a blind and automatic – robot-like – reaction to physical stimuli? Descartes' theory is that the bird is merely this kind of a well adapted mechanism: it has no more understanding of the need for the nest it is building than a tree has of the need for the leaves and fruit which it produces in an analogous way.

But what about the case of a woman who decides to join a political party and works hard to collect money for projects aimed at preventing harm to future generations? Is it in any way plausible to suggest that her behaviour is also explicable as a blind response to present stimuli? Descartes' theory is that it is not. Here there is clearly *something else* going on, something which no mechanical process can capture: the woman, we might say, can *think about* things, as opposed to merely reacting to them: she has 'understanding'. According to Descartes, no animal, no matter how clever (i.e. no matter how intricate and sophisticated its mechanism) can *understand* anything at all.

(2) Similarly, according to Descartes no animal can ever make a *choice*. My cat is a good illustration. Sometimes it so happens that a piece of fried haddock comes within range of her sensory apparatus, and when it does she gets very excited and makes a noise like a duck. If I offer her a piece of the haddock (yes, I know I shouldn't, but never mind) when I put it in front of her, she is often so overwhelmed by the sight and smell of the big piece she can see but can't have, that she is quite unable to eat the small piece, which she has also seen, and which she can have if she wants it. She is simply transfixed by the attraction of the big piece of fish, and even though she knows the small one is there and is available, she is just incapable of turning her attention away from the large one until it is gone, or until the small one is pushed right in front of her nose so that she has to eat it to get it out of the way.

My cat may, of course (for all the undeniable charm of her duck impersonations), be a particularly stupid example of the species. But compare her behaviour with that of a tempted but dedicated priest who has sworn a vow of chastity; or an athlete who is offered beer and chocolate. In at least some instances, it seems, people are able to override their instincts in a way that cats never are. Is it possible to give a mechanical explanation for such choices? It could, of course, be just that the athlete is more frightened of her coach than attracted by the beer and the chocolate – i.e. that one of the immediate stimuli is stronger than the other. But there are also cases where it seems as if it is not some present stimulus that is controlling her behaviour, but a *choice* she has made. Is it possible to give a mechanical explanation of a case of that kind? Descartes' answer is again no: whereas all animals are driven by present stimuli, *some* of the things which human beings can do involve the ability to stand back from those stimuli, to consider alternatives, and to make *choices* between them.

(3) Here is a third example of a related kind. Human beings can *abstract*, which is something no animal can do, and which again no mechanical process can account for. For example, a dog might know its way to the post office, and be able to distinguish it from the hairdresser's next door. You could even train your dog to go to the post office and buy stamps. But even if you did that, and even if it could collect your granny's pension at the same time, it would still have no *concept* of the post office, because it isn't able to abstract from that particular building and think about what such buildings have in common. That is why animals have no true language as such. They have signs, of course, which they can recognise and respond to, but they don't have language, because they aren't able to abstract from a sign to its meaning.

As a result, human beings can know a whole mass of things that no animal can conceive of. No animal has the concept of God, and it is hard to see how any mechanically produced state of the physical organism could ever account for an idea of that kind. If that example doesn't convince you, what about the case of mathematics? Animals, although some of them may react differently to, for example, three attackers rather than one, are not able to count; counting involves the ability to abstract from what we meet with in the world, which animals, because they are mechanical systems of cause and effect, can never do. The same goes for other abstract concepts, such as beauty, love, or goodness: could any mechanical (or, for that matter, any electrochemical) system have a knowledge of such things?

(4) Finally, there is the simple and striking fact of consciousness. Animals are very often aware of their surroundings; but they are not *aware* of that awareness. The thing which all people have and which no robot can ever possess is that subjectivity, or *self*-awareness. Whatever may be true of my physical being, whatever the most perfect anatomical investigation might discover, there will always be something additional to it, something which no purely physical description can ever capture. Whatever may be true of the various bits and pieces of which

I am made up, whatever state they may be in or however they may behave, there is something more: there is what it *feels like* to be me. Ask yourself: if there were a perfect anatomist, who knew all there was to know about brain functions, and had a perfect knowledge of your body and brain, would she know what it felt like to be you?[1] With a robot, on the other hand, no matter how complex and sophisticated it may be, there is nothing of the kind: there is *nothing it is like* to be a robot, just as there is nothing it is like to be a brick, or a screwdriver, or a puff of wind. According to Descartes, every living creature other than a human being is in this sense a robot; there is nothing it is like to be anything on earth, except a person.

I have tried to show that whether or not Descartes is right to deny a materialistic or mechanistic account of human beings, his position is by no means a stupid or an unnatural one. There *are* very significant differences between human beings and even the most intelligent of animals. In Cartesian terms, we possess Understanding – which covers both awareness of things, as opposed to mere reactions to stimuli, and our ability to consider what is not given by our surroundings – and Will – the ability to choose, to initiate events, to produce something which is not simply the product of causes acting on us. He therefore concludes that there is more to a human being than our bodily mechanisms, which are not significantly different from those of other things. There must be, in addition to that bodily mechanism, another thing of a different, non-material kind, which is responsible for the 'faculties' of Will and Understanding. And that thing Descartes calls a 'mind' or 'soul'.

Are you convinced? Or do you think those differences between animals and other creatures can be explained as just a consequence of their different physiology and bigger brains?

Descartes is convinced that they can't. So how does he think these immaterial minds stand in relation to the substance/mode distinction we saw earlier? Is each mind an individual thing, a substance in its own right? Or is it just an aspect, part, or activity of some larger whole, as all physical objects turned out to be modes of extended matter?

A lot hangs on this question. Which seems to you the more

plausible answer? Is your mind really just a part of a larger continuum of mental activity, in the way that your body can be seen as
just a part of the material world? Or do you have some essential
individuality, a substantiality, which no mere material thing
can possess? To put it another way, would it make sense to see the
boundary between your mind and mine as merely a conventional
one, analogous to that between an estuary and the sea?

Descartes' answer is that each individual person's mind is a
separate thing, and so has the same status as the material world as
a whole. It is an individual substance, created and maintained
in existence by God, but independent of everything else in the
universe. As long as you are alive, your immaterial mind is
intimately connected with the area of matter that is your physical
body (he suggested that the pineal gland, at the centre of the brain,
might be the locus of communication between the two), but when
the body dies and begins to break up, the connection is broken,
and the mind continues in a 'disembodied' form.

What then will be the modes of this mental substance, which
stand to the mind as individual material objects stand to matter
as a whole? The answer is its particular thoughts – its acts of
willing and understanding. Just like those individual objects,
those thoughts are real, but are not independent – they depend on
the mind for their existence.

We can now see the whole story of the nature of human beings
in Descartes' philosophy. It is the view which is usually referred to
as 'Cartesian Dualism' because of the way he represents us as a
combination of two elements, but in fact as a complete metaphysical account of what there is it is really a kind of unequal
trilogy of existants. The basic reality of all being is God, the one
true substance, which creates and recreates at every moment two
distinct types of dependent substances or pseudo-substances.
On the one side there is the one material continuum, which
we see as the three-dimensional world of objects in space and
time, and which is correctly describable only in the language of
mathematics; and on the other side there is an indefinite number
of individual human minds, each one expressly created at the time
of the conception of the body, and united from that moment on
until the death of the individual with that one particular area of
the material world.

Reading

Descartes' *Description of the Human Body* sets out his mechanistic physiology. He discusses the differences between animals and humans in *Discourse on Method* 5. His view of animals as mere machines was always controversial, and comes up often in his *Correspondence*.

Questions to ask

(1) Would a perfect anatomist be able to find out what it feels like to be you?

(2) Is talk of animal *language* a misnomer?

(3) If human beings had no free will, would that mean that all their 'actions' are in fact the result of causes outside them, and therefore that people don't actually do anything at all?

Chapter 5

Selling the picture
Descartes' story of doubt and discovery

Selling the picture

So far I have tried to show that Descartes had a wonderfully subtle and carefully thought-out account of Nature, God and Man, all of which had some continuities with, but were very importantly different from, what had been accepted before. His opinion of his predecessors, and of the contemporary authorities, was very low: he thought not only that their conclusions were wrong – they didn't understand what the world was really like, and mistook appearance for reality – but that their methods actually prevented learning, and could only lead people to a negative and backward-looking scepticism, because the fact that the so-called experts were so obviously mistaken, corrupt and stupid could only lend credence to the increasingly fashionable idea that human beings could know nothing of how the world really is, and should simply accept what they were told because they had no way of finding anything better (see Box 5.1).

Descartes was convinced that knowledge was possible, but that

---

Box 5.1

Scepticism

'Scepticism' is one of those words that philosophers use a lot, and that means a whole variety of different things in different contexts. The basic idea is a denial that we can know something we normally think we know – or sometimes the denial that we can ever know anything at all. Here are some of the ways the term has been used, both in relation to our authors and more widely.

Although in the modern era Scepticism in all its forms is generally seen in purely negative terms, for the first, Greek, Sceptics it seems to have been a much more positive doctrine. The basic idea was that all bad things come from holding opinions.

Wars and conflicts of all kinds are an obvious example, since it's hard to see what people could argue about if no-one believed anything. Disappointment is another evil for which beliefs were held to be responsible – you are disappointed when you form some belief, some expectation, about what might happen, and then it doesn't. So if you could only avoid forming any expectations about what would happen, you would never be disappointed, would you? And perhaps you can argue that *any* kind of sadness has the same cause, in that it derives ultimately from the mismatch between what you expect, and what you get – between how you think things will be, or hoped they would be, or convince yourself they *should* be, and how things actually are. If you could only avoid believing anything at all about how things were or would or should be, if you could suspend your judgement on all questions, then perhaps you could achieve true peace of mind.

The Sceptics therefore worked out a series of belief-avoidance strategies – lists of arguments to the effect that human knowledge is weak or non-existent, which you could run through whenever you felt a belief coming on, so to speak, in order to remind yourself that however obvious something seemed to be, you could always if you tried find a reason for doubting it, and so maintain your suspension of judgement (*epoche*), and therefore your peace of mind (*ataraxia*).

The works of the Greek Sceptics were rediscovered in the Renaissance, and caused quite a stir in a rapidly changing, conflict-ridden Europe in which established authorities were being called into question. Sceptical arguments became quite fashionable, and were used in all kinds of ways: Catholics used them against

Protestants (since we can know nothing, we must accept the Word of God as propounded by the Church), and Protestants used them against Catholics (since we can know nothing, we must accept the Word of God as we find it in the Scriptures). And fashionable young men known as the *Libertins Erudits* affected to deny all learning on sceptical grounds. Whether or not it is true to say that there was a 'sceptical crisis' in European thought at this time,[1] it is certainly true that authors like Descartes and Spinoza, committed to the view that science can give us lasting knowledge of the way things really are, felt the need to deny the fashionable sceptical opinions of the time in order to sell their revolutionary account of how that knowledge could be achieved.

Later, though, as is the way of these things, the confidence of those early revolutionaries leaked away, and the new science itself came to be seen by later generations as being itself a Sceptical force. Its invention of the World of Reality underlying the World of Appearance came to be thought by some (e.g. Berkeley – see Part 5) as cutting us off from reality, despite the Cartesian arguments to the contrary. Locke's conviction that genuine science was beyond our reach (pp. 169–73), and his failure in some people's eyes to get beyond the Veil of Ideas (p. 157), seemed to put us on a downward path to which Hume's triumphant negativity was the only possible outcome (ch. 20).

Nowadays, the original conception of Scepticism has been largely forgotten, and when philosophers today use the term it is usually some kind of Cartesian picture that they have in mind. The position that is sometimes called global, total, or 'Cartesian' Scepticism is something like that reached by Descartes at the end of Meditation 1: what if there were no real world around me? What if all my life were a kind of complex dream, or an illusion created by an Evil Demon – or perhaps by a mad scientist, who has destroyed my body and is feeding messages to my disembodied brain, which he or she is keeping alive in a vat in a laboratory? If that were true, how could I ever know it was true? What test could I possibly apply to show that I am here in the world I think I'm in, that couldn't equally well be read as showing that I was a brain in a vat, or an Evil Demon's plaything? If I can't remove that doubt, then it seems that all of what I normally call my knowledge of the world is thrown into doubt, and that really I can't know anything at all.

> This sceptical doubt is an invented position, which no-one actually believes, and which probably no-one ever has believed. (As we shall see, Berkeley's position is related but importantly different.) Yet philosophers still feel the need to argue against it. A sure sign, perhaps, that something is not right in our understanding of ourselves and our relation to the world around us.

in order to achieve it a wholesale revolution in attitudes and methods was necessary. Somehow we have to sweep away our old beliefs, escape from common-sense experience as a guide to reality, overthrow the established authorities who sought to preserve and explain that experience, and accept instead new authorities using new techniques which he thought he could show would necessarily be a sure guide to the truth. In his writings he therefore tries to establish:

(1) That the accepted authorities are wrong.
(2) That secure and lasting knowledge – what we would call scientific knowledge – is nevertheless possible.
(3) *How* such knowledge is possible.
(4) What in outline the world is really like; and
(5) That this new approach does not damage, but actually strengthens, Christianity.

His whole creative life was devoted to persuading people of the truth of those five propositions. In his huge output of letters and publications you can see him trying to get that message across – bypassing the authorities where possible, placating them where necessary, opposing them where he thought he could get away with it, and building his network of like-minded supporters. In his different writings the emphasis is on different parts of the story: his master work, his formal presentation of his system, is the four-volume *Principles of Philosophy*, which was intended for the specialist reader and concentrates chiefly on point 4. His more detailed treatises like the *Treatise on Man* and *The World* are more polemical, more intended for the lay reader, and concentrate on both points 4 and 1. But nowadays we tend to disagree with the detail of his account of nature, so we look chiefly at his other books, especially the *Discourse on Method*, which was written as a preface to his *Optics*, *Meteorology* and *Geometry* and deals with points 1, 2, 3 and a little of 4, and most of all his *Meditations on Philosophy* (or on First Philosophy, or on Metaphysics, depending on the translator), which is concerned mainly with points 1 and 2.

Descartes' fictional quest

Over the years Descartes developed a standard way of presenting his ideas, which you can see in *Principles*, *Discourse* and best of all in *Meditations*, and which is meant simultaneously to explain his ideas and to persuade a non-technical reader of their truth. He presents it as a story of discovery, a fictional journey of thought which he claims to have taken, and which he invites his readers to follow through with him. It is short, and, astonishingly for a piece of seventeenth-century philosophy, immediately compelling to a non-specialist reader even today. If you haven't read it, you should. I shall make no attempt here to recapture the excitement, the anxiety, the genuine fear it can still provoke in a reader, but in this section and the next I will try to set out the content of the tale, try to explain some of its more puzzling sections, and concentrate on showing how it relates to the overall philosophical position I have been trying to present.

The *Meditations* is presented as the story of a retreat, a spiritual exercise of the kind in which people still engage. Descartes withdraws from the world for a week in order to sort his head out – to think through what he believes and doesn't believe, whom he can trust, what he truly values, and how he should live his life. Manuals of such retreats, as it were guidebooks to help people through this process of spiritual regeneration, were a fairly common literary/religious genre at the time, and Descartes aims to write a new one as a means of showing people how natural, indeed how inevitable, his view of things really is: if only you will take the time to think it through clearly, he is saying to us, you will find the truth of his view of things is inescapable.[2] In the course of his retreat, Descartes seeks to recapitulate the work of God: in his six days of labour he will create the world anew, by clearing his head of accumulated errors and doubts, and thinking his way through to a clear understanding of his own nature and of his relation to God and to the world.

The reason the *Meditations* is such an approachable text even today is that he succeeds in thinking his way into the position of the troubled seeker after truth that he is pretending to be. He begins his quest by setting himself a question, and simply thinks his way through to an answer to it, step by step, stage by stage. At the end of each day he takes stock of where he has got to, then pauses to let his thoughts settle and to accustom himself to his new discoveries, before beginning again on the following day on the next stage of this imagined but very plausible journey. The reader is invited to follow him along his path, to share his doubts and his discoveries, in the belief that we will in the end come to realise that the only view we can reasonably hold is the one which Descartes himself has been convinced of all along, and which I have tried to sketch in the previous sections.

Emptying the barrel: the doubt

The first step in sorting our heads out is to clear them of all the falsehoods we have come to believe – conventional wisdom, things accepted on trust from people around us, the sayings of various authorities, conclusions jumped to on the basis of how things appear, and so on. When you think about it, an awful lot of the things we all take for granted come into one or other of these categories. The trouble is, we wouldn't believe these things if we could see that they weren't true; how are we going to sort out the false beliefs we've cluttered up our minds with from the true ones which we really *ought* to believe? Descartes' solution is radical: he says that for the purposes of his retreat he will begin by clearing his mind of *all* his beliefs, and he will then reintroduce only those things he has satisfied himself he can rely on. He uses various analogies to explain this process; he talks of knocking down the house of knowledge and rebuilding it on a firm foundation, and compares it to the way you proceed when you suspect there are some rotten apples in your apple barrel: the only thing to do is to tip out *all* the apples, and put back only those which on close inspection are shown to be sound.[3] And that is what he proceeds to do in Meditation 1: he tries to imagine that everything he has ever believed is actually false, in order to see what he can rely on as the basis for a secure understanding.

The first thing he does is to chop away all his observational knowledge of the world – everything he believes because he has seen it, heard it, felt it, or whatever (his simple 'empirical' knowledge, what he knows from his 'senses'). Can I rely on my observational knowledge? Most of the time I do, of course . . . but then sometimes I make mistakes. I see a friend in the street and it turns out to be someone else; my uncle's brown car turns out to have been pink all along. Obviously I can't trust all such beliefs. So I shall be on the safe side, and pretend they're all false – let's pretend that every person I've ever seen has actually been someone else, that everything I believe to be one colour is actually a different one, and so on, and so on.

Where does that leave us? Only with our most immediate, most obvious sensory judgements, perhaps. I make mistakes about people seen in crowds, but not when I'm talking to them in good light; I misremember the colour of cars, but there's no way I'm wrong about the colour of the wall of the room I'm sitting in now. So can I at least accept things like that?

Well, I suppose I could be wrong about them. I could dream I'm looking at a green wall, when really it's pink or yellow. I can dream I'm talking to my friend, when really I'm asleep in bed and she's in Guatemala. A pretty implausible suggestion, of course – but then, this isn't a practical enquiry. I'm trying to decide what kind of belief I can always depend on, as a basis for a new understanding of the world, not trying to decide who is who, or what colour to paint my living room. So: let's imagine that even these immediate observational judgements are all false – my wallpaper's really purple, I'm not really writing this stuff, I'm in Guatemala, this isn't my hand in front of my face, it's a fish, and so on and so on and so on.

What am I left with?

Think about it. I'm trying to imagine that everything I believe about the world around me on the basis of what I see and feel is false. Would there be anything I could rely on?

Well, perhaps there is. Think about understanding, rather than knowledge as such. Even if everything I am inclined to say about the world is false, don't I at least know what it *means*? Perhaps the wall I think is green is really purple – but at least I know what green and purple are, and how they differ. Perhaps the sun isn't shining as I think it is – but at least I know what sunshine is, and that if it's sunny it isn't overcast, and so on. Perhaps this page isn't really rectangular – but at least I know rectangles have four sides, don't I? Even if I give up on everything I take to be a fact of the world, and in fact even if I give up on the world itself, and pretend the Evil Demon has destroyed it and left me nothing but the imaginings of my disordered mind, *still* my understanding of the kind of thing that *could* exist isn't endangered, is it?

Descartes then tries to threaten even that. It isn't just our particular beliefs about what's what in the world that he wants us to put into doubt; he believes the very categories in terms of which we understand the world are inadequate. So he brings in the Ultimate Doubt, which threatens literally *everything* I believe. What if I am just made in such a way that *whatever* I believe is actually false? Or what if, as his most famous formulation of the problem puts it, there is some Evil Demon who is watching over me, and every time she sees a thought forming in my mind, she alters either the thought or the world in such a way that the belief I end up with is a mistake? Isn't that at least conceivable?

That is the point at which the first day of Descartes' retreat ends. We are primed: we have knocked down the house of knowledge, shaken all the apples out of the barrel. *Everything* is in doubt, *nothing* can be taken for granted. In four pages he has overthrown centuries of learning and shaken us out of our comfortable assumptions; we are ready to start the rebuilding process, and to replace the jumble of ideas we started out with by the Cartesian system we saw earlier.

Are you convinced? Is everything now thrown into doubt and confusion? When it is done by the master himself it is a brilliant device which still today reads as fresh and worrying. In fact, the problem with it is that it is if anything rather *too* successful. Most people who read it find that the doubts he raises are insuperable; they are convinced by his doubts, but not by the way in which he tries to overcome them. As a result, it is this *story* of Descartes', this device to popularise his philosophy, which has come to be the main focus of work done on him in the last 200 years or so. In fact we are so interested in the medium – the story of the *Meditations* – that there is a danger that we lose sight of the message – the metaphysical picture it was intended to present.[4] But we must press on to the next part of the story.

Re-establishing the world

By the beginning of Day Two of his fictional retreat, then, Descartes is in a mess. He has deliberately chopped away everything he ever believed, and is confronted by the possibility that Scepticism is the only option that remains. 'So what remains true? Perhaps just the one fact that nothing is certain'.[5] But although his fictional self confronts that ultimate doubt – and so do we, as we follow his train of reasoning – his intention in doing so is to show that knowledge is indeed possible, if only we start again, and start to think scientifically. This section will set out the story of the remaining five days of the retreat, as Descartes tries to get us to think our way through to the certainty of the new world he has discovered.

The cogito and its consequences

The device which Descartes employs to disprove scepticism and set himself back on the upward path is the most famous single moment in the whole of Western Philosophy – *cogito ergo sum*. What he needs to show is that there are some things that just *can't* be false, even on the desperate assumptions he has made so far. And he finds such a thing in his own existence. Even if I am made in such a way that I go wrong at every turn; even if there is an evil demon of infinite power whose only business in life is to make sure that everything I believe is false; even then it must still be the case that I exist – because if I didn't exist, I couldn't even make mistakes. I must exist in order to possess this deeply flawed nature, or in order to be deceived by this creature. The mere fact that I think at all, even if I always think badly, proves beyond doubt that I exist: I think, therefore I am.

Can you deny it? Can you see any way in which your belief that you yourself exist could in fact be false? Descartes says you can't. And from that fact, he wants to derive three conclusions.

(1) The first is that scepticism is instantly disproved. We *do* have some reliable knowledge, because the cogito shows that even on the most unfavourable and exaggerated assumptions, we can still have some unshakeable, certain knowledge.
(2) But that isn't enough for Descartes. The second thing he wants to draw from the cogito is an account of *how* we can have knowledge. Ask yourself: if the cogito is true, *why* is it true? How do you *know* it is true?

In a sense, there is no answer to that question. I know there's a squirrel outside because I can see it; I know that Leicester City lost the 1949 FA Cup Final because I've read about it . . . but what evidence can I point to to convince someone that if I think, I must exist, and that if I didn't exist, I couldn't even make mistakes? I can't find anything. It seems to be just something I can't deny, something I can see, just by thinking about it, *cannot* be false. It doesn't *need* any evidence. I can, as it were, hold the whole assertion in my mind at once, and see that there is obviously no alternative to its being true. In Descartes' terms, it is a 'clear and distinct idea'. Elsewhere he calls an idea of this kind an 'intuition' – something you can just see immediately is true, without having to derive that knowledge from something else. Another example he uses is that 2 and 3 make 5. Can you deny that, or is it another indubitable intuition, like the cogito?

Descartes says the latter. And you can see why. Of course, the symbols 2, 3 and 5 might have been used differently, to stand for different numbers, and then writing '2 + 3 = 5' would have been a mistake. But that doesn't cast doubt on the truth of *what we currently mean* when we write it. Or again, we might have had a different mathematics, in which the operation called addition was significantly different from the one we have; but again, that wouldn't mean that what *we, now* mean by '2 + 3 = 5' was in fact false, would it?

What about the Evil Demon hypothesis? Does that cast any doubt on a case like this? Well, the evil demon could destroy the world, so it could presumably play a very nasty trick on me; every time I tried to put three apples together with two apples to make five apples, it could destroy one of the apples, so that I ended up with only four. Would *that* falsify my belief that two and three make five? Well, no. It might mean that if I want to get my hands on five apples I will have to go about it a different way, but it wouldn't mean that two and three didn't really make five, would it? If that is true, then much of what I abandoned to the evil demon in my initial panic on Day 1 can in fact be reclaimed. I now realise, says Descartes, that there are some things I just *can't* doubt – rational, intuitive truths, things which I can't help thinking just *have* to be true.[6]

It is an enormous step that Descartes is trying to make here. In terms of the progress of his ideas on his fictional retreat, it is essential, because we now have not a single truth, but a whole class of things we can't doubt. But in respect of his overall philosophical position, it is even more important, because what he is asserting here is that the way to achieve genuine certain knowledge and not mere opinion, which is vulnerable to sceptical doubt, is not to look casually around us, but to *think*, to work out the *implications* of what we see – i.e. to abandon the sense-based theories of antiquity and adopt the new science of Descartes and his friends.

At various points he compares the relation between the rational, scientific thinking he is advocating and the common-sense observational knowledge he is rejecting to that between a grown-up and a gullible child, who takes everything at face value. He uses the example of the stick which is half in and half out of the water, and so looks bent because of the refraction of light by the water. The child thinks the stick is bent; the adult knows it isn't. But *how* does the adult know that? If you look at the stick, it looks bent; if you run your hand along it, it feels straight. That, and similar observations in other cases, is all the information your senses can provide; on their own they can't tell you which answer is the correct one. In order to know that, you need something which neither looking nor touching can give you – you need to *work out*, intellectually, which appearance is the correct one. And that process of not merely looking at the world, but using our intellect to look beyond the appearance to the hidden reality, is a matter of seeing the logical relations between observations, seeing what is implied by the things we see. And that kind of rational insight is the kind of move which the cogito has demonstrated as lying beyond the reach of doubt.[7]

(3) And there is yet a third conclusion Descartes wants to draw from this wonderful rhetorical device of the cogito. Having used it to show *that* he is, he now uses it again to establish *what* he is.

As we have seen, he regards himself and all human beings as consisting essentially in an immaterial mind united with an area of the material continuum. That too, he claims, is indicated by the cogito. After all, we saw that it proved beyond doubt that he existed, even when he had assumed that the whole material world had been destroyed by the Evil Demon. Doesn't that show that he himself, the real Descartes, is not any part of that material world, but must be a separate, immaterial being? The conclusion he claims follows directly from his proof of his own existence; and what is more, it follows by precisely the kind of rational, intuitive step which the cogito has shown to be reliable.[8]

God

How is he doing so far? Are you happy to accept that Descartes has shown that we do have certain knowledge, that rational intuitions can't be doubted, and that the self is something separate from the material world? If not, can you say exactly where you think his chain of reasoning breaks down, and why?

Whatever your conclusion, Descartes takes himself to have laid down a foundation, and he proceeds to put the sound apples back into the barrel by going on to establish on this basis the existence of God, and the outline of the mechanical universe, which we saw in Chapter 2. (And this is the stage at which many people, nowadays and at the time, have thought the story really breaks down.)

Can the existence of God be proved? Harder yet, can it be proved using only the materials which Descartes has so far given himself, i.e. the certainty of his own existence and the reliability of his rational intuitions? Descartes thinks he has a way – in fact two ways.

Here is the first. I know that I exist, and that my rational intuitions can't be doubted. Now, among the ideas I have in my mind is that of an ultimate reality, an infinite substance on which everything else depends and from which everything derives: the truth that underlies the world, the reality behind all appearances, on which everything else depends. And that is what I call 'God'. Is there anything corresponding to that idea, or is it just something I've made up?

Well, let's think. I know that *I* am not an infinite substance on whom everything else depends. My limitations and weaknesses are all too obvious. (Of course, I could be wrong about the kind of thing I am – but that in itself would prove that I wasn't an infinite substance, wouldn't it? Because how could such a thing make mistakes? Who or what could mislead it?) But, then if I'm not myself an infinite substance, where did I get the *idea* of such a thing from? I can't have made it up all by myself, he says, because something that wasn't an infinite substance could never create the idea of something that was.

Well, how could it? It would be like making something out of nothing – or at least making more out of less. To create the idea of something, you have to be as it were on a par with that thing. So I could imagine the existence of something like myself – another person, say – even if such a thing didn't exist. And I could imagine something that was less than I am – such as a part of a person, or something a person did, or thought. But how could my imagination move *up* the scale of existence, as it were? How could I come up with the idea of something of a kind which is beyond me, and of which I have never had experience? Yet I *do* have the idea of God . . . and if I haven't made it up for myself, it must somehow have been put into my mind by something else. And for exactly the same reason, that thing itself, if it wasn't an infinite substance, couldn't have created the idea either.

There is only one conclusion: the idea can only have originated with something that *is* an infinite substance, i.e. with God himself, and it must have been passed to me either directly or through some intermediary. So there must be a God, as the only possible explanation of the fact that I have the idea of him.[9]

Convinced? Many people are not. But if it doesn't work, can you say what exactly is wrong with it?

In Meditation 5 Descartes comes back to the question of God's existence, and he produces another argument, which again begins from the fact of his having an idea of God, but this time focuses on the content of that idea, rather than on its origin. My idea of God, he says, is of an absolute reality, something limitless, unbounded, lacking in nothing, absolute perfection and the source of all being. But wait: if the idea of God is the idea of something that lacks nothing, then God must necessarily exist – because if he didn't, he would lack a great deal. So in fact, when you think about it, it's actually a contradiction to think that God doesn't exist: to think that God didn't exist would be as crazy as thinking that the thing which lacked nothing lacked something, or that the thing that was perfect was imperfect, or that the ultimate reality was unreal – which is absurd.[10]

The world

The reception of these two arguments in Descartes' own time, and their subsequent history, seem to suggest that Descartes was mistaken in thinking of them as conclusive proofs. You will have to make up your own mind as to their worth. What use does Descartes make of them in the rest of his fictional journey?

His first move is to use the existence of God to expand the circle of his certainty. Until now all we can be sure of are rational intuitions – not because they are somehow guaranteed, but just because, as with the cogito, when I think them I find it can make no sense to doubt them. But if there is an all-good God who created me, and who made me such that I couldn't doubt these things, then I have more than just these momentary certainties, and I can say in general that my mental faculties can be relied on. As long as I think things through rationally – as we would say, scientifically – and don't jump to conclusions on the basis of how things look to the uneducated, I can achieve a reliable knowledge of how things really are.[11]

And now the story is almost complete. The only thing that's left, is everything: I now know for certain that I exist, and can if I follow my God-given reason and ignore the delusions of my senses establish a true science of nature. But how do I know that there is actually a real physical world out there, corresponding to the ideas I have of it? The existence of God again supplies the answer: I can't help but think when I look around me that there are real material objects in the world. It seems to be something automatic, inescapable, a belief we all form quite *naturally*. And if God gave me my nature, then what I believe naturally must surely be true. The world is not at all the way it looks to be – it looks like independently existing objects possessing sensory qualities, but really it's a single continuum describable only in the language of mathematics – but it's really there.[12]

And that is the end of Descartes' fictional journey. Are you convinced? If not, where exactly does he go wrong? And where does the path really lead? Down the years the attempt to answer those questions has spawned a whole philosophical industry, expanding, expounding, analysing and contradicting every step he took. In Descartes' own eyes, he thinks the story has shown:

(1) That we can have a secure and lasting knowledge of how things are, whatever the sceptics might claim.

(2) But that secure knowledge is achievable only if we sweep away the traditional, observation-based learning of the universities and accept that the world is not as it appears to common sense. We must escape from the deceptive appearances of everyday life, and strive instead for a rational, scientific view of things.

(3) When we do that, we find that nature as known to the scientist, to the eye of reason, is not a rich and confusing world of objects and qualities, but a vast material continuum generated out of simple deterministic laws and correctly describable only in the language of mathematics.

(4) Human beings are in that world, but not of it; they are essentially separate, immaterial and enduring entities who operate in that natural world but who are also capable of rising above it to recapitulate in their own small way the understanding and willing of the divine intelligence.

The story Descartes tells is still compelling, even today. The picture it is designed to sell us has been massively influential, and still dominates many of the ways we think and speak and act. It came as a great revelation to many people, including Baruch Spinoza, a young man growing up in the Jewish enclave of Amsterdam, who was eighteen when Descartes died. He was completely convinced by the first three of these claims by Descartes, but came to believe that he was very seriously wrong about the last one.

Reading

The *Meditations* is nowadays Descartes' most frequently read text. Something of the same story is also told in the *Discourse on Method*, especially Part 4, and even more of it in Part 1 of the *Principles*.

Questions to ask

(1) If it is possible that the material world doesn't exist, but not possible that I don't exist, does that prove that my consciousness is not part of the material world, but a separate thing which *could* exist without it?

(2) God is by definition wholly perfect. A non-existent thing is less than wholly perfect. Therefore it is a contradiction to say that God doesn't exist, isn't it?

(3) Descartes thinks we can know the contents of our own minds independently of knowing anything else. Is that true? Could you know what the word 'pig' meant if you could never know whether it was correctly applied?

PART 2
Baruch Spinoza

Biography

Baruch Spinoza (or Spinosa, or Espinosa, or d'Espinosa; Latinised as Benedictus de Spinoza) was born in 1632, in the year when Rembrandt painted *The Anatomy Lesson of Dr Tulp*, and five years before Descartes published his *Discourse on Method*. He was ten when Louis XIV came to the throne of France, twelve when Descartes published the *Principles*, and twenty-seven when Pepys began his *Diary*. He died in 1677, the year in which William of Orange married Mary, daughter of the future James II. His main work is the *Ethics*, published in 1677, after his death.

He was born in the Spanish-speaking Jewish community of Amster-dam (founded some forty years before by refugees from the Inquisition in Spain and Portugal), but was excommunicated at the age of twenty-four for having unorthodox views and refusing to keep them to himself. He lived simply, on a small inheritance and on the money he made as a lens-maker, and became a well-known figure in intellectual and political circles in the Dutch Republic.[1] He never married, and died at the age of forty-six (perhaps in part as a result of inhaling glass dust as he worked) in The Hague, where he had lived since 1670.

His thought, like his life, can be seen as a combination of mediaeval Judaism and then-contemporary Cartesianism. He was a strong advocate of freedom of speech and of conscience, and an important reinterpreter of the Bible. Despite his fame, and his friendship with some of the leading figures of his time, he lived quietly. He published little (in part because some of what he did publish was publicly burned) and devoted himself to polishing and refining his master work, which during his lifetime was seen only by his immediate circle.

His work is a union of science and religion, dismissive of ignorance and superstition, insisting on freedom of thought and presenting the need for rational understanding as the only thing of any lasting political, psychological, moral or religious value. As a result he was reviled as a heretic Jew, and his name became a byword for wickedness and atheism, especially among people who had never read anything he wrote. He was rediscovered in the late eighteenth century, and (mis-)cast as a hero of the new Romantic tradition.

Chapter 6

God, or Nature?

Spinoza's pantheism

Overview

Descartes built a whole new world on the basis of his mathematical science of nature, explaining the hidden reality which lies behind the misleading appearances of our lives. He then explained the place of God and of human beings in that new world, and how they were related. Spinoza, some twenty years later, was convinced that Descartes was right about the reality of the world around us, but completely wrong about God and people. He therefore set about trying to create a system in which not only the natural world, but also human thought, and even God himself, are explicable by the same mathematical science that Descartes brought to bear on the material world. The result is startling, puzzling, strange; it seems as if he is muddling up natural science, human feelings and religion all in a single mysterious mishmash. The big question is: is that because he was confused, or because *we* are?

Reading Spinoza is very much harder than reading Descartes.

Descartes was a salesman, a populariser, devoted to getting his message across, and he formulated a variety of clever ways of presenting it. Spinoza by contrast worked for years to refine and develop the one perfect expression of his view of life, the universe, and everything into a single compressed treatise which he continually recast and reworked in order to get it exactly right. And the result is so dense and obscure as to be almost unreadable without a little help. His ideas too sometimes strike people as a little strange, and he has a certain reputation as a difficult philosopher. But if you can understand what Descartes is up to, you can understand Spinoza, because essentially what Spinoza does is to take the work of Descartes that we have just seen and to develop it to its logical – and ultimately very un-Cartesian – conclusion. We will look first at his central – indeed in a sense his only – idea, which he calls 'God or Nature', and try to understand what sense it makes both of nature, and of God (ch. 6). Then we will try to make some sense of his revolutionary science of the mind (ch. 7), and finally take a quick tour of the way he derives from that account of what we are a view as to how we ought to live (ch. 8).

Spinoza's pantheism

In trying to see the world as Spinoza saw it, we have to start with God. None of our philosophers, not even Bishop Berkeley (whose philosophy, as we shall see, was as theocentric as his profession) makes God so central to his view of the world and our place in it as does Spinoza. He was truly 'a man drunk on God',[2] a man for whom, quite literally, God was everything. And yet, amazingly, Spinoza is often hailed as the great prophet of the Enlightenment, a thinker whose rational, scientific approach to the study of the world (and especially of people), intolerance of superstition and ruthless insistence on taking a dispassionate, objective view of human life in general and of religion in particular make him in many ways the most modern of all the philosophers we will be looking at. The biggest question that his ideas raise for people of our time is which of those two stories we take as being the real Spinoza; or whether, just possibly, he could in some way combine the two.

The key to answering that question, and to the whole of Spinoza's philosophy, is an understanding of his pantheism. In some sense or other Spinoza holds that God is everything, and everything is God – or rather, more exactly, that everything that is is what he calls 'God or Nature'.[3] In this chapter I will first try to say what that means as an understanding of Nature in general, and then I will ask you to consider the difficult question of whether, given what we see here, Spinoza's God is really a notion of *God* at all. The next two chapters will look in more detail at what his account amounts to as a description of human beings, and of the lives we can lead.

God or Nature

As with a great deal of what Spinoza says, the simplest way to understand his account of God or Nature is to begin with Descartes, and to extend it way beyond anything Descartes ever considered.

We saw that on one reading of Descartes – what I called the God of science as opposed to God the clock-maker – God is not a separate creator of the world, but the underlying reality of it. To recap: a particular part of matter – such as what we call an object – depends on matter both for its existence and for its nature. That is to say, if matter did not exist, that particular object wouldn't; and to understand what the object is and how it behaves, we have to look outside the object itself, at the laws of matter in general. In a similar way, on this reading, according to Descartes the whole material world, like each individual human mind, depends on God both for its existence and for its nature – if God ceased to exist, matter and minds would cease to exist; and to understand them, we have to look beyond them, to the nature of God himself.

But nowhere does Descartes deny a more traditional theology. In addition to being that kind of substantial reality both of the material world and of every mind, the God of Descartes is also, it would appear, a personal God. Like each one of us, God is a mind. We, of course, are limited, imperfect, fallen, incomplete, finite minds, whereas God is infinite, perfect, complete and all-good. But we resemble him in that just as we can understand and will, so too can God. God freely chose to create the world and all that is in it; he understands it through his infinite wisdom, and he conserves it through his infinite power. And what he knows, he loves: he takes an interest in every one of us, and wants the best for us. He is pained, even angered, by our errors and our wanton disregard of what our God-given understanding can tell us, and he is pleased by our praise and our good deeds and our rational understanding. It is not obvious how those two aspects of the divine nature fit together. Descartes himself, ever careful to avoid legal or religious censure, tends to keep clear of such subjects and to leave them to the theologians. Spinoza, though, is simply, self-destructively, outspoken.[4] With characteristic ruthlessness and lack of sentimentality he simply eliminates the second half of this Cartesian picture. God or Nature, the one substance of the world, he says, has *no* human attributes, *no* personality of any kind. To think that it does, he says, is mere childish anthropomorphism – like people who think that when the wind blows the Wind God is puffing out his cheeks. If you want to use words like 'understanding' and 'will' to refer to God, he says, you must remember that to apply those words to God and to a human being is about as misleading as to use the word 'dog' both for the Dog Star up in the sky and for the annoying little creature that runs around your garden and bites the neighbours' children.[5] To anyone who feels that God *must* be a personal God who loves and cares for his creatures, Spinoza witheringly replies that no doubt in the same way if triangles could speak they would say that God must be eminently triangular, and a circle that he must be perfectly circular.[6]

We will look later at the question of whether this kind of depersonalised infinite substance can still meaningfully be called a God; for the moment, we need to see more of what the idea means as an account of nature.

Descartes, you will remember, held that God is the only true substance; but extended matter and individual human minds were as it were pseudo-substances, which depend only on God. Spinoza will have nothing to do with these pseudo-substances, and claims instead that Extension and Thought are only two of the infinite number of 'Attributes' of the one substance which is God or Nature, each of which is itself infinite.

And what exactly does that mean? We will look here at the

Attribute of Extension, in order to get a grasp of the kind of thing Spinoza's God is supposed to be. In the next chapter we will consider the Attribute of Thought.

The Attribute of Extension

Again, the best way to make sense of it is to start with Descartes. Spinoza's Attribute of Extension is everything that Descartes' extended substance is. As for Descartes, in reality there is no such thing as a vacuum, because an area with no substance is an area with no reality, i.e. it is unreal, or imaginary.[7] As for Descartes, in reality there is no such thing as an individual object, only areas of a material continuum differentiated by motion and governed by simple mechanical laws of the conservation and communication of that motion. As for Descartes, everything in that material world is explicable solely by those mechanistic, deterministic laws, and to understand any physical event correctly, as it is in reality – i.e. to see it with the eye of reason, to see it in its eternal aspect – is to see it not as a collision between separate objects in time, but as an expression of a timeless mathematically statable law.

With a few minor adjustments, then, we can say that everything in Descartes' extended pseudo substance is paralleled in Spinoza's Attribute of Extension. It is what lies outside it that makes the biggest difference between them. What is outside Descartes' material continuum?

In a sense, you could say that nothing is. Descartes' material world doesn't have edges, or sides, or boundaries, which some things could lie beyond. If something were outside the continuum, it would be a certain distance outside it: but to say there is distance is to say there is extension, and anywhere there is extension is necessarily *inside* the continuum of extended substance. At the same time, though, there are some important things which the extended world does not include – not in the sense that they are positioned somewhere outside it, but in the sense that they are not at all material, they have no dimensions, and therefore they have no spatial location at all. God, and created minds, are in that category; they are not in the extended world, not because they are somewhere outside it, but because they are not the sort of thing that can be *anywhere at all*.[8]

Spinoza will have none of that. His Attribute of Extension (like all his attributes) is 'infinite' – boundless, unrestricted, all-encompassing – there is nothing that is located outside it, but in addition there is nothing that is real and which is not in some way or other included in it. For Spinoza, in other words, dimensionality or materiality is a fundamental, irreducible characteristic of *everything* that exists, without exception. Reality just is extended; so if God and minds were not in some way or other included in extension, they would be unreal; but they are real, therefore '. . . the mind and the body, are one and the same individual',[9] and 'God is an extended thing'.[10]

The logic of that move is very simple; it is a working out of the by now familiar Cartesian position. But the consequences of it were unthinkable for a Cartesian, and were disastrous for Spinoza's chances of being accepted by his contemporaries, even in the enlightened Netherlands. If the mind is in some way or other material, then it can at least in theory be broken up, and so destroyed by natural means, and so is not immortal. And if God is material, then he too, it would seem, will be corruptible, divisible, destructible, imperfect.[11]

No wonder Spinoza's books were burned and he was derided as an atheist and a materialist for over a century after his death. He was known as the person who called all things God, and his ideas were standardly mocked. If all things are God, people said, then a cockroach is God, plagues are God, and murderers and deformities and the dirt under your fingernails are God. And what could be more irreligious, and indeed more absurd, than that?

But to make these objections is really to misunderstand Spinoza's God, and how it relates to the things around us. If we look more closely, we find that buried beneath the archaisms, obscurities and technicalities of Spinoza's system lies a picture of surprising power, beauty – and even perhaps relevance.

The main point to grasp is that Spinoza's pantheism does not take the form of regarding God under the Attribute of Extension as just the sum total of everything that exists, taken as consisting of just one great material object. For Spinoza, to say that God is everything does *not* mean simply that God is the sum total of everything that exists – in the way, for example, that your match-box collection is just the sum total of all the matchboxes you own. Spinoza's Attribute of Extension, after all, is a variant of Descartes' material substance, so for Spinoza as for Descartes there is a good sense in which really there is no such thing as an individual material object at all. Take a stone, for instance, as a good example of a material object, and follow it back through its history. There was a time when that stone was just a lot of grains of sand spread over a substantial area under the ground, until they came together, were squeezed and heated by the movements of earth and water into what we call a stone. At present that stone may be sitting in the wall of a house; each day the wind and the rain wear it slightly, but it changes very little. Eventually, though, the house will fall or be pulled down, and the stone might be reused, or might be broken up, and smashed into rubble which blows away in the breeze. The stone itself came into being and has now gone out of existence; the stuff of which it was composed, though, continues to exist, only now it is doing other things than making up a stone. The stone comes into being and passes away; it is a temporary manifestation of the nature of matter, a useful way of talking about one particular episode in the history of space.

Matter, on this view, is like a child's lump of clay, out of which he or she makes animals, soldiers, flowers, houses, sausages – each of them existing for a time, and then getting squashed back into the lump and turned into something else. If you think of every-thing that is ever made out of that lump of clay – the sum total of everything that ever exists in the world, throughout all of time – then we are starting to get closer to Spinoza's conception of God or Nature. What we have arrived at here is what Spinoza refers to as *Natura Naturata* – God or Nature as Effect – in the material world.

To stop at *Natura Naturata*, though, is not yet to understand what Spinoza means by the Attribute of Extension. Anyone who knew *only Natura Naturata*, although they would thereby know everything that had ever existed in the whole universe over all time, would not know God or Nature under the Attribute of Extension, because he or she would not know *why* those things had existed as and when they did. In order to know *why* the world is as it is, we need to know more than everything *that* it is, everything it ever has been and ever will be – we have to know what produced those things, the cause of their being as they are. But according to Spinoza (as perhaps for Descartes), to know that cause is not to know some *other* thing, some further being which produced all the phenomena of nature; it is to know *the world itself* better, by knowing the laws which govern its operations.

Here our analogy of the child's clay breaks down, because to understand the things made out of the clay we need to look beyond the clay itself to the child who plays with it; but that is not so with the things that are made out of matter. To understand the history of the stone we have just talked about we need to understand, not something else, which produces it, but just the nature of matter itself, as described by the laws of its operation. Thus in order to understand the stone we have to understand the laws of nature which produced it and which govern its behaviour, and in general we can say that in order to understand the products of nature we have to look beyond those individual things themselves, which are mere temporary *expressions* of Nature, to Nature itself, and the laws of its operation. We have to look beyond God or Nature as Effect, or *Natura Naturata*, to God or Nature as Cause, or *Natura Naturans*.

Does that story make any sense at all? At first sight it reads very oddly. But if we think about it we can I think see that it is in fact surprisingly close to an idea of nature that we ourselves still use.

The Ideal of a Unified Science

The idea we need to consider is what philosophers refer to as the Ideal of a Unified Science. We commonly think that knowledge progresses, that science advances and pushes back the frontiers of understanding, gradually discovering more and more about the world we inhabit. And it seems reasonable to think that the knowledge which science is revealing to us is not a piecemeal collection of bits and scraps of information, but an integrated system, a hierarchy of laws from the most general truths about the nature of matter down to the most particular laws about the behaviour of particular creatures in particular circumstances, so that to know everything would be not to have an endless list of disconnected truths, but to grasp a systematic body of interrelated facts.

Now, assume for the moment that we are right in that; and imagine what it would be like if the process of the development of that Unified Science could ever be completed. We would then know absolutely everything: we would know why the butterfly beat its wings in just that way at just that time, and we would be able to derive our understanding of its behaviour from our knowledge of the underlying laws about the nature of animals, and those in turn ultimately from more basic laws about the nature of matter itself. How different would such an understanding be from what Spinoza calls a knowledge of *Natura Naturans*, the World of Reality, under-lying and explaining all the phenomena of *Natura Naturata*, the World of Appearance?

The answer to that question, I think, will turn on what you take to be the relation between the facts of experience on the one hand, and the system of laws that explains them on the other. If you think that the facts of nature, the individual things and their behaviour, are the reality of the world, and that the laws which govern them are mere generalisations or abstractions – higher-level descriptions of what goes on – then your view of a unified science is not like Spinoza's. Spinoza, like Descartes, looks at things the other way round. For him the laws of nature – God or Nature as Cause – offer the only accurate description of the world as it really is; what we call the 'facts' of nature, the things of the world, the events we see around us, are only the *expression* or *manifestation in time* of that unchanging, eternal reality.

Pantheism or atheism – God, or Nature?

So far I have tried to show what kind of a thing it is that Spinoza calls God or Nature under the Attribute of Extension, and how it relates to the material world as we know it. In the next section I will try to make some sense of that same story as applied to the mental world, but before we come to that I want first to deal with a question that I have put off and which by now is probably crying out for an answer. If what Spinoza means by the infinite Attribute of Extension of the single infinite substance is what we would mean by the world itself as a completed physical science would describe it, then why on earth doesn't he just say so? Why, in particular, does he insist on referring to that underlying reality as God? Some people think his system is really a kind of disguised atheism: either he knowingly misrepresented his account by talking about God when in reality he was interested in a purely mechanistic, non-spiritual, naturalistic reality, or he was stumbling towards that kind of atheistic, naturalistic view of the world but had not quite succeeded in emancipating himself from the theistic language of his predecessors and contemporaries. The startling thing is, though, that when you look closely at this thing Spinoza talks about, it turns out to be very much closer to what we normally think of as God than at first meets the eye.

To see this, draw up a list of all the characteristics that a traditional Judaeo-Christian God possesses; when you've done that, I will work through my list and try to see how many of them can – sometimes it must be said with a bit of re-interpretation – be attributed to Spinoza's God or Nature. You can then decide for yourself whether you think it really is a God, or just a strange way of talking about Nature.

Here then is my list of the characteristics which are standardly applied to God in the kind of non-specialist, non-practising mainstream Christian tradition in which most of us at present live. God is:

- Infinite
- Eternal
- Perfect
- Necessarily existent
- Omnipresent
- Omnipotent
- Omniscient
- All-good
- All-loving
- Creator of the world
- Who inspired the prophets
- And chose the Jews
- And whom to love is perfect freedom.

GOD OR NATURE? SPINOZA'S PANTHEISM

Is there anything you think I've missed out?

Now, how many of those characteristics can plausibly be attributed to Spinoza's scientific reality?

- Well, God or Nature is certainly *infinite* in Spinoza's sense, because there is nothing that is real and that is not God. It has no boundaries, limitations or edges – it is all-encompassing, limitless, all-pervasive. It is the reality, of which everything we ever experience is the appearance.

- It is also *eternal:* not merely in the sense that it does not come to an end, but in the stronger sense that it *could* not come to an end. After all, how could reality end? Imagine that the universe as we know it could suddenly cease to exist – a kind of giant reversal of the Big Bang (the Big Pop?), in which everything in existence collapsed down in a massive implosion into a lump of inconceivably dense matter no larger than a pea. And imagine (if you can) that the process then continued, so that even that last remaining thing were squeezed out of existence, leaving a completely empty world. Would that mean that reality had ceased to exist, that Spinoza's God or Nature was no more?

No. Because if it happened, then it would be true that it had happened (even though there would of course be no-one around to *realise* that it was true); and if there is truth, there is a way things are, and there is an explanation of why they are that way. The situation we have imagined is one in which the underlying laws of nature produce an empty world in place of the rich and complex universe they produce at present – but it is not one in which there is no reality. Reality, remember, is not the sequence of events *in* time, but the timeless laws which *explain* those events.

- *Perfection* is a slippery notion, not easy to pin down. Sometimes we use it to mean *morally* perfect, in which case it means the same as all-good, which we will consider below. Interestingly, the Latin word that is translated as perfect and is the ancestor of our word is in fact derived from the verb *facere*, to make, and means something more like finished, completed, actualised, or realised. Spinoza actually uses the words 'reality' and 'perfection' interchangeably, and in

71

that sense God or Nature, as the one reality, is obviously completely perfect.[12]

- God or Nature also *exists necessarily*. As we saw above, it is impossible to imagine a situation in which there is no reality, or in which God or Nature does not exist.[13]

- *Omnipresence* is pretty easy to deal with: there is nowhere that reality is not. *Omnipotence* is a little harder. Nature or reality is omnipotent at least in the sense that everything that happens is something that Nature does, or Nature does all things.[14] It is also omnipotent in the sense that it does everything that *can* be done. Reality, Nature, is the basic facts about the world; those basic facts are what determine what is and is not possible – if it is not possible in Reality, then it is not really possible. So Nature does everything that can be done – i.e. it is omnipotent.

- *Omniscience* is complicated, because it is tied in with what we understand by knowledge, which takes us into material covered in the next chapter. For the moment we can only say that the Attribute of Thought contains the idea of everything that exists in the Attribute of Extension, and so in that sense God is omniscient.

- God or Nature is also the *cause of the world*, in the sense that everything that makes up what we know as the world, everything we see around us, is a part of *Natura Naturata*, i.e. is a consequence or expression of the underlying facts of nature as a completed science would know them – of *Natura Naturans*.

- God or Nature also *inspired the prophets* and *chose the Jews*, according to Spinoza. The prophets, he claims, were in fact philosophers, who understood the way things really are, or glimpsed the true character of God or Nature, and the consequences of that for mankind. It was that knowledge which led them to say and write what they did – although of course since they were attempting to teach practical lessons to uneducated people they were forced to speak in simple, childish language, as if – absurdly – God were something like a very wise and powerful king.

- And to know God or Nature is *perfect freedom*, in the sense that (as we will see later) to know reality, to know the truth about the world and your own place in it, and thereby to understand the true causes of your own decisions, provides you with a kind of control over your own actions which is the only freedom of which human beings are capable.

We will see in what follows something of what this conception means as a view of the world and of our place in it; for the moment I want only to point out that all the characteristics I have just listed are ones which Spinoza can with at least some plausibility claim to be possessed by his God or Nature – and indeed by nothing else. All that is missing from the list I gave above are the human, or at least pseudo-human, anthropomorphic, qualities of being all-good and all-loving. Spinoza states quite plainly that we should love God – but he also says that we are crazy if we expect God to love us in return.[15] Only people, or things that are similar to people, can love; and Spinoza is insistent that God is not at all like a person, any more (as we saw) than it is like a triangle.

So where does that leave you? Is it a God, or isn't it? The question is a big one, because if you are at all persuaded that it is not altogether unreasonable to call this one substance which a unified science would reveal by the name God, then it seems we will have to conclude that Spinoza has achieved the Holy Grail of many philosophers and has proved the existence of God. (And in doing so he has unified science and religion.) If you think he hasn't done those things, it will presumably be because for you those human characteristics that our traditional God has are essential to any conception of a God. Is that because you have a clear understanding of the concept of God? Or is it only because, like the Children of Israel of whom Spinoza speaks, you find it hard to think in abstractions, and far easier to deal with the imaginative language of the prophets, and so tend – absurdly – to think of God as a kindly old man in the sky?

Reading

Reading Spinoza is a painful process, because his single great work, the *Ethics*, is presented in axiomatic form. Each section begins with a set of definitions and foundational axioms, and he proceeds to present all his philosophy as a set of propositions, each remorselessly deduced from those and from the earlier propositions (with a few additions along the way). The intention is to make his work dispassionate, objective, rational and self-explanatory; its effect is to make it almost unreadable. Take your time, don't worry too much at first about the proofs, but concentrate on the propositions, notes and appendices. The account of God and God's relation to nature is contained primarily in Book 1. The *Theologico-Political Treatise* – fortunately written non-axiomatically – helps make some sense of it.

Questions to ask

(1) Is Spinoza's God God?

(2) Is there any good reason to believe in the possibility of a unified science?

(3) Are the laws of nature merely descriptions of how objects as a matter of fact behave? Or do they specify how objects *must* behave? If the latter, where does that necessity derive from? If the former, is it just a coincidence that they all behave the same way?

Chapter 7

The attribute of thought

In the last chapter I was trying to show you what Spinoza's conception of God or Nature amounts to as an account of the natural, physical world. I also tried to ask whether it could make any sense to regard such a thing as God. But regardless of whether or not you are convinced of the Godliness of Nature, we need now to extend the picture a little and to see what it amounts to as an explanation of the mind. Again, the way to approach it is as an extension of the ideas of Descartes.

Descartes on the mind

For Descartes, as we saw, among created things there exist, in addition to the material continuum, an indefinite number of individual human minds. (And also non-human minds, such as those of angels.) Those minds stand to their thoughts in the same relation as the material continuum stands to individual material objects: the thoughts are modes or modifications of the minds, and without the minds can neither be nor be conceived. Diagrammatically, you can represent the story like this:

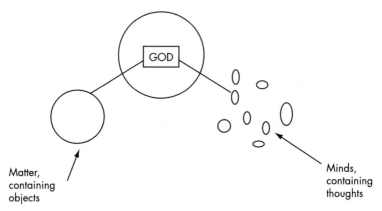

Matter, containing objects

Minds, containing thoughts

Figure 7.1 Descartes' 'Dualism'

I haven't drawn boundaries around the objects or the thoughts, because those boundaries are only conventional – there is no one correct answer to the question of where one object or thought ends and another begins. The God–Matter and God–Minds relation is very hard to represent. On the one hand, in so far as God is for Descartes the only true substance, it should be a relation of containment like that between matter and objects or between minds and thoughts. But on the other hand, in so far as finite minds and matter are independent productions of the divine nature, they need to be separate. Think of the arrows linking God to matter and minds as lines of emanation, or flowing forth, like the light flowing out of a lamp.

Looking at that picture from Spinoza's point of view, the first thing we see is how asymmetrical it is – one substance on the left-hand side, and an indefinite number on the right. That doesn't just mean that it's ugly – it reveals what for Spinoza is the big weakness of the Cartesian philosophy, which is that it provides no possibility of a science of human beings.

Descartes, for all his radicalism and insistence on a rational explanation of natural phenomena, made a science of the mind impossible. Why? Well, consider first matter or extension as a whole. Any individual material thing can and must be explained by seeing it as a local manifestation of the nature of matter itself, through the laws of materiality. But what about matter itself? How is that to be explained? The answer is that it can't be explained naturalistically, scientifically, or as the appearance of an underlying reality – it can only be explained as something which God freely chose to produce, for reasons to do with God's nature and intentions. Beyond that, there is and can be no explanation of matter and mechanism themselves – we just have to accept that they are as they are, and see how they serve to explain everything else in the non-human world.

For a mechanist like Descartes, that is not much of a limitation on our understanding of nature. But look now at the right-hand side of the diagram. How can we explain the human mind? The answer again is that necessarily we can't. Minds flow from God in the same way as matter does – they are individual productions of his, which he saw it as good to create. The explanation of your mind is simply that – that God chose to create it, and while we can talk further about God's purposes and nature, there is nothing more to be said in the way of explaining what the mind is. Within the mind, it is true, there is the possibility of explanation, in that the thoughts I have can in theory be traced back to the nature of my mind in a way which is analogous to the way in which indi- vidual objects can be explained through their derivation from the nature of extended material substance. In practice, though, Descartes does little in this direction. While he does write a trea- tise on the *Passions of the Soul*, it is as much a work of physiology as of psychology, and he nowhere makes any sustained effort to analyse mental phenomena and re-describe them in terms of an underlying reality as he does in the material sphere. The universal and defining characteristic of the mind (its 'principal attribute') is thought,[1] which can be divided into willing and understanding. And what is, for example, willing? Well, it is what you do when you choose. And understanding? What you do when you understand. Whereas in the material realm even the most basic concepts like solidity are explained away as the mere appearance of a world which is correctly describable only in mathematical terms, the most basic features of the mental world turn out to be – well, just what they seem to be.

For Spinoza, that position is quite intolerable, indeed absurd. If the mind is real, it must be part of the one reality that science reveals. There must therefore be a way of presenting a naturalistic, scientific explanation of minds just as there is of bodies – the human mind, remarkable though it is, different from the minds of animals though it may be, must be a part of nature unless it is purely illusory. With typical, ruthless, brutal logic, therefore, he sets about constructing a view of the mind exactly parallel to that of body.

Spinoza's panpsychism: the mind as part of nature

The details of his account therefore directly match those of his picture of extension. Thought, he tells us, like Extension, is an infinite attribute of the one substance. For every individual object in the Attribute of Extension – every physical object, that is – there is also a corresponding 'object' – an 'idea', or mode of thought – in the Attribute of Thought. There is something called an Immediate Infinite Mode of thought, which is Understanding, and there is also a Mediate Infinite Mode, the 'Infinite Idea of God'. There are, he says, no causal relations between objects of different attributes (no thought is ever caused by anything material, or vice versa), and in fact each object in the one attribute is identical with its equivalent in the other. What does all that mean?

I have set out the technicalities in Box 7.1. We will look in the next chapter at what it means in terms of the lives we can and should lead – the psychological, moral and political system which Spinoza derives from his metaphysical structure. For the moment, we need to look more closely at that metaphysical structure itself to try to see how he seeks to make sense of the nature of mind, and its relation to matter, and to God or Nature. The way to do this is through taking seriously the parallelism between mind and matter, the Attribute of Thought and the Attribute of Extension: if we can see the form of explanation that is being offered in the one field, we can grasp at least the outline of what Spinoza is trying to do in the other.

In giving his account of Extension, what Spinoza, following

Box 7.1

Substance, attribute and mode in Spinoza

Separating fact and interpretation in Spinoza is more than usually difficult. This box aims to lay out what I think are the agreed facts underlying the interpretation I have given. The bits in Roman type are things I think most commentators would agree on; the italic bits are how I suggest you try to make sense of it.

There is one substance, which is infinite and eternal: *The universe as we know it is the appearance of a single Reality, the result of a single set of timeless laws.*	GOD
It has an infinite number of ATTRIBUTES, of which we know only two: *Those fundamental laws generate phenomena which we can grasp in either of two ways. Any other way of understanding which any other creature might possess would not be a grasp of a different reality, but another way of grasping this one.*	EXTENSION and THOUGHT
Each attribute is coextensive with God, and therefore with every other attribute – i.e. the whole of God is expressed in every attribute. *Extension and thought (and all the other attributes there might be) are irreducible features of everything that is. Neither is reducible to, or more fundamental than, the other.*	
Each attribute has an IMMEDIATE INFINITE MODE:	Motion/Rest Understanding

All physical phenomena can be explained through laws of motion; all mental phenomena through laws of thought.		
– and a MEDIATE INFINITE MODE:		
Those laws generate all physical and mental phenomena – the whole history of the universe in time, or Nature as Effect.	The Face of the Whole Universe	The Infinite Idea of God
– and an uncountable number of FINITE MODES, among which are:	My Body and	My Mind
For each finite mode in one attribute there is a finite mode in every other attribute, with which it is identical. *So my mind is my body, and vice versa; every body has its mind, and every mind has its body.*	Mode Identity	
So everything that exists in one attribute is exactly mirrored in every other – but nothing in one attribute causes anything in any other. *Mental phenomena have to be explained through mental laws; physical ones through physical laws.*	The Parallelism of the Attributes	

Descartes, has done in effect is to transform the then common-sense notion of a physical object. For their Aristotelian predecessors, with their sophisticated, refined, common-sense science based on sensory categories, the notion of 'body' or material substance was equivalent to that of a solid object – like a stone, for example. It made sense, therefore, for them to extend that notion of a material body to a fluid body, such as a quantity of water, for example, or even a cloud. But it was a major development to go beyond that and to say, as many in the seventeenth century were doing, that the air, too, was material – a kind of layer of very thin, very fluid liquid which sits on top of the earth and through which the birds swim around as the fish swim in the sea. What Descartes, Spinoza and others did was to stretch that notion of matter to the ultimate degree. Forget about such properties as colour, hardness or softness, solidity and weight, which are properties which things like stones, and even bowls of water, possess. Those, the new philosophers are saying, are not properties which belong to matter *as such*, but only to *certain kinds* of matter, or more accurately to matter when it is *arranged* in certain ways. The *only* properties which belong to matter as such are the mathematical properties of extension (dimensionality) and movement. So although it may seem to common sense that nothing could be more unlike a lump of rock than is the light of the sun, or the spaces between the planets, nevertheless we have to learn that to the eye of reason they are really the same thing, differentiated only by motions in the continuum. In this way the concept of material substance, or solid body, has been transformed into the substance or Attribute of Extension, or dimensionality. Matter, body, or corporeality, it turns out, is a property possessed by everything that is spatial; the only difference between what we used to call solid objects and other material things is that the matter in them is arranged differently.

All of that should be familiar from the earlier sections. The significance of it here is that Spinoza's Attribute of Thought represents an attempt at the same kind of transformation of the notion of mind, directly parallel to his and Descartes' transformation of the notion of material substance into Extension. Descartes and Spinoza both wanted in effect to say that the notion of a solid object was a sense-based concept which functions in the world of appearance but which has no application in the world of Reality. Spinoza, unlike Descartes, wanted to say something exactly analogous about the notion of Mind. To us now the suggestion that a piece of stone is no more material than is air or light – a crazy-sounding suggestion which Descartes struggled long and hard to defend – seems perfectly obvious, but Spinoza's corresponding move in the area of thought still seems intuitively far less plausible. The challenge that Spinoza presents, therefore, is to make us ask whether that implausibility is due to the fact that the move simply does not work in this case, or whether it is just that we, like many of his contemporaries in relation to matter, cannot get our heads round such a radical departure from what we have grown up with.

Spinoza's basic move, then, is to say that just as it is a mistake to think that there is no matter where there is nothing obviously solid, so it is an exactly analogous mistake to think that there is no mind where there is nothing obviously thinking. To the ignorant person, to the person who doesn't try to understand natural phenomena but is content merely to gaze at them like a fool,[2] a person has a mind, whereas a brick is completely mindless and inert – just as a brick is solid while a ray of sunlight is not. To the man of reason, though, according to Spinoza, just as the immateriality and insubstantiality of the light is merely apparent, so is the mindlessness and thoughtlessness of the brick. Thought, mind-stuff, is not something that occurs inexplicably only in the minds of people, any more than materiality is something that occurs inexplicably only in solid objects like bricks; thought is a universal and an irreducible feature of the world. The difference between a human being and a brick is not that one has mind and the other lacks it, but that the mind-stuff in the human being is arranged in such a way as to be obvious to the casual observer, while that in the brick is not – just like the difference between the brick and the air in an 'empty' room.

Spinoza, in other words, is a *panpsychist*: he holds that every-thing that is, is mental, or has mentality.[3] The idea strikes us as crazy – that bricks should have minds makes it sound as if he were espousing some kind of primitive animism or childish anthropo-morphism – as if the brick might get up and dance if it only felt like it. The intention behind it, though, is quite the opposite: Spinoza is saying that the human mind is not something that is magically breathed into a human being by God at conception, as Descartes thought, but is a natural phenomenon like any other, and as such is to be explained in the same way as anything else in nature. And is it really any more crazy to say that bricks have rudimentary mental properties than it is to say that sunbeams are solid? In the next chapter I will examine whether this panpsychist metaphysic can make any sense of life as we experience it; now I will try to finish the basic picture.

Mind, like matter, is an irreducible property of everything that is real. Just as in the physical world (or, more accurately, the world understood physically) if you had a complete knowledge of everything that had ever been thought, you would have a complete knowledge of Nature. But that knowledge would be only a knowledge of *Natura Naturata*, of everything that Nature does; to understand it we would have to understand the underlying laws of thought which are responsible for that history – to understand *Natura Naturans*. The two systems, then, Extension and Thought, are exactly parallel. And so they must be, because they are in fact not two systems, but one. There is only one world, one Nature, but it is expressed in different ways – both as matter and as mind.[4]

There are any number of questions to be asked as to how if at all this story can be filled out satisfactorily. All we can ask here is whether something along these lines might be made to make sense of what we know about what it is like to be a human being. We will ask that in the next chapter.

Reading

Spinoza's metaphysics of the mind is given in Book 2 of the *Ethics*. Note particularly the material inserted between propositions 13 and 14, where he sketches out the broadly Cartesian physical system to which his mental world is parallel.

Questions to ask

(1) Can a dualist account of human beings ever permit a science of mind?

(2) Could it ever make sense to say that a mind can be generated from a purely material system? Or should we say that any

system from which a mind can be generated must be one which has mental, or protomental, characteristics?

(3) Is it conceivable that there should be another reality, parallel to ours but incompatible with it? Or must we say that reality by definition is unitary, because everything that isn't part of it must be unreal?

Chapter 8

Spinoza's ethics
Metaphysics and the life of man

Ethics and the *Ethics*: metaphysics and the life of man

We have seen that, compared to Spinoza at least, Descartes was very conservative in his metaphysics of mind. He was conservative in other ways, too. His whole effort was to introduce his new framework for a science of nature without incurring political, moral or religious censure, and as a result he says very little about religion, morality or politics – and what he does say is traditional, uncontroversial stuff. Spinoza, again, is much more radical. He wrote a *Political Treatise*, and a *Theologico-Political Treatise*. In addition, his master work, the *Ethics*, is an astonishing feat of miniaturisation which, in a little over 200 densely packed and closely argued pages, presents a moral and political theory based on a naturalistic account of human nature which is itself grounded in a complete metaphysical and epistemological system. Book 1, *God*, lays out the basics of metaphysics, the structure of reality as a whole. Book 2, *The Nature and Origin of the Mind*, then explains the place of man within that metaphysical framework, by setting out the fundamentals of Spinoza's philosophy of mind and episte-mology. In Book 3, *The Origin and Nature of the Emotions*, he builds on that picture to present a detailed theory of psychology, and then in Books 4 and 5, *Human Bondage, or the Power of the Emotions*, and *Human Freedom*, we have an extensive working out of what this new, scientifically based understanding of human beings amounts to in terms of the good life for man, both at the individual and at the social level. It is a truly amazing piece of work: astonishing in its scope and completeness, almost beautiful in the austere, remorseless way it works through the exposition of his passionate vision, and magnificently, naively courageous in the simple, honest radicalism of his views. A pity then that it is such hard going as to be almost unreadable.

I will try to put over here something of that vision as he derives it from the framework we have seen, first as an account of the life of the individual, then in its social aspect.

The mind and consciousness

The first conclusion we can derive from the metaphysical structure we have seen is that for Spinoza there is more to mind than con-sciousness. Descartes' thinking substance is a conscious mind, fully aware of itself and of all its contents. Spinoza's area of the mental continuum is much more complex.

For every part of my body there is its corresponding idea in my mind: my mind is the aggregate of all the thoughts that make it up, just as my body is the aggregate of all its parts, and every part of my body has its corresponding idea in my mind. Thus my mind is the idea of my body, and there is in my mind an idea of my big toe, of each hair on my head, and so on. And every event that occurs in my body also occurs in my mind. The digestive pro-cesses in my stomach, for example, the beating of my heart or the browning of my skin by the sun – all of them have their corre-sponding ideas in my mind, or my mind 'knows' them. Obviously, though, I am not *conscious* of all these things. Some of them I am conscious of – being poked in the eye with a stick, for example; others I can *become* conscious of – such as the feeling of my clothes against my skin – but others I have never been and never will be conscious of – the growing of my fingernails. Yet all of these thoughts, according to Spinoza, are in my mind, and they all play their part in making me what I am, just as each physical part of my body, however insignificant, plays a part in making up my body as a whole. The contents of my conscious mind, the ideas I am actually aware of, are therefore only a small proportion of the total number of ideas in my mind, and the fact that all the other ideas that exist in my mind are not obvious is no reason for anyone who thinks carefully about these things to deny that they exist, any more than the fact that many parts of my body are (thankfully) not visible to the casual observer is a reason to deny that *they* exist.

I am not claiming here that Spinoza has invented the Freudian unconscious, but he certainly has invented a theory of the mind which represents large parts of that mind as being below the level of consciousness – exactly as both he and Descartes have presented theories of matter according to which the great majority of material things are neither visible nor touchable. One obvious advantage of this kind of story of consciousness is the way it permits a better account of the minds of non-human animals. For Descartes, you will remember, mentality was an all or nothing affair: either you are an immaterial, thinking substance endowed with intellect and will, or you are a completely inert, mindless robot. Spinoza's universal Attribute of Thought allows for a much more nuanced picture. There are no purely immaterial thinking substances such as Cartesian minds are supposed to be, because as we have seen, for every idea in the Attribute of Thought there is an object in the Attribute of Extension. For exactly the same reason, there are no completely unthinking objects, either. This means that we have a kind of spectrum of cases of different kinds of mind. At one end of the range of cases we encounter human beings, with their complex interrelated systems of thoughts; at the other extreme are the things we think of as completely mindless, such as grains of sand. In between are all the intermediate levels of consciousness, from the apes and dolphins down through dogs and cats to the rudimentary sensory system of the sea slug, and on down to bacteria, and finally down to the 'inert' sand and stones. All of them are mental, some of them are conscious, and there is no clear dividing line between the two.

Psycho-physical parallelism?

This expanded notion of mind also helps to make sense of Spinoza's otherwise puzzling account of action. In everyday life we regularly explain the physical by the mental, and vice versa: we say the physical event of my punching my neighbour in the eye was caused by the mental event of my feeling angry about all the noise he was making, or we explain the mental event of my feeling a pain in the buttock by the physical event of my sitting on a dried sea anemone. This kind of intersubstantial causation – the apparent interaction between mental and material substances – was a big problem for the Cartesians: how can the rule-governed, deterministic physical continuum affect or be affected by something which is immaterial, and so by definition cannot operate mechanically?[1]

Nowadays people tend to regard this problem as outdated and quaint. People tend to assume that in some way or other the mind is reducible to some kind of physical process in the brain – that just as atomic explosions, the growth of plants and the progress of diseases can be traced back ultimately to the law-governed behaviour of material particles (as Descartes and Spinoza would have maintained), so too the love-life of an opera singer or the infinite compassion of a saint can ultimately be traced back to some underlying physical process. In practice this kind of Materialism is surprisingly difficult to explain or to defend, but it is one of the unexamined assumptions that currently structure our lives and thought. In the seventeenth century it was one contender among many in the struggle to reconceptualise the place of human beings in the world after the failure of the Aristotelian orthodoxy.

Spinoza, as we have seen, denies materialism, just as he denies Descartes' dualism, and he mocks his attempt to account for mind/body interaction.[2] Rather mysteriously, he insists instead on the Parallelism of the Attributes: he says that all mental events must be explained through other mental events, and all physical events through other physical events – but also that the two systems, as we have seen, are in reality identical.[3]

This theory of 'psycho-physical parallelism' seems deeply weird; but I think we can make some sense of it by taking account of the extended notion of Mind that Spinoza has adopted. If I lash out at someone in anger, the motion of my arm has to be explained, he is saying, not directly by reference to my feeling of anger, but through the physiology of my arm and hand, and the brain and neural processes that underlie them. In that way we can describe and explain the whole event, from start to finish, just as the materialists would claim. The fact is, though, that over and above all those physical interactions, there was surely something else going on – there was how it *felt* to do those things: the build up of anger, the release of it through violent action, perhaps feelings of shame and remorse when it was over – and none of these things seems to be captured by the purely physical story we have just told. In order to do that, we surely need some kind of (as we would say) *psychological* theory: we need to understand how anger is related to fear, to unacknowledged desires, to half- – or even completely – forgotten memories, to pride and to love; and we need to know what shame and remorse are, how they are related to anger, and to sorrow, to hope and to loss. Spinoza's story is that this second kind of explanation is just as necessary as the first: that human subject-ivity cannot simply be explained away by the scientific viewpoint, but must be incorporated into it. At the same time, though, that psychological account does not refer to some other thing, over and above the physical organism as described by the materialist: the emotional, thinking being is one and the same as the physical mechanism, its complex systems and subsystems of awareness are identical with, but not reducible to, the material body.

Spinozan psychology

I don't know how much sense that story makes at first sight. (Or even later?) What it is meant to be is a metaphysical framework for a scientific account of people which does justice to subjectivity, to what it is like to be alive. The materialism of Spinoza's con-temporary Thomas Hobbes – like modern-day materialism – explains away our subjectivity as being not fundamental, not necessary to a complete understanding of how the world really is; Descartes' dualism avoids that drawback at the cost of making the mind necessarily magical, supernatural, inexplicable; Spinoza's parallelism, strange though it seems at first sight, is an attempt to improve on both.

But Spinoza doesn't stop at the level of the metaphysical frame-work: just as Descartes' mechanism had laid out the basic structure for a complete science of matter, so Spinoza in Part 3 of the *Ethics* sketches out the outline of a complete science of mind. I can't go into much detail here, but the basic outline of the system is not complicated. The central idea is that of effort, striving, or wanting-to-be: in Latin *conatus*.[4] This at first strange-seeming concept is what you might think of as a thing's nature, or essence – what makes it what it is. Take a stone, for example. It may sound strange to think of a stone as striving, or exerting an effort; but a stone does have a nature, or an essence, which is responsible for its being what it is. Left to itself, of course, a stone is pretty dull: it doesn't melt, or sing, or turn into a flower – it just sits there in (stony) silence, being hard, grey, inert, stable, unmoving. Why does it do those things and not others? Because of the sort of thing it is, because of its nature; because the laws of nature determine that if you are a stone, that is what you do. The stone, then, exerts an effort, or exhibits a tendency, or has a conatus, to go on being a stone. Now compare that stone with a seed. A seed is a massively more complex system of parts, put together in such a way that, unlike the stone, if it is left to itself, it changes. The essence, or nature, or conatus of the seed is to grow, to develop, in a certain way – to become a tree, a flower, or whatever. Given appropriate conditions, that is what it will do, because that is what it is. In just the same way, a human being also has a conatus, a nature, which makes it what it is. We have natural tendencies, deriving from the basic laws of nature, which lead us to behave in certain ways and not in others. Some of these tendencies – some parts of our conatus – are common to our whole species; some are particular to us.

Does that make any sense at all? A conatus is a nature, a character, a tendency to develop in certain directions rather than others; everything has one, from the smallest speck of sand to the universe as a whole; the only difference is that some are more interesting than others.

That notion becomes the centrepiece of Spinoza's psychology, because it accounts for the most basic of all emotions, which is Desire. Desire is simply the direction in which a conatus leads, the expression of a nature. Thus the stone 'desires' to sit around and be a stone, the seed 'desires' to grow and bear fruit, and the person desires – all kinds of things: football, flowers, poetry, coat hangers . . . and all the other things that people can wish for. Some of these desires we are conscious of, some not; some are natural, basic, inherent – sex, food, warmth, for example – some derivative, acquired, learned – designer trainers, compound interest, longer eyelashes. All of them have the same source: the nature of the person, striving to be itself.

When we are conscious of a desire, and conscious of achieving it, we feel good; when we are aware of a desire which is thwarted, we feel bad; thus Spinoza, in his remorseless, naturalistic way, defines the other two primary emotions of pleasure and pain.[5] And on the basis of those three primary emotions, he proceeds to explain all the other emotions as built up from them in various ways.

Life, death and the individual

Some people object to Spinoza's account of the mind on the grounds that he denies our essential individuality. As we have seen, whereas for Descartes the mind was an indivisible, indissoluble unity, for Spinoza its status is comparable to that of a Cartesian material object: it is a temporary local concentration of thought, conventionally distinguished from other areas of the mental continuum. Does that work as an account of what we are?

First, let's be clear exactly what is being said. Spinoza is not claiming there is really no such thing as me or you, any more than Descartes is claiming there is no such thing as Mont Blanc. The fact that we cannot say without arbitrariness where Mont Blanc ends and its neighbours begin doesn't mean it isn't there, or isn't in our modern sense a real thing (though it *does* mean that in the Cartesian or Spinozan sense it isn't a Real Substance). It is an identifiable, long-lasting part of the world; but if we want to understand it we have to look beyond it, to the laws of matter which compose it and through which it is explained. That is precisely the status which Spinoza accords to you. Is that plausible? It means:

BARUCH SPINOZA

(1) You are a real person whom we can pick out and refer to and distinguish from other people; but the boundaries between you and other things are not perfectly sharp, but are conventional. (Remember that when we talk about 'you' here we are talking about more than just your conscious mind; your mind is the net result of the 'ideas' of every little part of your body, and just as it is not always clear whether a particular flake of skin is or is not currently part of your body, so it is not clear whether the idea of such a thing is part of your mind.)[6]

(2) Perhaps more surprisingly, you are nothing over and above the sum total of your thoughts. Just as Mont Blanc is not something over and above all the parts that make it up, so your mind is not a Cartesian *thing* which *has* thoughts, but is only the integrated totality of the thoughts that make you up; your thoughts are *in* your mind not as the tea is in the cup, but as a player is in a team, or a cog is in a machine.

(3) Your identity over time is therefore also not straightforward: there is no continuing element or container that unites your thoughts and makes them all the thoughts of one and the same person; we say you are the same person now as you were ten years ago because of the continuities and commonalities and causal relations within the developing network of ideas that make up you – rather in the way we say this is the same football club as the one which was founded 100 years ago, even though the name has changed, the people have all changed, it is in a different part of the city and it started out playing rugby.

(4) And since there is nothing more to you than that gradually developing system of thoughts, so when you die the integration of that system is broken up, all your ideas slip back below the threshold of consciousness, the parts of your body and their individual ideas separate out, and – although the individual ideas which made up all the thoughts you ever had don't cease to exist, any more than the atoms which made up your body cease to exist – you as an identifiable individual agent go out of existence. You were formed out of pre-existing ideas; you came to consciousness and lived your life, and for a while you were a force to be reckoned with, an identifiable individual; then you broke up and dissipated – like an eddy in a stream, or a storm in a teacup.

92

Ethics and the good life for people

I hope you are beginning to get some feel for the mixture of passion and austerity that characterises Spinoza's view of the world. It is a relentless insistence on the power of science and of rational understanding, but with none of the dehumanising elements that we have come to associate with that kind of approach. We see it again most clearly in the two faces of his moral theory.

For Descartes one of the defining characteristics of the human soul was its free will: whereas animals merely obey the promptings of their mechanical natures, human beings, in imitation of the divine nature, can make decisions. To Spinoza this idea is simply nonsensical. What it means in effect is that human action is necessarily incomprehensible: whereas the behaviour of a dog can be explained through an understanding of its mechanical construction, and so subsumed under general laws and seen as part of a greater whole, the behaviour of an individual person cannot. The categories of experience cannot be transcended when dealing with the human mind as they can and must be when producing a scientific account of the body, and so the only possible explanation for why I did what I did was that I chose to do so: my nature, my personality, my will must necessarily be the stopping point for all such explanations.

Spinoza's first move – in his usual tactless, uncompromising style – is absolutely to deny any such freedom.[7] Human beings are parts of nature, and must be understood as such – i.e. they must be understood in the only way that anything can be understood, which is by seeing it as an inevitable consequence of the underlying facts of nature. To say that I did it because it was my will, or my choice, is as naive and unscientific as saying that opium puts you to sleep because it has a dormitive virtue (see Box 15.1): all it does is to restate the problem. What we need to know is *why* I chose as I did: what are the underlying facts about the sort of creature I am that made that choice in those circumstances as inevitable as the yapping of the dog when the doorbell rings, or the breaking of the window when the stone hits it?

Views of this kind, of course, tend to be unpopular – then as now. A classic argument which is always used in opposition to any determinism of this kind is that it leaves no room for morality: if

my actions are the inevitable result of my nature and circumstances, people say, then it can make no more sense to say that
I shouldn't steal my neighbour's bicycle helmet than it does to
say that lions really ought not to eat wildebeest, or that rain is
wrong to fall on cricket matches (which it is). If all my actions
can be understood naturalistically as being in some way or other
expressions of my conatus, it is argued, then it makes no more
sense to praise the surgeon for saving the patient's life than it does
to praise the knife she uses to save it with; and instead of blaming
the hooligan for trampling on the flower bed, we could just as
meaningfully blame his boots. Determinism and morality, people
say, just do not mix.

Spinoza is aware of this problem, and responds to it with his
customary ruthlessness. Faced with an incompatibility between a
concern for morality and a scientific understanding of human
beings, he simply abandons any concern with morality (but see
below). Morality, he says, is a mistake, or a political device. No-one
ever does anything because it is good, or avoids doing it because it
is wrong; on the contrary, we call something good because we want
to do it, and bad because we want to avoid it.[8]

This theory is a natural development of the psychology we saw
earlier. A desire is an expression of a thing's nature, or conatus;
the dog wants to bark, the stone to be stony, the merchant banker
to make money. The only difference between these cases is that
the banker is conscious of her desire, can think about it in the
abstract, and name it as something desirable, something good. She
can even, if she is a philosopher, invent a theory as to why it is
good for her to make money, and can use that theory to persuade
other people to agree with her, and to persuade them to give her
honours (and more money). Theft, by contrast, she will see as a
threat to her position; she will label it a bad thing, as wrong, and
she will seek to punish those who engage in it – just as the dog sees
the postman's hand in the letter box as an invasion of its territory,
and tries to bite it if it can.[9]

This attempt by Spinoza to give a purely scientific, neutral
account of moral judgements has never been very popular. It
goes along with his demystified account of religion as merely
the superstitious misinterpretation of metaphysical and social
teachings, and his denial of personal immortality, to explain why

his writings have been so unpopular for so long. His political philosophy too is clear-eyed and unsentimental: no plea for Justice and Equality or anything of the kind, but a simple, pragmatic approach to the problems of enabling people of differing wants and needs to co-operate. For some people, this is Spinoza the scientist, who has given up on any concern with what is good and what is noble in human life in favour of a cold-eyed explanation of why they do what they do.

But to see that side of Spinoza is to see only half the story. Earlier (ch. 6) we saw how Spinoza seemed to combine a purely naturalistic account of God with something surprisingly close to a deeply religious view; in the last section we saw also how he seemed to want to combine a concern for an objective account of human action with an insistence on preserving the role of human subjectivity in a way that we now find very difficult to accept. And here again something analogous happens. As you read your way through the painful, remorseless grinding out of consequences from his crabbed and constricting definitions, a strange thing occurs: out of his objective, dispassionate account of the human animal there slowly arises a vision of human freedom and of the good life which we have learned not to associate with such a view. How does he do it?

He describes the life of human beings in the last two books of the *Ethics* in terms of enslavement, and freedom. Book 3 has given his painstaking analysis of all our emotions as being built up out of the basic elements of desire, pleasure and pain, and Book 4 builds on that to show what a sad and sorry affair the life of human beings necessarily is. We are weak, finite creatures, at the mercy of a whole range of forces which are beyond our control. Those forces include obvious external agencies which dominate us and force us into unhappiness by preventing us from doing what we desire and making us do and undergo what we want to avoid – such things as fire, flood, disease, the state, invading armies, noisy neighbours, etc. etc. – but also other, less obvious opponents.

The first of these is our ignorance. As we saw back in the Introduction, we live most of our lives in the world of appearance: our senses provide us, just as Descartes said, not with an accurate understanding of the world around us, but only with a feeling of its impact on us. Those impressions from the outside world are fragmentary, disordered, incomplete, and the beliefs we base on them are unreliable and apt to mislead. In so far as we live the life of common sense, therefore (and in so far as we base our understanding of the world on the sense-based Aristotelianism of traditional learning), we are enslaved – the ideas that fill our minds are planted there by our casual interactions with the rest of nature, out of our control. Their haphazard nature means they are unreliable: some of them will be pleasant – i.e. will enable us to fulfil our natures – and some not; but because we have no control over them the pleasures they provide will be short-lasting and unreliable, and their misleading character will give us only a poor understanding of how things really are, which means it will be all the harder for us to achieve our ends, because we don't understand either ourselves or the world around us.

The second kind of enslavement is an enslavement to our own feelings. Time and again, the emotions which Spinoza has so carefully anatomised in Book 3 get in the way of our achieving our ends, developing our natures and so achieving pleasure. We get angry with someone, upset them, and so make it much less likely that they will do what we want; we are distracted by short-term, easy pleasures, and lose sight of our longer-term aims which are more deeply grounded in our natures and would have brought us longer-lasting happiness; we are afraid of failing, of being humiliated, and so our fear and our pride prevent us from trying to do what we really want; we are afraid of death, and so live our lives in a weak and cowardly way. The examples could be multiplied indefinitely; the underlying thought is that negative emotions, like ignorance, provide false needs and shallow pleasures which prevent us from achieving our more important goals and more lasting joys.

The picture that emerges at the end of Book 4 of the *Ethics*, then, is a very negative one. Book 5 provides the more optimistic part of the story. As Descartes said, we can escape from the world of appearance through science. In so far as we think rationally, Spinoza says, the conclusions we come to are not foisted on us by external forces, but are a natural, logical development of ideas that we already possess. So the scientific investigation of nature, which consists in systematic, orderly observations, and the rational working out of their implications, not only leads to a true understanding of the world, so that we can more easily achieve our desires, but is also in itself pleasurable and productive, since it consists in the working out of our own ideas, the development of our own understanding, and so the perfection of our natures.[10]

The point to notice here is that this is again an instance of Spinoza's mixing together what seem to us very different things. His theory is not what it might appear – the advocacy of pure intellect, the cold, remorseless use of reason to overcome the delusions of the senses and the distractions of the emotions. Some people have advocated that line, both before Spinoza (Stoicism), and since (Mr Spock in *Star Trek*). But that is quite clearly *not* Spinoza's position. He does not make a distinction between the intellect and the emotions, and simply say that one is preferable to the other; his distinction is between rational, positive emotional states which result in deep-seated, long-lasting satisfaction, and irrational, disordered, misleading emotions which blind us to the truth, prevent us from achieving our real ends, and provide at best only shallow, short-term pleasures. The astonishing thing about the theory is that it equates the former with the rational understanding of science, and also with the life of service to God.

And there is one more rabbit to pull out of the hat. Not only does the life of reason unite the pursuit of science, the truly religious life and the pursuit of happiness, but it also turns out to explain all our social and moral obligations as well. Because reason and truth are universal, they can provide the basis for agreement between people. To the extent that we are misled by appearances and driven by destructive emotions we will be in conflict with other people and will harm one another; but to the extent that we think clearly, understand ourselves and the world we live in, we will necessarily agree.

It is an extraordinary story: truly a complete answer to most of the questions of philosophy – What are we? Where do we come from? How should we live? It is an answer which to us seems paradoxical: we should love God without being religious; we must die, but can achieve immortality; we must live the life of reason, and be very emotional; there is no morality, but there is a good way to live, and so on. Is Spinoza's story incoherent, or is it merely that, like his contemporaries, we are too trapped in our deep-seated misconceptions to appreciate it?

Leibniz was fourteen years younger than Spinoza. The two corresponded, and met to discuss philosophy. Spinoza seems to have regarded him as a young man on the make, and warned his friends to be careful what they said to him. Leibniz thought Spinoza was wrong about most things, but had some important insights – but then he thought that about everyone.

Reading

Spinoza's psychology is contained primarily in Book 3 of the *Ethics*, where he explains the basic emotions and the way they combine to produce others. Book 4 describes the life which follows from that account, and Book 5 explains the ways in which through understanding we can achieve a measure of self-determination and a more stable and happier life.

Questions to ask

(1) According to Descartes and Spinoza, your body is not a unique individual, but a constantly changing mass of particles which it is convenient for us to refer to as if it were one thing. According to Spinoza (but not Descartes) the same is true of your mind. Which account, Descartes' or Spinoza's, seems to you a better description of the human mind, and why?

(2) Does Spinoza's conception of freedom provide a convincing account of the good life which is compatible with his determinism?

(3) Does Spinoza's psycho-physical parallelism open up the possibility of an understanding of human subjectivity in a way that no dualist or materialist account ever could?

PART 3
Gottfried Wilhelm Leibniz

Biography

Gottfried Wilhelm von Leibniz (or Leibnitz, or Leibnits, or Libnits) was born in 1646, when Descartes was fifty, Spinoza was thirteen, and Isaac Newton was three. He was twenty when the Great Fire of London occurred, forty when Newton published his *Mathematical Principles of Natural Philosophy*, and sixty when Benjamin Franklin was born. He died in Hanover in 1716. He was an extremely prolific writer, but produced no definitive statement of his ideas. The *Discourse on Metaphysics* of 1686, and the work which has come to be known as the *Monadology* (probably written 1714, but published after his death) are the best short summaries of his views.

He was born in Leipzig, where his father was a university professor. He himself changed his mind about an academic career, and for most of his life he was employed in a variety of posts (including teacher, historian, mining engineer, librarian and diplomat) by a number of European noble houses, often several at the same time. He spent his life travelling around Europe, meeting and/or corresponding with all the

GOTTFRIED WILHELM LEIBNIZ

leading intellectuals of the day (including Spinoza and Locke), and trying to pursue his own interests while struggling to keep his various employers off his back and complaining about lack of money, time, and recognition. He never married.

Leibniz was a polymath, who thought and wrote on more or less every subject you can think of, most famously on mathematics. In philosophy he is the great reconciler, who claims to bring together the best of Catholic and Protestant, Plato and Aristotle, Ancient and Modern, Descartes, Spinoza and Locke, and to have discovered the ultimate truth which all other philosophers had been working towards.

Probably no-one ever bought into Leibniz's views wholesale, but he was enormously influential in Germany in the eighteenth century, and therefore in the work of Kant. In the English-speaking world his ideas were rediscovered in the early twentieth century by philosophers convinced of the importance of logic in philosophy, most famously in the work of Bertrand Russell.

Chapter 9

The Principle of Sufficient Reason

Overview

Spinoza developed Descartes' mathematical science of nature to the ultimate degree, claiming that a completed natural science would reveal the single reality underlying all of existence, natural, human and divine. Leibniz accepts and reinforces the requirement for complete explicability, and is driven by that to suggest that the reality that lies behind all the appearances of the world is an infinite universe of self-sufficient reasons, unified in the infinite understanding of something much more like a traditional Christian God.

His writings are in many ways the opposite of Spinoza's. Where Spinoza laboured for years to perfect a single master work encompassing everything he wanted to say, Leibniz gives us instead a mass of letters and short articles attacking other views, holding back his own, and all the while claiming to agree with everyone he writes about – provided that we interpret their opinions in the correct, i.e. Leibnizian, way. The only general presentations we have are some very compressed summaries or snapshots of his gradually evolving views, which it is not always easy to reconcile with his more detailed treatment of particular topics. The way to make sense of it all, I think, is to begin with his central conviction that everything that is true must be fully explicable, and to work through the conclusions he comes to in working out the consequences of that belief. I will start by setting out that central belief in explicability, and some of the reasons he offers for it, to let you decide how far you are willing to agree with him (ch. 9). We will then follow his working out of that conviction by looking at the only kind of explanation he thinks is possible (ch. 10), the kind of reality he thinks must underlie the phenomena of experience (ch. 11), and the way human beings fit into that extraordinary story (ch. 12). It is a strange journey, and few people have ever been persuaded to accept the conclusions Leibniz claims are inevitable. The challenge is to say where and why you think he goes wrong.

Explicability and its limits

In order to get a grasp of what Leibniz is saying here, we need first of all to be clear on what we ourselves think, so that we can appreciate Leibniz's different point of view. So we begin by asking a question: do we live in a rational, explicable world? Does the world around us make any sense? Do things that happen happen for a reason, or are they just random?

Most of us, I think, would say that the world does make sense, it is intelligible, at least up to a point. Consider this example. A lift breaks down, and someone is injured. We investigate, but can find no explanation for the fault: everything seems to be in perfect working order; the lift was in good condition, and well maintained, but now, suddenly, it has gone wrong. And we don't know why. What are we going to say? How would you respond if someone – perhaps a lift engineer – said that since she had proved that there was nothing at all wrong with the lift, it must follow that there was no reason for the malfunction, that it had no cause?

Most of us I think would deny it: we would say that although we don't know *why* it happened, although we can't *find* the cause, there must have been one. Things don't just happen for no reason;

in a simple mechanical/electrical system like a lift, everything that happens can be explained, if only we know enough about it. It *couldn't* be the case that the lift just fell, with no mechanical cause, or that one of its components just malfunctioned, with no explanation in terms of faulty manufacture, wear and tear, damage, some hitherto unknown property of the materials, or something of the kind. A lift, surely, is *deterministic* – everything that happens in such a system is the inevitable consequence of what happened before. And as a result it is *explicable* – it is always in theory possible to explain every event by reference to preceding events and the laws which govern them.

And it isn't only man-made systems towards which we take this attitude. Ever since the seventeenth century we have believed, just as Descartes tried to convince us, that the whole of nature is an orderly, deterministic system in which everything that happens happens for a reason. Why does the wind blow? Something to do with atmospheric pressure. Why does the seed grow? Something to do with the chemistry of plants. Why does the sun shine? Something to do with nuclear fusion, and perhaps the structure of the human eye. In all these and similar areas we may not be sure that we know what the precise answer is, but we are quite convinced that there is an answer: if someone suggested that tornadoes for example just happen for no reason at all, most of us would deny it.[1] There are two points we need to get clear in relation to this conviction of ours that the world around us is an explicable, deterministic system.

The first is just to ask why we believe it. Can you prove it? If you believe it, *why* do you believe it? You perhaps feel that it is proved to us every day – that you only have to look around to see that nature, at least at the macroscopic level, is a deterministic system. After all, things *don't* just happen for no reason, do they? And when things do go wrong, we generally find out why.

But do we?

What happens in practice when something goes wrong? When your car breaks down, for example, you take it to a garage. And the mechanic replaces what's broken, or replaces parts that may have contributed to the fault, until it goes away. She then reports that the cylinder head was cracked, or the condenser had packed up – but she doesn't tell you *why* those things had happened.

Everything in a mechanic's life is more or less consistent with our faith in a deterministic universe; but isn't it equally consistent with a belief in a universe which is deterministic most of the time, but which contains a few random elements? Your experienced mechanic generally knows what kind of things happen to what kind of car – on this one the front suspension arms tend to give out after a few thousand miles, and need replacing; that one often has trouble with its electrics. But she will also be able if asked to tell you a long list of surprises she has come across: the car whose back axle just gave way at the traffic lights for no apparent reason; the ongoing case of the car with the intermittent fuel problem which has never been solved, or the mysterious case of the fractured gudgeon pin.

In all these cases we *assume* that there is some reason why they happen, that if we committed sufficient resources to the inquiry into why the gudgeon pin fractured, we would eventually find that there was some cause, and it wasn't really an anomalous event that occurred for no reason. And that may well be true (though the history of air accident investigations doesn't always bear it out). The point I am trying to make is only that it is not obvious that our belief in a deterministic universe is founded on what we observe: it seems quite possible that it isn't in fact a generalisation from what we observe to be the case around us, but is in fact a deeper, metaphysical belief that we *bring to* our experience, rather than something we *derive from* it, and that the belief in intermittent randomness is every bit as well justified by what we see.

The second point I want to make about our belief that everything is explicable – in order to set up Leibniz's importantly different assumption – is that this faith of ours is not unlimited. Here are four ways in which we allow – or at least some of us do – the world to be inexplicable.

- *Perhaps not everything is deterministic.* While things like lifts and car engines are generally held to be deterministic systems, other things we are less sure about. Quantum phenomena are now standardly held to be *in*deterministic – while we can predict with a high degree of accuracy that in a certain length of time a certain number of alpha particles will be emitted by a certain object, for example, there is *nothing* that determines whether a given particle will or will not be emitted at a given time: it simply happens or it doesn't, and there is no reason why – or so a lot of people now claim. And of course not everyone believes that human beings are deterministic systems; many people – including Leibniz, as we shall see – believe that human action is at least sometimes the result of a free choice, and that such choices are *not* simply determined by pre-existing conditions in the world.

- *The deterministic system of nature is not itself explicable.* We understand the natural world by tracing back the causes of events; but how far back can such explanation go? Is there a first cause, which started the whole process? If not, then the search for explanations simply goes on to infinity, and it begins to look as if nothing is ever really explained. But if there is a first cause, and if all explanation is through tracing causes, then the first cause must necessarily be inexplicable, mustn't it? But if that is the case, then surely the whole world is, ultimately, beyond explanation – the most we could ever say is that a given event is the necessary consequence of something that in the end we can never make sense of.[2]

- *We can't explain why things are determined as they are.* Whatever you think about that, there is another way in which our faith in the explicability of nature is limited. We explain events through laws – the stone fell because of the regular feature of the world we know as gravity. But why does gravity operate as it does? If as Newton said objects attract each other with a force which is (among other things) inversely proportional to the square of the distance between them, then why isn't it inversely proportional to the *cube* of that distance? Or if, as Einstein says, $E = MC^2$, why doesn't $E = MC^{17}$? In general, it surely makes sense for us to ask *why* the world is as it is – why stones don't fall upwards, and why light doesn't travel in wavy lines instead of straight ones. *Some* of those laws and regularities we may be able to explain by reference to other laws on which they depend; but then we are going to encounter another regress just like the last one – a regress, not of causes, this time, but of regularities. Just as before, if there is no basic truth or fundamental regularity – some Ultimate

Fact about How Things Are – then it seems as if the way they are is just an accident, just the way things *happen* to be. And if there *is* such a fundamental truth, then, since it is ultimate, it will be forever inexplicable, just a big mystery on which everything else non-mysteriously depends.

• *Coincidences have no explanation.* There is one more point to bring out before I explain why I am going on about these things, and how they relate to the work of Leibniz. Consider coincidences. We can perhaps explain more or less why the brick fell off the house; but can we explain why it fell off just at the moment when someone was walking along the pavement underneath, and in just such a way as to tear the end off his nose? And moreover, can we explain why this bizarre accident happened to *this particular person*, and to no-one else?

Most people I guess would say there is no reason for an event of that kind. There is a reason why the brick fell, and why it fell as it did; and there is a reason why the man was there when it happened; but there is no reason for the fact that the brick fell when he was passing, any more than there is a reason why the brick fell at the exact moment that a sheep bleated on the other side of the world, or in the year when Leicester City won the FA Cup. Each event has its own explanation; the fact that they happen at the same time is just *chance*, isn't it?

The conclusion I want to draw from these thoughts is simply that the metaphysical view in terms of which we tend today to make sense of the world around us perhaps isn't as obvious as it looks, and tolerates a certain level of contingency, of inexplicability. We assume that at the macroscopic level at least, and with the debatable exception of human minds, the world is a deterministic system; but we also allow that we can't explain that system as a whole – either why it exists, or why it is as it is. And neither is there any explanation for particular combinations of events within it.

Our belief in explicability, then, is not easy to prove, and indeed it is quite hard to defend once you have recognised it; but since it is not obviously inconsistent with most of our day-to-day lives, we don't question it, because it allows us to go about our business with no major problems. The main point to grasp about Leibniz, and what I think is the key to all the strange ideas we are going to meet with in his work, is that to him this common-sense metaphysic of ours is completely unacceptable, and indeed quite absurd.

The Principle of Sufficient Reason

Leibniz would regard our attitude that the world is explicable *up to a point* in a way which is analogous to that in which I suggested we would regard the lift engineer who said that since the lift was in good condition the accident must have been an inexplicable, random, uncaused event. That idea seemed to us crazy, because we feel it can't be the case that some things are explicable, and some not, that there is randomness within the deterministic system of the natural, macroscopic world. Leibniz would say that it is equally crazy – indeed more so – for us to hold that although events in that natural, macroscopic world are explicable, the system as a whole, and particular types of event and combinations of events within it, are not. According to Leibniz, for everything that is the case there must be a Sufficient Reason – a reason why it is as it is and not otherwise. If it is true, therefore, that the world exists, and that stones fall downwards and not upwards, then there must be a comprehensible *reason* why those things are true; and if it is true that the stone that fell off the roof tore off the nose of a man named Walter who lived in Darjeeling, then there must again be a *reason* why that is so and not otherwise. Explanation, according to Leibniz, is an all or nothing affair: either the universe is explicable, or it is not, and to say that it is explicable in parts, or up to a point, or to a certain extent, is the kind of lazy compromise which is perhaps comfortable for a child, or for a very ignorant and unthinking person, but is completely unacceptable – indeed unintelligible – to a philosopher.

Does that seem to you to make sense as an attitude to take to the world? Can you see any way of defending our common-sense view against it?

The Principle of Contradiction

As I shall try to show in the next section, all the oddities of Leibnizian metaphysics and epistemology flow directly or indirectly from that central conviction that for everything that is, there is a reason why it is thus and not otherwise. For the kind of truth we have been discussing so far – things like that the world exists, that stones fall downwards, that poor old Walter lost his nose – the explanation takes the form of a Sufficient Reason, of a kind I shall be setting out in the next section. But before we go on to that we need to take account of a second kind of explanation, and the second great principle of Leibniz's world.[3]

Think about this question: why do triangles have three sides? Why don't they have four, or seven, or sometimes two and sometimes eight?

The answer, I guess, is just that that's what a triangle is. A triangle just *is* a three-sided figure; that's what the word 'triangle' means. Therefore, while Leibniz may be right that there will always be an explanation as to why some particular object – a field, say, or an earring – is a triangle, i.e. it is *triangular*, there can surely never be an explanation as to why, given that something *is* triangular, it has three sides. To ask that question is like asking why is a triangle a triangle – and how do you answer that? Why is a tree a tree? Why is the capital of Namibia the capital of Namibia? Why was Karl Marx Karl Marx? Surely, any such question is just nonsense. As we saw with Descartes' rational intuitions (ch. 5), there is no explanation for any of these things; you can't give a reason for why a tree is a tree, or a bicycle is a bicycle, because they *couldn't have been anything else*, so their being what they are stands in no need of being explained.

Leibniz puts the same point slightly differently: he maintains the Principle of Sufficient Reason, that for everything that is true there is a reason why it is true, but he says that in cases like these that Sufficient Reason is to be found in what he calls the Principle of Contradiction. The statement 'A triangle is a triangle' is true because to deny it would be a contradiction – and contradictions are always false. And 'A triangle has three sides' is true for the same reason: a triangle is a three-sided figure, so this is equivalent to saying that a figure which has three sides has three sides; and to deny that would mean saying that a figure that has three sides does not have three sides – which is a contradiction.

According to Leibniz all of what he calls these 'necessary truths' or 'truths of reason' are true in the same way – and this includes all of mathematics. Thus the reason that '1 + 1 = 2' is true is just that if we analyse the idea of 2 we can reduce it to 1 and 1, and the reason why $17^2 = 289$ is true is that again, if you analyse both sides you can reduce them down to a simple identity statement, which it would be a contradiction to deny.

But what kind of Sufficient Reason can there be for things which are *not* necessary?

Box 9.1

Occasionalism

How far can a scientific explanation go? Can science tell us *why* things happen, or only *how* they happen?

Consider: a biologist might tell me why the grass doesn't grow in my garden, in the sense of explaining what processes are involved, what laws are instantiated, what factors play a part. But she would make no attempt (qua biologist, at least) at answering the *really* important questions, like why there is grass in the first place, and why it doesn't grow just where you want it to; why *those particular* laws operate, and not ones which are more convenient for lazy gardeners like me; and why it is *my* garden that the grass doesn't grow in, and not the garden of the man next door, who wears those horrible striped shorts and has the silly little dog that yaps all the time. None of those things, we think, is it the job of the scientist to explain.

All our six philosophers would *agree* with us about that. What is striking, though, is that for many of them that fact was taken as evidence that a scientific explanation wasn't enough, and wasn't all we should aim for. While we tend to be content with the explanation of *how* the grass grows, and not to push for an answer to the question of *why* it does so, some of our authors thought that once we had done the scientific job, we had completed only half the task of explaining natural phenomena: as it was often put, *physics* had to be supplemented by *metaphysics* (see p. 123).

Descartes, as we saw, said little about metaphysics in this sense. He thought of God as stirring up the great soup of being at creation, and thereafter as continually conserving or recreating it at every moment in accordance with his three laws of motion. Any further explanation would therefore be an investigation into why God chose to act as he did – and that was just the sort of area into which Descartes was very reluctant to enter.[4] Spinoza's position was very different. Part of what seems to us the very modern feel of his work is precisely that for him the question of why things are as they are has no sense: once we have seen the unchanging reality which lies behind the phenomena of experience, there is nothing more to be asked.

Other people, though, took the issue much more seriously, and one classic example of the attempt to buttress physics with metaphysics is the theory of Occasionalism, most famously exemplified in the work of Nicolas Malebranche.[5]

Malebranche was a convinced Cartesian, but felt that Descartes had left the story incomplete. If the created world is a continual creation or activity of the divine substance (cf. p. 31), then no mechanical explanation of nature can ever be satisfactory in itself. When one billiard ball rolls into another, for example, and the second ball starts to move, we must of course analyse the event as Descartes had said in terms of the laws of motion which it instantiates. But when we have done that, we haven't really *explained* the motion of the second ball at all, so much as set out more fully what event it is that stands in need of explanation: we have given the *how* of it, but haven't begun to give the *why*. To say that the rolling ball is the cause of the motion of the second ball is crazy, according to Malebranche. The rolling ball can do nothing. It is an inert, completely passive area of the material continuum through which the motion implanted by God at creation is transmitted. There is no necessary connection, as he puts it, between the motion of the first ball and the motion of the second. True, impacts of that kind are regularly followed by movements of the kind we see in this case, but there is no reason why it *has* to be so. There would be no contradiction involved if the second ball stayed where it was, or the first one passed through it, or both balls moved off in opposite directions. The fact that we must focus on, then, if we really want to understand what goes on in a case like this, is that God, in recreating the world in the moment after the impact, chooses to create a world in which the second ball moves in a certain direction and with a certain speed. The laws of motion, in other words, are just as Descartes says they are; but they are descriptions, not of the way matter behaves (as if mere matter could *behave* in any way at all), but of the choices God makes in conserving the world from minute to minute. That is the only true explanation of the motion of the second ball – that God chose to recreate the world in that way and not in another. (And the regular and unchanging character of the laws of nature is only appropriate to the constant and unchanging nature of God, who has no whims, and doesn't change his mind.)

The way Malebranche presents this view is in terms of a distinction between what he calls natural or secondary causes, like our example of the rolling ball, and true causes – or rather, *the* one true cause, which is the will of God. Natural causes are what science reveals, and a knowledge of them is what enables us to improve our lives and to some extent to predict the future. But really, natural causes *cause* nothing at all. A natural cause like the impact of a rolling ball is not the true *cause* of the motion of the ball that it hits, so much as the *reason* why God chooses to recreate the world with a rolling ball in it, i.e. it is *because of*, or in view of, the impact that God decides to act as he does. But to put it like that is misleading – as if God simply observed what happened in the world and acted accordingly, when in reality, of course, he knows in advance everything that can ever occur. So Malebranche typically says not that natural causes are the *reason* why God acts as he does, but that they are the *occasion* for his so acting. Natural causes are therefore 'occasional' causes – not in the sense of being intermittent, but in the sense that they are the grounds for his action, or the features of the world at one moment which God takes account of in making his decision as to how it should be in the next. Hence the name of the Theory of Occasionalism.

Malebranche's theocentric ideas were enormously influential. In particular, their effects can be seen to different extents and in different ways in the work of Leibniz, Berkeley, and even the atheist Hume.

Reading

References to the Principle of Sufficient Reason are scattered throughout Leibniz's work, including *Discourse on Metaphysics* 13, *Monadology* 33–6, *Specimen of Discoveries*, *Primary Truths* and the correspondence with Clarke.

Questions to ask

(1) Is the belief that nature is a deterministic system something we discover from experience, or is it an assumption which we bring to our experience, and which no experience could ever disprove?

(2) Is it true that the hypothesis of a Big Bang can never provide a complete explanation for how things are?

(3) Leibniz claims that necessary truths are not just truths of language: even if there had never been a language, it would still have been true that all triangles have three sides. Do you agree?

Chapter 10

The best of all possible worlds

So far all we have done is to say that for everything that is true, there must be a reason why it is true, and that in the case of a necessary truth that reason lies in the Principle of Contradiction. But most of the things we want to explain are simple contingencies – things which are true, but which *might* have been false; as Leibniz puts it, things which are true in this actual world in which we live, but which in other worlds which *might* have existed – in other possible worlds – could have been false. Why did it rain today? Why did my child die? How do trees know it's time to drop their leaves? Why does $E = MC^2$? Why are we here, and what is it all for? Leibniz doesn't pretend that he knows the answer to all these questions, of course; but he does claim that he knows the *form* which the answers to them must take; he knows the general *kind* of Sufficient Reason which must ultimately be given for contingent truths.

The God of reason

The first step is the existence of God. For Leibniz, as for Descartes and Spinoza, the idea that God might not exist is quite literally *unthinkable*. Both Descartes and Spinoza, as we saw, hold that God exists necessarily – that given what God is, it is nonsensical to suggest that God could not be. How could that which is completely perfect lack existence? How could the underlying reality not be real? For Leibniz the idea is rather that God is required by the Principle of Sufficient Reason: that without God, nothing would be intelligible, nothing could be explained.[1]

The argument is close to the one I gave above as number three in my list of reasons why our belief in the intelligibility of the world is limited. Let's assume there is no First Cause – that explanations just go on to infinity: A is caused by B, B is caused by C, C by D, and so on without end through an infinite number of alphabets. Leibniz says that even if you think that is possible, and you can explain an event by reference to an infinite chain of causes without the need for a First Cause which explains them all, you *still* won't avoid the need for God as the ultimate explanation. Otherwise, while every individual event in your infinite series will be explained, there will be no explanation for the series as a whole, nor for any smaller series within it. Because even if we can explain A by B and so on, surely it still makes sense to ask *why* B explains A: yes, the window broke because the stone hit it . . . but *why* does hitting a window with a stone cause it to break? Surely we can imagine a world in which stones simply passed through windows, or bounced off them, or caused them to sing the Marseillaise; and if that is so, why don't those things happen in *this* world, or why do we inhabit a world in which they don't? And if your answer is simply that we just *don't* live in such a world, and that's all there is to it, then as we saw, Leibniz will say that you have abandoned all attempt at understanding, because it makes no sense to say that the world is intelligible, but only in parts, or only up to a point.

Leibniz concludes that however long the chain of causes may be, there must inevitably be something that lies *outside* that chain in order to explain it – and that thing is God.[2]

But how does that solve the problem? Doesn't the same problem arise all over again? If we say that God explains the whole sequence of contingent truths, then surely we can ask what is it that explains God? Because, if God has no explanation, then we are back with just the kind of partial intelligibility that Leibniz has rejected: the natural world is explained by God, but God itself just *is* – for no reason. But if God *does* have an explanation, then the regress just begins all over again. In other words, bringing God into the picture is just a cop-out: however you try to deal with these problems, you end up with something inexplicable, with an end to the possibility of understanding; sooner or later you reach something that must just be accepted. Isn't it just an empty gesture to call that something 'God'? All Leibniz is doing, surely, is giving a religious name to what he doesn't understand.

Leibniz does have a reply to this charge, and you must decide for yourself how successful it is. God, he claims, *does* have an explanation . . . but that explanation lies not in some further thing, but is internal to God himself, and so puts an end to the regress of explanation. God, in other words, is his own cause; as we would put it, God is *self-explanatory*.

The thinking here is very close both to Descartes' argument that since God is completely perfect he could not fail to exist, and to Spinoza's thought that it is self-contradictory to deny the existence of the one reality. The idea is that whereas for everything else in the world you can ask for an explanation of its existence, for God you can't, because once you understand *what* God is, it simply makes no sense to ask *why* it is – because you see at once that God *could not fail* to exist. God is substance, God is reality, God is perfect and perfected, God is infinite and all-powerful. Given that such a thing *could* exist, therefore, it *must* exist.[3] After all, what could possibly prevent it?

How God explains the world

According to Leibniz, then, if we know what God is, we know that God exists, and why he exists. More importantly, he claims that if we know what God is, we know in outline the explanation of everything else, because everything else is as it is only *because God decided that it should be so.*

Again this may sound like a rather trivial cop-out on Leibniz's part. What has become of the impressive-sounding Principle of Sufficient Reason if all it boils down to is the unenlightening claim that for everything that is true, it is true because God chose it? Is that what he means by an explanation? Is that all that the intelligibility of the world amounts to? The answer is that the principle is much more interesting than that, because according to Leibniz if we think about it carefully enough we can understand of everything that is true not only *that* God chose that it should be so, but also in good measure *why* he chose it.

The job of metaphysics, then, for Leibniz, is nothing less than that of trying to understand God's decisions. God is infinitely powerful, and all-knowing. He can do – not whatever he *wants* to do, exactly, because to want something is to lack it, to be short of it, and God lacks for nothing – but whatever he freely *chooses* to do, God can do. So why did God create the world? And why *this* particular world, of all the hugely many different worlds that could have been created?

Consider an example. God could have created a universe which consisted only of one thing – a small grey stone, for example. Such a universe is perfectly possible: there is no contradiction involved in conceiving it, and it is clearly within the power of God to create such a thing. So why is there more in existence than that?

The answer, according to Leibniz, cannot be chance: when you are dealing with an omniscient and omnipotent being, *nothing* happens by chance. God knew that the grey stone world was possible, just as he knew this world was possible; and God could bring it into existence every bit as easily as he brought into existence this world. (Since God has infinite power, nothing is more difficult than anything else.) So why did he choose this one and not that one? God has no whims, and he doesn't throw dice: every decision is a rational choice, made for some good reason. So there must be some reason why this world is *better* than that one, so that an all-good being such as God would naturally prefer to create it.

The question then becomes this: what is wrong with the grey stone universe? Why did it lose out when its merits were assessed by the divine intelligence? And the answer is simply that it was too boring to exist. When God makes his choices, he is looking for the best world to create, of all the possible worlds he can understand (which is all of them). And part of what makes one world better than another is the richness and diversity of the phenomena it contains.

This is what Leibniz calls the Principle of Plenitude. Existence, he says, is clearly better than non-existence: Being is better than Nothingness, because being is the completion, actualisation or perfecting of potential, and non-being is its denial or thwarting, or failure. So the more being a world contains, the more rich and diverse its contents, the better that world is. It follows that the grey stone universe never had a hope of coming into existence, because it was insufficiently perfect. Leibniz sometimes talks of this decision on God's part as if it were a competition between all these different possible worlds, all striving for his attention, vying to be selected in the struggle for existence, the strength of their claims being in exact proportion to their worthiness or perfection. In this battle of the 'striving compossibles', the grey stone universe didn't stand a chance – it was easily defeated, for example, by its close relative the possible world which consisted of *two* grey stones, which was at least twice as rich and diverse. But the Two Grey Stone universe itself was no competitor for the Three Grey Stone universe, which lost out to the Four Grey Stone universe, which was easily defeated by the Four Grey And Two Pink stones universe, which in turn was no match for the Four Grey And Two Pink Stones With Complex Laws Of Interaction Between Them universe . . . and so on and so on and so on.

There is of course an unthinkably large number of these striving compossibles. But that is no problem to an infinite intelligence. He considered them all.

But so far we have seen only half of the story. From what we have seen so far, the calculus of perfection of worlds is a simple matter – the more diverse and complex the world, the better it is. The best world, therefore, would be a world of unthinkable complexity and diversity. So for example, a world exactly like ours but with twice the number of spiders would necessarily be better. And one in which those spiders suddenly and with extreme speed mutated into lobsters on a regular basis would be better yet. And a world in which nothing remained constant, but $E = MC^2$ on Mondays, MC^3 on Tuesdays and MC^{17} for a short time on a Friday afternoon would be still better. The problem, of course, is that such a world would be very hard to make sense of – natural laws which change every few seconds in accordance with an extremely complex and constantly changing principle are as good as no laws at all when it comes to trying to make sense of the world around us. So there is a second part of God's calculation of perfection, parallel to the Principle of Plenitude, which Leibniz calls the Principle of Economy – that a world which has simple principles is better, other things being equal, than one which has complex rules. After all, simplicity makes for intelligibility, and makes for elegance. A watch, for example, which has 25,000 cogs, wheels and levers is not as good as one which does exactly the same work with only three. Not because it is cheaper to produce, but because it is a more rational engineering solution to the problem of keeping good time. For the same reason, a world which achieves its diversity and richness at the cost of a massively complex and constantly changing set of rules is less good than one which (like Descartes' world) achieves the same effect from three simple mechanical principles.

If this fantastic chain of reasoning is making any sense to you at all, it should be clear that these two principles, those of Plenitude and Economy, pull in opposite directions. Our old friend the Grey Stone universe now starts to look like a real contender, because although it may be dull, it is certainly simple, whereas its cousin the Three Grey Stone world is starting to look far too complicated for a rational God to choose.

So how does God make the choice between these competing demands? The answer is that although the two principles pull in opposite directions, there is a *best possible resolution* of them. Like an engineer who has to work out a trade-off between the strength of a bridge, say, and the weight of the materials that go into it, or an architect who tries to make a room as spacious as possible without having the roof fall in, God works out the best possible combination of Plenitude and Economy in what Leibniz calls the Principle of Perfection, or the Principle of the Best. Human examples like architects and engineers are therefore little gods, recapitulating in their small-scale, finite intelligences the original act of God's creation.

Crazy as it may seem, according to Leibniz this Principle of Perfection, with its opposed subsidiary principles of Plenitude and Economy, provides the ultimate metaphysical explanation for everything that is – the Sufficient Reason for every contingent truth. Why is there a world at all? Why is there something rather than nothing? Easy – as the Principle of Plenitude states, existence is objectively better than non-existence, so God has a reason to actualise one of the possible worlds. But why *this* world, the one that actually exists? The world, that is, in which $E = MC^2$, in which stones fall downwards and not upwards, Walter from Darjeeling lost his nose and that spot of rain fell exactly there on that leaf and not half a millimetre to the right or left – why is *that* the world that exists, and not one of the uncountably many alternatives?

In one sense we can never know the answer to that question, because we finite minds can never carry out the necessary calculations. We would need, for instance, to follow out all the knock-on effects of that half-millimetre difference in the fall of the raindrop: all the incalculable consequences that would ultimately follow from it over the course of time, and also all the adjustments that would have to be made to the previous states of the world – to the way the wind was blowing, or the position of the cloud, or the way the laws of meteorology and gravity interact, or whatever – which would have made it possible for that raindrop to fall just that bit further away. We human beings can never do a fraction of that calculation: but we do know that if we could work it out, we would see, for every one of those uncountable alternative scenarios, that at some point it came out worse on the calculation of Plenitude and Economy than this actual world. In other words, we know, just because this world actually exists, that it is the Best of All Possible Worlds.[4]

It's an odd story, isn't it? And as we will see in the next chapter, it gets odder still. The challenge it presents to us all the time is that while we may not like this way of making sense of why things are as they are, it is hard to find an alternative. And can we really defend our common-sense belief that not everything is explicable against Leibniz's charge that it amounts to admitting that nothing makes sense at all?

Before we go on to see where his convictions take Leibniz next, there are three further points we need to clear up about the idea that everything is for the best in the Best of All Possible Worlds.

God and the calculus

Consider carefully the kind of trade-off calculation God has to perform in order to decide which is the best possible world.[5] We can represent all possible worlds as lying on a curve on a graph, as in Fig. 10.1 As you can see from the graph, World 5 has maximal Plenitude – it is unthinkably rich, varied and complex – and therefore has minimal Economy, because the principles of its operation are inconceivably complex. At the opposite end of the line, World 1 is the simplest, most economical world possible (simpler even than Grey Stone World) – and so has absolutely no Plenitude. Worlds 2–4 lie somewhere in between those extremes. Which one is the best? Well, we can see from the slope of the curve that World 2 is definitely an improvement on World 1: its Plenitude is far higher, and the comparative loss of Economy is quite small, so the overall perfection of this world is clearly greater. In moving from World 2 to World 3 the comparison is similar: the gain in Plenitude is less now, and the cost in terms of lost Economy is higher, but still the Plenitude gain outweighs the Economy loss, so World 3 is more perfect overall than World 2. However, if we go on in the same direction, from World 3 to World 4, the gain in Plenitude is now

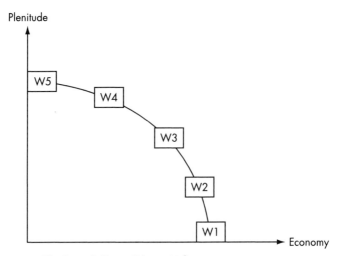

Figure 10.1 The best of all possible worlds[6]

actually less than the consequential loss of Economy, so every world we meet from now on will be *less* perfect than the one before. World 3, therefore, is the one God will choose – the Best of All Possible Worlds – and that is the one we inhabit. This world is the best because all the worlds to the right of it on the line have too much Economy for their level of Plenitude, while all those to the left of it have too much Plenitude for their level of Economy. At that precise point on the line, therefore, the two requirements are perfectly balanced: the over-economical worlds have run out, and we are not yet into the over-plenitudinous ones.

Any mathematician will recognise this kind of calculation as an example of the application of the Differential Calculus – the technique of calculating the slope of a curve at a point. And the Differential Calculus, of course, was invented by Leibniz.[7]

Theodicy and Dr Pangloss

Another aspect of this Principle of the Best is Leibniz's solution to the Problem of Evil. Christianity is always vulnerable to the argument that because bad things happen in the world, God cannot be both all-powerful and all-good. If he is all-good, then he wants nothing bad to happen. But 'evil' does happen – both human evil (like the actions of Dinsdale Piranha, who used to nail people's heads to coffee tables) and natural evil, like earthquakes and wet holidays. That must mean that God can't prevent evil, and so is not all-powerful. Alternatively, if God is all-powerful, then he has the power to prevent bad things from happening and chooses not to – and so he isn't all-good.

One traditional response to this problem is to say that, contrary to appearances, evil doesn't really happen – that while something like a person's having his head nailed to a coffee table may seem to us, from our limited perspective, to be a Very Bad Thing, nevertheless in reality, from God's omniscient point of view, that tragic event could be seen to be part of a greater plan in which the good outweighs the bad. When we rail against God because of the existence of evil, it is said, we are like children who wish it would never rain so that they could always go out to play – they don't realise that from a wider perspective rain is in fact a Good Thing. Leibniz's story was intended in part to put some flesh onto that kind of defence. God could very easily have created a world in which no-one was ever killed by an earthquake, for example – perhaps by making the laws of nature such that whenever a human being was likely to be endangered by an earthquake, some mechanism prevented it from happening. But in considering whether to create a world of that kind, God, who sees at a glance the whole history of each one in advance, can see that every one of them is either too complex to be economical enough, or too simple to be rich enough.

Whatever you may think of this defence against the Problem of Evil, it is clear that there is at least a little more to it than simply the pious assurance that we should just accept the world as it is because God must have his reasons – it is a much more central and reasoned part of Leibniz's theory than that. But that didn't stop Voltaire in *Candide* from satirising the theory through the character of Dr Pangloss, who happily glossed over all the most terrible disasters like the great Lisbon earthquake with the bland conviction that 'everything is for the best in the best of all possible worlds'.

Physics and metaphysics

The final point to make about the theory of the best of all possible worlds follows on from the last one. Just as Leibniz does not see God's will as replacing the possibility of an intelligible interpretation, in the same way he does not see this whole paraphernalia of metaphysical principles as an alternative to a naturalistic, scientific explanation. He is emphatically *not* proposing that what we should do in trying to understand the science of dynamics, for example (which he invented), is to concentrate on God's choices and the interrelation of Plenitude and Economy. On the contrary, he insists that natural phenomena should be given a purely naturalistic, mechanical explanation, just as Descartes had suggested. The explanation of nature in terms of God's choices is intended not to replace mechanical explanation, but to supplement it. As we saw earlier (pp. 114–15), it provides the *metaphysical*

THE BEST OF ALL POSSIBLE WORLDS

explanation which has to be added on to any purely *physical* explanation if the world is not to be left as purely contingent, accidental and unintelligible.

Reading

The Argument from Contingency and the Principle of Perfection can both be seen in *Monadology* (45 and 58), but are clearer in, for example, *On the Ultimate Origination of Things*.

Questions to ask

(1) Does Leibniz's Argument from Contingency work?
(2) If God were self-explanatory, would that solve the problem of the Regress of Explanations? Is God self-explanatory?
(3) Does Leibniz have any good answer to the Problem of Evil?

Chapter 11

The world as explicable
Monadology

I have tried so far to show that Leibniz's absolute faith in the possibility of understanding led him to the conclusion that the only possible explanation was via the rational decision of an omniscient God, and that the form which that decision took was a comparison, perceived via the calculus, of the respective worthiness of all possible worlds. I want now to show how that view of the possibility and nature of understanding translates into an ontology – an account of what there is. In essence, the story is that, like Descartes and Spinoza before him, Leibniz represents the world we know as a world of Appearance; but whereas Descartes held that the world of Reality which lies behind it was a world of mathematical sequences, and Spinoza that it was a world of timeless natural laws, Leibniz claimed that it was nothing but *a universe of reasons*.

It is a strange world we are about to enter, but not perhaps as odd as it first appears. Leibniz argues that, strange though it may be, it is the only possible way to make sense of the world. Unless (like our contemporary common sense) you are willing to say that ultimately the world makes no sense at all, then he claims it *must* be as he says it is. So the thread to hang on to as you enter the Labyrinth of the Continuum and the Labyrinth of Freedom and discover the windowless monads that they contain is that Leibniz's extraordinary account of what *is* the case is, he claims, the only possible view of what *must be* the case in order for the world to make sense.[1]

Individual substances and the pre-established harmony of mind and body

Leibniz's first public presentation of his metaphysical ideas was in relation to the then hot topic of mind/body interaction.[2] As we have seen, the Cartesian theory that mind and body are separate things led to problems as to how they could interact. Leibniz took advantage of this well-known difficulty to try out a version of his controversial and eccentric metaphysical views.

Like most of his contemporaries Leibniz claims that the traditional, pseudo-Aristotelian view that when mind and body interact something passes from the one into the other (there is a flowing-in, or 'influx', from one into the other) is nonsensical. But at the same time he claims that the then-fashionable theory of Occasionalism[3] is equally untenable. Instead he proposes his own new 'Theory of Agreements' or theory of 'Pre-established Harmony'.

The name sounds very odd; and the theory is even odder. He claims that the reason why, for example, my mind has the idea of a banana when my eyeballs are struck by the light bouncing off a banana is *not* because visible species from the banana flow into my mind (influx theory), *nor* because on the occasion of my eyes' being struck in that way God chooses to reveal to me something of his idea of a banana (Occasionalism). In reality, according to Leibniz, the banana idea in my mind is not produced by any external agency at all, but is *generated by my mind itself*: the banana idea is a perfectly natural, law-governed development of ideas that were already in my mind, though not clearly perceived. It unfolds, or develops, from within the recesses of my mind at *just the very moment* when the light affects my eyes, but there is no other kind of connection between the two events. My mind is pre-programmed, as we would now say, to have that idea at that moment, and has been so since the moment of its creation.

And the same thing happens (or should I say *doesn't* happen?) in the opposite direction, when as we would say an event in my mind causes an event in my body. If my leg swings as a result of my decision to kick the cat, there is again no flow of energy or the like from my mind into the muscles of my leg, and there is no intervention by God in the workings of my leg to take account of the decision I have made (as the Occasionalists would claim). Rather, the cause of the movement is wholly internal to my body, which has been pre-programmed from all eternity to swing its leg at just that moment. The swinging of the leg and the decision to kick the cat are perfectly synchronised, but quite separate: mind and body are two completely independent things, each acting out its own pre-programmed course. But those courses, those programmes, have been designed by God to take account of one another, so that there is a perfect 'concomitance' or 'agreement' between the events in one realm and those in the other – a 'Pre-established Harmony' between the two quite separate sequences of events.

What are we to make of this bizarre story? The first thing to get clear is that Leibniz is certainly *not* denying the kind of account that we today might give of the same events. He would *completely agree* with our suggestion that I have the idea of a banana in virtue of a sequence of events in my brain and nervous system. (Though he might think of that as a mechanical process, whereas we would think of it as electrochemical.) And he would also *entirely agree* that those brain and nerve events were a consequence of the effects of light on my eyes. (Though he might talk about pressure waves in a plenum, whereas we would think in terms of bombarding with photons, or whatever.) And he would be as horrified as we would be if someone were to claim that we should abandon this kind of detailed physical or psycho-physical explanation and say simply that it was the will of God that it should happen. So why does he deny that there is any real causal process involved, and what does he think is really going on? The answer, as I tried to suggest above, is that our story gives no account of *why it is* that the light fell on the banana in the first place, and *why it is* that when my eye is stimulated in that particular way those particular brain processes follow, and that particular idea comes into my mind. To those metaphysical questions, we offer no answer at all. We say it is *just a brute fact* that the banana was there, and I was looking at it; it is *just how things are* that eyes react to light in that way; banana ideas are *just the sort of thing you have* when things like that happen to you, and that's all there is to it. For Leibniz, by contrast, that is only the beginning of the story, and a story which stopped at that point, as ours does, would be no kind of intelligible story at all.

Here is an analogy which may make the point more clearly. A child is taken on a tour of the inner workings of a large public clock. She is shown all the weights and pulleys and levers, and sees in some detail how the turning of the wheel releases the lever which allows the spring to unwind so as to move the hammer and strike the bell. Later, she explains the whole process to the girl who lives next door. She knows exactly why the bell rang, she says: 'There was this great big wheel with a kind of lump on one side, and that lump held up this big piece of wood. But then the wheel turned round and so the bit of wood fell off. But the end of the bit of wood was holding this other wheel, so when it fell off the other wheel went round and round and round, and that pulled this great big hammer up in the air – and then it dropped it, and it landed on the bell and went DOINNG.'

Now (as is probably obvious), I don't know much about the workings of clocks, and I know even less about the workings of children, but I think you can see how if you told this story well the child's account could be a perfectly accurate description of what happened inside the clock. Would the child then have given a good explanation as to why the bell rang?

Think about it. How would the clock-maker respond to this account?

What I am trying to suggest is that the child may have a perfect knowledge of what happened, but she has absolutely no understanding of *why* it happened as it did. Her story makes the whole process sound like some kind of wonderful *accident* – as if the wheel just happened to turn and release the lever which just happened to be restraining the wheel which turned out to be connected to the hammer which ended up falling on the bell – like the kind of thing you sometimes see in a comedy film, where the vicar falls out of the window onto one end of a see-saw which projects the bicycle through the window of the scantily-clad lady who drops the jelly onto the head of the bald man who . . . etc. The child's account of the chiming of the clock is true – but it is misleading, because although she sees what happens, and although she understands each stage of the process, she doesn't really know *why* it happens because she doesn't appreciate that it all occurs in accordance with a carefully worked out *design*.

The point of the analogy is that for Leibniz a scientist who correctly understands a natural causal process as a deterministic, mechanical operation is in the same position as the child with the chiming of the clock – the position of having a good understanding of *how* that causal process occurs, but no idea at all of *why*. We see the events of the world around us, and we work out the rules of their operation; but until we grasp the *design* they instantiate – the rational principles which account for their being as they are, their Sufficient Reason – we have no true understanding of them. The chiming of the clock is *more* than just a simple causal chain because it is a *designed system*, and if you understand it as a simple causal process, as the child does, then you don't really know what's going on. According to Leibniz, all the causal processes of nature are of the same kind.

In fact, in a designed system it is in a sense misleading to talk of causal processes at all. We naturally explain the chiming of the bell as the child does, by reference to the hammer that hits it. But we could equally well do the same in reverse. It is true to say the bell rings because the hammer hits it; but isn't it also true to say that the hammer falls because it is going to hit the bell? In the mind of the designer, certainly, both are true. The clock wouldn't have a hammer if it didn't have a bell, so we can say that the hammer is there because the bell is there. And the hammer wouldn't move like that if it wasn't in order to strike the bell; so we can say that it is because of the ringing of the bell that the hammer falls, with just as much accuracy as we can say that it is because the hammer falls that the bell rings. As long as we are talking about the *design* of the clock, the explanation can run in either direction. The bell is where it is and as it is because of the hammer that is going to strike it, and the hammer is the length it is and made of the material it is because of the bell it is going to strike.

All this means that if you were an expert clock-maker, you could read off from a knowledge of the bell quite a lot about the hammer that hit it, as well as the mechanism that powered it, and the building that housed it. Being struck by that kind of hammer in that kind of way is not an accidental, contingent fact about the bell, but something internal to the bell itself, in the sense that the bell wouldn't exist, and wouldn't have the characteristics it does have, if it weren't going to be hit in that way, by that kind of hammer. In Leibnizian language, being struck by the hammer is *internal* to the bell, or happens to it *spontaneously*.

I hope the point of this rather long-winded analogy is now becoming clear. For Leibniz, God is the ultimate clock-maker, and I am a perfectly engineered clock. Therefore, what is true of the hammer and the bell in the clock is true to an infinitely greater extent of my mind and my body. It is therefore a mistake to say that I had the idea of a banana because the light from it fell on my retinas, just as it is a mistake to say that the bell rang because the hammer hit it; as in the case of the clock, we could just as accurately say that the light fell on my retinas because I was going to have the idea of the banana. Of course it is true that I wouldn't have had that idea if my retinas hadn't been affected in that way – but then, they wouldn't have been affected in that way unless I had been going to have that idea, because that is the way it was *planned*. Again therefore, the point is that because there must be a sufficient reason for everything that is true, and because that reason can only be found in the rational decisions of an all-good God, the events in my mind and my body, like the events in the clock, can only be truly understood by reference to the design of the whole system, i.e. to the reasons why God found a world in which the light from the banana hit my eyes and I had the idea of a banana to be a better world than any of the unthinkable number of alternatives in which the event did not occur, or occurred differently.

That, then, is the explanation of Leibniz's strange-sounding story of the pre-established harmony between mind and body. It is a mistake, he says, to talk of my mind's causing my body to move or my body's causing my mind to feel, because both are parts of a perfectly engineered system in which each element does what it does only in virtue of its position and role in the whole system, and its relation to all the other parts. That is the real sense in which he claims that the idea of the banana is spontaneous in my mind: that it arises because of the particular mind God has given me, chosen from all the others because of the way it relates to (among other things) my body.

The analogy of the clock breaks down, of course, because humans are imperfect. You could build a clock which fell apart, or was abducted by aliens, before the first blow of the hammer fell. But the same is not true of mechanisms produced by an omniscient and omnipotent God. In just the way that many features of the design of the clock can be read off from a knowledge of the bell, so *all* the features of my body could be read off from a perfect knowledge of my mind. Just as the bell would not have existed if it had not been for the purpose of its being struck by the hammer, so my mind would not have existed if it had not been for the purpose of receiving impressions from my body. Just as the function and operation of the bell in being struck is therefore not accidental but 'spontaneous', or built into the nature of the bell it is, so every little thing that happens in my mind in virtue of its relation to my body is in the same way spontaneous, built in, pre-programmed from its creation. And everything that is true of my mind in relation to my body is true of my body in relation to my mind: in the perfect mechanism which God has produced, nothing is left to chance, nothing is wasted, but each part acts out its destiny as he saw that it would, in order to realise the best of all possible worlds. My mind and my body are therefore made for each other, perfectly synchronised or harmonised, and it is a childish mistake to think that what happens in the one of them is somehow brought about merely by what happens in the other.

Complete concepts and the *Monadology*

If that account of mind and body makes any sense at all, then we are well on the way to understanding the 'fantastic fairy tale'[4] that is Leibniz's metaphysics as summarised in one of his latest works, now commonly referred to as the *Monadology*.

Although Leibniz makes out the story of pre-established harmony in relation to the 'communication' as he calls it between mind and body, that is in fact only one particular application of a theory which is completely general. The story we have told in relation to my mind and my body applies equally well to any two things in the universe which are as we would say causally related.[5]

Take for example a flea which bites a cat. We tend to say that the biting of the flea causes the cat to itch; according to Leibniz, that is true at the practical level, but in terms of metaphysics, just as with the bell and the hammer, or my mind and my body, the cause of the itch is something entirely 'internal' to the cat. God in his infinite wisdom chose to bring into existence a world in which just that flea, at just that time, bit just that cat in just that way, producing just that very particular kind of itch. The reason why he chose to create a world with those ingredients is that he considered all the other possible worlds in which that particular event didn't happen, or happened differently, and he found that somewhere along the line every one of them was inferior to this one. That being the case, we can say that one of the functions of the cat, one of the reasons why that particular cat exists, indeed, is to be bitten by that flea in that way at that time. A complete understanding of that cat would include knowing why it sat where it did, why it had skin of that particular thickness and a nervous system of such a kind that it would undergo that experience in those circumstances. In that sense, therefore, the event was pre-programmed into the cat, a natural and inevitable consequence of its having been created in preference to a different cat with a different constitution and/or a different life history. It is *wrong* to say that the flea bit the cat – not because it is false, but because it overlooks the fact that the cat existed in order (among other things) to be bitten by that flea. And what goes for the flea bite, of course, goes for every other event in the life history of the cat – every one of them, properly understood, can be seen as part of the nature of the cat, and therefore in Leibniz's terms as arising spontaneously within it.

But if all that is true, then another conclusion seems to follow. Consider that flea bite once again. We have said that in choosing a world in which that precise event happened, God had to consider the whole life history of the cat in order to put it in a position to receive the bite, and the whole design of the cat's nervous system to produce that particular result. But the same is obviously true of the flea: the event is only possible if the flea is in the right place at the right time, and if the structure of the flea and the nature of fleas in general are both such as to make it behave in that way. But then, if God had to consider the whole life history of that particular flea, and the whole nature of the race of fleas, before he could choose that particular cat, then it follows that all those things are part of the nature of the cat, too, so that from a complete understanding of the cat a sufficiently intelligent mind would be able to read off a complete knowledge of the nature of fleas. But of course, an understanding of the life cycle of the flea involves an understanding of all the other creatures their lives intersect with, and *their* life histories, and *their* natures, and *their* environments – and so on and so on without end. And so we arrive at Leibniz's extraordinary conclusion: that a complete understanding of that one particular cat would involve a complete understanding of the whole universe.

Leibniz puts this by saying that in essence the cat is what he calls at various times an individual substance, an entelechy, a Substantial Form, or a *monad*. It is an individual thing which has been brought into existence to play a very particular role in the pre-arranged system which is the best of all possible worlds. As such it is completely 'windowless', in the sense that it has no means of communicating with the rest of the world, because everything that ever happens to it is part of its design, an integral part of its being the thing that it is. At the same time, though, this windowless monad is a 'perfect living mirror' of the whole universe, in the sense that just as the nature of the clock could in theory be read off from the nature of the bell, so a knowledge of the whole universe could be read off from a sufficient knowledge of this one cat – from what Leibniz calls its 'complete concept'. The cat, therefore, like every other individual substance or monad, mirrors, reflects or 'expresses' the whole universe from its own point of view. We poor humans, of course, do not know those complete concepts or true natures which contain the entire destiny of the monad and its surroundings – we know only a tiny fraction of the nature of the cat, because we see only the appearance of it. But if we did possess the complete concept of the cat, we would be able to deduce everything that would ever happen to it, and everything that had ever happened in the entire universe, as certainly as we can deduce the geometrical properties of a triangle from an understanding of the basic definitions of geometry.[6]

And there we have it. By following out the thread of explicability, we have proceeded by what seem like perhaps strange but surely not entirely incomprehensible steps to a world of windowless monads, incapable of causal interaction, yet each one mirroring the entire universe from its own point of view. What does it all add up to as a description of the world as we know it?

Reading

Leibniz's account of mind/body relations is set out in the *New System of the Nature of Substances and their Communication*. The notion of Complete Concepts is clearer in the *Discourse on Metaphysics*. The ontology of monads is summarised in *Monadology*.

Questions to ask

(1) Is the belief in Leibnizian Complete Concepts the only alternative to thinking that ultimately the world cannot be explained?
(2) Is it true that physics can never explain the world unless it is supplemented by metaphysics?
(3) Is Leibniz's theory of pre-established harmony just occasionalism by another name?

Chapter 12

Matter, mind and human life
The world as monadic

Leibniz's conviction that there must be a reason for every-thing that is has driven us step by step to a world which con-sists ultimately of nothing but a vast series of interlocking and perfectly synchronised reasons. How does that strange fairy-tale world of windowless monads relate to the world as we know it?

The material world

The details of Leibniz's account of matter and its relation to mind are obscure and much debated, but I think we can make sense of the general position.[1] Consider for example an individual material thing, like a tree. Nowadays we tend to assume that the most accurate description of the tree, the one which tells us what it is really like in itself, is a materialistic one which represents the tree as a collection of atoms which are themselves made up of smaller, subatomic parts. Leibniz, like Descartes and Spinoza, thinks any such account is obviously wrong: no atomistic account can ever provide an explanation of matter, because if the most fundamental subatomic particles are still material objects, then however small they are they have some determinate size, and so are not ultimate, but built up out of something smaller, and so on ad infinitum. And if the smallest particles are not themselves material objects, then atomism is not in fact a materialistic account after all, and we need some explanation of what those particles are, and how matter arises from them (cf. p. 271, footnote 6).

What, then, is Leibniz's alternative account of the true nature of the tree? The tree is, of course, a material mechanism, as Descartes had said; but for Leibniz any account of that kind, like the child's description of the clock, will be inadequate and misleading. The only true, complete account of the tree is given by its complete concept, which as we have seen mirrors or expresses the entire universe from the tree's own point of view. Thus the tree is to the right of the street lamp, opposite the school. And the school is on the main road into town, and the town is 20 miles from the city, and the city is . . . etc. etc.: the tree's position can be specified by reference to any and every object in the rest of the universe. And what is the thing that is to be found at that location? Well, it is an ash tree, and the ash is a member of such-and-such a family of trees, and trees are a certain kind of plant, and plants are a subset of living things, and living things are related to non-living things in these ways . . . and so on: the classification of the tree, like its location, can be made out with reference to everything else in the universe. And for Leibniz the life history of the tree is of the same kind. The tree was planted by this person, whose mother was this woman, who built that house, which is next to that factory, which makes this kind of product . . .; and the tree was attacked by these insects, which . . .; and it will one day be cut down by this builder, who . . . – the life of the tree is a window on the world, and we can follow up the ramifications of its life endlessly, as they bear with gradually diminishing directness on everything that has ever happened, anywhere in the universe. And *that* is Leibniz's account of what the tree is. It is *that* unique individual part of the universe, that individual substance, or that monad. In itself, you might almost say, it is nothing – nothing but a perspective, a point of view, a way of seeing the universe.

Note that a consequence of this way of seeing the world is that the monad which provides the ultimate explanation of the tree, like every other monad, is eternal. Just as it would be possible now, if only we knew enough, to describe everything that exists from the point of view of a future historian, it would also be possible to describe the whole universe in relation to a mouse which will be born in a thousand years' time; although our actual tree came into existence at a certain time and will one day cease to exist, its *point of view*, its perspective on the world, has always existed, and will always exist. Part of what it is to be that tree, after all, is to have been planted exactly 1,898 years after the death of Julius Caesar, just as part of what it is to be Caesar is to have died exactly 1,898 years before the planting of the tree. Perspectives, points of view, monads, do not come into and go out of existence, they merely feature more or less prominently in the experience of other monads. Thus the tree looms large in our lives, because we can see it, shelter under it, drive our cars into it; its relations to Julius Caesar are no less real, no less definitive of its nature, but very much less obvious to him. He never found any need to refer to the tree at all (or to me, or to you), any more than do people who currently live on the other side of the world, or those who will be around in 1,898 years' time. We therefore speak loosely when we say that the tree 'did not exist' in Caesar's day: it existed, but its existence was tacit, hidden, obscure to people such as Caesar. In the timeless understanding of God, which is the only true description of how things are, it was then and always will be every bit as prominent as it is now.

If all of that can be said of the tree, what do we say of the individual leaves of the tree? Essentially we tell just the same kind of story. Each leaf, too, is ultimately an individual thing, an organic unity, a monad, a perspective on the universe. While it is growing each leaf is also, in addition to being an individual in its own right, an integral part of the tree itself. We could describe the whole tree in terms of its relations to one leaf, or vice versa, but because of the kinds of way in which we relate to the tree and to the leaf it is more convenient and more economical to talk of the leaf as part of the tree than to talk of the tree as the leaf-bearer; in Leibniz's terminology, the tree is the 'dominant' monad, to which the leaf is subservient, i.e. the tree is an integrated system, of which the leaf is a subsystem. But for all that subservience, the leaf, like the tree, is still at bottom an eternal viewpoint on the universe, a living mirror, a monad. And what goes for the tree and its parts which are the leaves goes also for the constituent parts of the leaf itself. Leibniz was very deeply impressed by the work of seventeenth-century microscopists and their discoveries of such things as spermatozoa, and the hitherto unsuspected creatures living within the purest water, and he saw this as proof that what the tree is to the leaf, so the leaf is to its organic parts, and they to their own, and so on for ever: worlds within worlds within worlds without end.[2]

It is a strange place that the material world has turned out to be: a world of explanations, of reasons, of perspectives, which tends to leave people with the strange feeling that somehow there is nothing left to explain: what has happened to reality, to materiality itself? The answer is that it has been reduced to sets of relations. Time and space have both evaporated in the world as God knows it: it is true of the tree that it is near the tobacconist's and a long way from the Taj Mahal, and that is all it means to say that space is real; it is true that the tree grew after the death of Julius Caesar and before Leicester City won the European Cup, and that is all it means to say that time is real. And to say that time and space are real is what it means to say that there is a material world: matter is real in the sense that spatial relations and material interactions are not imaginary; but it is not substantial, not part of the ultimate, most accurate description of what there is. In the last analysis, what there is is not matter, not lumps of stuff, but reasons why lumps of stuff are as they are and not otherwise.

Leibniz on mind

Matter, then, Leibniz explains away as real but not ultimate, a consequence of monads and of their complete concepts. Does he do the same with minds? The short answer is yes and no: if by minds we mean centres of consciousness, then yes; but if we mean centres of perception, then no.

For Leibniz, as we have seen, everything that exists is either a monad, or an aggregation of monads. And every monad reflects, mirrors, expresses or perceives the entire universe from its own point of view. Therefore everything that exists is a perceiver, or has a mind. But of course, not all of these 'minds' are of the same kind, and in particular Leibniz is certainly *not* saying that everything that exists is a mind in the same way that a human being is a mind. Think of a flea again; and now think of the unthinkably tiny thing which makes up the thousandth part of the thousandth part of a cell of the flea's body. That thing, too, if it is a real thing, is a monad, just as an elephant is a monad; it exists, and is as it is, only because of the way it relates to everything else in the universe, and in that sense it feels the effects of the whole universe, or it perceives it. But it feels those effects only very dimly and indirectly. Remember what we said earlier about Julius Caesar and the tree in front of the school which was planted long after his death – God had that tree very clearly in mind when deciding to create Caesar, and he would not have been the monad who crossed the Rubicon exactly 1,958 years and some days before that tree was cut down to make way for the by-pass if instead it had died a natural death some years later. But the effect of the cutting-down of the tree on Caesar – his perception of it – is negligible, undetectable to us, and even to him. In Leibniz's language, Caesar does perceive the cutting-down of the tree, but dimly, confusedly. Now, the thing which is the thousandth thousandth part of the cell of the flea's body perceives the whole macroscopic world that we experience in the way that Caesar perceives the tree: it is virtually unaffected by it, to all intents and purposes, it is inert; nothing that we do will have any detectable effect on it, but it perceives it just the same.

Now move back up the size-scale of monads to the cat on which the flea lives, and *its* perceptions of the world. The cat is in some respects similar, and in some respects different. It is no more affected by such things as the success or failure of football teams, quadratic equations and Third World debt than is the particle of a flea's leg: it perceives all those things, of course, in the sense that it wouldn't be the cat it is if any of them were in the slightest respect different. But for practical purposes it is unaffected by them. Contrast that with something like the smell of fish, for example. To things like that the cat is very much more sensitive: if the smell of fish reaches it, even when it is asleep, the cat becomes excited, and its whole body and all its actions become focused on finding the source of the smell. The cat is fitted with receptors which in Leibniz's terminology 'focus' and heighten the effects of the air particles deriving from the fish as its eyes focus rays of light, with the result that the presence of the fish produces a very obvious reaction in it, whereas the success or failure of Leicester City leave it (astonishingly) unmoved. The cat not only perceives the fish, as it perceives everything else in the universe, but it has 'sensations' or heightened perceptions of it.

In this way animal and human feeling – 'sensation' – is explained by Leibniz as a special case of the universal quality of perception, expression, or mirroring. And in the same way he goes on to explain consciousness – or what he calls 'apperception' – as a special case of sensation. Like Spinoza, therefore, and unlike Descartes, he sees the human mind as a part of nature; just as a solid object has no more matter in it than does what the Aristotelian thinks of as an empty space, so the human mind has no more perception in it than does what the Aristotelian thinks of as inert, unperceiving matter. The human brain and nervous system are such that they can receive and store large numbers of sensations simultaneously; we can compare our feelings from moment to moment, learn from our sensations, and anticipate the future. Thought, consciousness or apperception is thus the product of systematic sets of simultaneous and successive sensations.

As an illustration of this he talks of hearing the sound of the wave crashing on the shore. That sound is actually made up of the undetectably small sounds of millions of tiny water drops landing together. We perceive every one of those sounds as 'tiny perceptions', but we are not conscious of them; all we are conscious of is their net result. In the same way, we receive messages from every area of our skin, reporting on its temperature, the feel of clothes against it, the pressure of the ground against our feet, and so on; but all we are conscious of, all we 'apperceive' is the net result of all these signals – a general feeling of cold, perhaps, which is not a further, separate sensation from all the tiny perceptions of all the parts of the skin, but the net result of a mass of sensations over a period of time.

Having a mind of this kind, or consciousness of this level, is the distinguishing feature of the human monad. There is only a difference in degree between the simple monad of a blade of grass, the simple soul of the animal and the rational mind of a human being; but it is a difference which builds up into a difference in kind. Because they are conscious, human beings can reason, can understand eternal truths of logic and mathematics. And because they can reason, and abstract from their immediate surroundings, they can consider alternatives and make choices, and are therefore responsible for their own acts in a way that animals can never be. Leibniz explains this by saying that human beings have a twofold relationship with God; whereas for the rest of creation God is the engineer, their maker and controller, for human beings he is also their sovereign; they enter into a moral relation with him, based on understanding and choice.

But that brings us to the great problem which Leibniz faced, and on which the viability of his whole system turns. If everything that happens in the universe happens because God, at the moment of creation, saw it as an ingredient in the best of all possible worlds, then what possible sense can it make to say that human beings are anything but clockwork monads, living out their pre-programmed existence in accordance with God's design?

Leibniz on freedom and necessity

This problem was raised against Leibniz from very early on in his philosophical life, and kept on recurring. He consistently replied that it was really no problem at all, but his readers took, and still take, a lot of convincing. We can divide the problem into two parts: the problem of necessity, and the problem of freedom.

Necessity

We saw earlier that Leibniz makes a distinction between necessary truths, which depend on the Principle of Contradiction, and contingent truths, which depend on the Principle of the Best. A triangle has three sides because if it had more or fewer it wouldn't be a triangle, and that would be a contradiction; an antelope has three legs, not because it is part of what it is to be an antelope to have three legs (as it is part of what it is to be a triangle to have three sides), but because the other one was bitten off by a crocodile. A triangle *has* to have three sides; that it has them is *necessarily true*: this antelope just *happens* to have three legs, and that it has them is *contingently* true.

The problem is that now that we have seen the kind of sufficient reason that lies behind these contingent truths, that simple-looking distinction seems to have evaporated. It is a contingent truth that the antelope has three legs as long as we think of it as we normally do – as that animal over there with the white patch on its nose and the tendency to hop a lot, for example. But if we possessed the complete concept of that antelope – if we knew it in its monadic unity, as God knows it – then we would know it as 'that monad which . . .' and there would follow a complete description of the entire universe, described in terms of its relation to that antelope. And somewhere in the middle of that unthinkably long description of the antelope, of course, would be an account of its losing its leg. But that means that the statement 'This antelope has three legs' is really just a shorthand for 'This monad, which is an antelope, which died 656,767 days after Caesar died and 17 years before Leicester City won the European Cup, which has a white spot on its nose, which has three legs after an encounter with a crocodile, etc. etc. etc. – has three legs'. And *that* statement will be necessarily true, because to deny it would be a contradiction.

Leibniz's answer to this is to say that there is still an important difference between necessary and contingent truths, even though it has turned out not to be quite the difference we thought it was. The point about the triangle example is that there is no possible world in which a thing could be a triangle and not have three sides.[3] Now, in the same way there is also no possible world in which *that particular antelope* (as specified by its complete concept) doesn't lose its leg; but there are many possible worlds in which God chooses not to bring that particular antelope, with that complete concept, into existence at all, and instead creates a different antelope, with a different life history. (Or no antelopes at all, or ones with special crocodile-resistant legs.) To know that a triangle has three sides you don't have to count them, you only have to know what a triangle is;[4] to know that the antelope has three legs without counting them you would need to know the respective advantages and disadvantages of all the other possible worlds, *and also* that God is good, and so chose to create only the best one. Therefore, although Leibniz holds that in every true statement the predicate is contained in the subject (e.g. 'has three legs' is contained in 'this antelope'), or as he puts it elsewhere, every truth has an a priori proof, there is still a difference between necessary and contingent, because only God possesses the complete concepts of things.

Freedom

If that was hard, the problem of human freedom seems to be even harder. Even if it makes sense to say that it's a contingent fact that Dinsdale Piranha nailed someone's head to a coffee table, how can it possibly make sense to say that he did it freely, given that the action is part of his complete concept, so that if he hadn't done it, he would have been a different monad? If there is an a priori proof that Dinsdale did it – even if that proof is available only to God – then surely he had no *choice* about doing it, did he? It may be true that a different Dinsdale could have acted differently – but surely *this* Dinsdale could no more choose not to nail people's heads to coffee tables than a clockwork train could choose not to run along its rails going 'choo-choo-choo'?

Again, though, Leibniz says no, by another piece of wonderfully clever (some would say sophistical) reasoning. To think that way, he says, is to confuse what he calls absolute and hypothetical necessity. It is *absolutely* necessary that *that particular Dinsdale* should nail people's heads to coffee tables, just as it is absolutely necessary that that particular antelope should have three legs; but it is *not* absolutely necessary that that particular Dinsdale should exist. That he does those things is *hypothetically* necessary, because it is necessary only *given* all the things that go to making him the person that he is. Given his personality and his upbringing and his values and his interests – and everything else that is true of him – *then* it is necessary that he does what he does. But that is only the same as saying that he freely chooses to act that way. Whereas the explanation of the three-leggedness of the antelope lies primarily in the crocodile, the explanation of the wickedness of Dinsdale Piranha lies primarily in Dinsdale himself. And that is what it means to say that he acted freely, isn't it?

It is true that anyone who possessed the complete concept of Dinsdale would know a priori what he was going to do; but none of us does possess that complete concept – not even Dinsdale himself. Therefore at the time of his unfortunate action Dinsdale, like the rest of us, is responsible for his own choice, because at the time of making it the future is open for him. He can understand the alternatives, and make a decision between them in the light of how he understands them, his expectations of their consequences, and the things he holds to be important. The fact that his social worker, and the Mounties who always get their man, can predict with a very high degree of probability what Dinsdale will do doesn't mean that he doesn't do it freely; and the fact that God can see with absolute certainty what he will do, and created him in the knowledge that he would do it, is according to Leibniz just the same.

Leibniz was a fantastically intelligent and creative thinker and writer, for ever pestering famous and important people with his new ideas and offering unsolicited comments on their work. Quite a few of them seem to have found him something of a pain. One of the people he latched on to in this way was John Locke.

Reading

Leibniz's account of matter can be seen in *Monadology*. There is a useful explanation of his theory of mind in the *New Essays on Human Understanding*, his reply to Locke. On freedom and necessity, see *Discourse on Metaphysics*, especially sections 13 and 30, and the *Correspondence with Arnauld* that it provoked.

Questions to ask

(1) Is it true that an atomistic theory can never give an explanation of matter?

(2) Does Leibniz succeed in explaining consciousness as a special case of universal perception, or mirroring?

(3) Does the idea of Complete Concepts exclude the possibility of free acts?

PART 4
John Locke

Biography

John Locke was born in 1632, the same year as Spinoza, and fourteen years before Leibniz. He was a schoolboy when Charles I was beheaded, and a tutor at Oxford when Charles II returned to the throne. He died in 1704, the year in which Newton published his *Optics* and J.S. Bach wrote his first cantata. His main philosophical works are *An Essay Concerning Human Understanding* of 1690, and the two *Treatises of Government*, published in 1689 but written much earlier.

He was born in Wrington in Somerset, the son of a lawyer and minor landowner who fought on the side of Parliament in the Civil War. He went to Oxford, and became a tutor there until he was bought out by Anthony Ashley Cooper, later the Earl of Shaftesbury, for whom he worked as physician, researcher, confidant and general adviser. In 1683 he fled to Holland when Shaftesbury seemed to be losing the religious, political and philosophical arguments over who should succeed Charles II, and he returned in 1689 after the overthrow of James II and the succession of William and Mary. He never married.

His work is a sustained argument for reasonableness and toleration in all areas. He examined the claims made by government, religion and science to the right to tell people what to think, and came to the conclusion that none of them had any foundation. He argued instead that their proclamations had authority only if and to the extent that they could be shown to be based on grounds which any reasonable person would accept for themselves.

His importance for Berkeley and Hume was enormous, but his real influence goes far beyond the thoughts of people who call themselves philosophers. His work perfectly encapsulates the liberal ideal. He was famous throughout the eighteenth century as a hero of the Enlightenment, much admired by, among others, the leaders of the American Revolution, and many of the ideas and attitudes he adopted have come down to us, built into the language that we speak and the institutions that we inhabit.

Chapter 13

On living in the world

Locke on the contents of the mind

Overview

All of the philosophers we have looked at so far have been concerned to tell us what the world is really like: to explain the reality which lies behind our experience. Locke is importantly different, not because he disagrees with his predecessors about the existence and importance of the distinction between appearance and reality, but because he begins from the other side of it. While they all began with what the world is like, and explained how our experience derived from it, Locke begins with what our experience is like, and shows how it connects – and in important respects how it doesn't connect – to the real world. Locke is therefore much more of a *social* philosopher than were his predecessors, both in the sense that his social and political writings were at least as influential as his more clearly theoretical ones, and also in the sense that his theoretical works themselves begin not from the objective facts as to how the world is, but from the subjective, engaged perspective of life in the world: not from metaphysics, but from epistemology – and politics. (See also Box 13.1.)

Box 13.1

Rationalism and Empiricism

The thinkers we are dealing with have traditionally been divided into two opposed camps, the Continental Rationalists (Descartes, Spinoza and Leibniz), versus the British Empiricists (Locke, Berkeley and Hume). The Rationalists are said to base everything on reason and seek to work out the nature of reality by thinking about it; the empiricists base everything on experience and try to discover what's what by looking around them.

The division was invented by Kant, who held that all of what we take to be reality derives from a combination of the nature of experience on the one hand, and the categories of our own thought on the other. He therefore presented his predecessors as having stressed only one side of this great divide which was finally overcome in his own work. Later writers, particularly in Britain, gave the distinction a more political and historical twist. They contrasted on the one hand the emotional, visionary, system-building continentals, producing their metaphysical visions of how the world must or should be, with the pragmatic, down-to-earth, practical Britons who kept their feet on the ground and took the world as they found it. (Thus the continentals had political theorists and revolutions, while the British had a series of political compromises and no written constitution.)

Until comparatively recently the history of modern philosophy was done in terms of these two schools of thought, usually interpreted as two different approaches to The Problem of Knowledge. The Rationalists, it was said, held that the Foundations of Knowledge lie in a priori certainties, while the Empiricists say that they are to be found rather in the data of experience. More recent work on the subject tends to be less schematic, more sensitive to the details of individual thinkers and their historical contexts. Seen from that point of view, there just doesn't seem to be some single all-embracing question that all six of our philosophers addressed but from two different standpoints, and whatever lower-level question you ask of them – be it concerning the nature and reality of knowledge or the nature of scientific inquiry – you get a variety of different answers which it is very hard to pigeon-hole into two opposed camps. All of

---

our six hold that rational intuitions are the most certain truths, which seems to make all of them rationalists; but none of them imagined for a moment that facts of nature could be discovered a priori, which makes them all empiricists. And all of them took Euclidean geometry as their model of what a completed science would look like, which would make them rationalists again, if it weren't for the fact that well-known empiricists like Newton and Boyle agreed with them.

But the terms are still used – more perhaps out of habit than because they are either philosophically or historically informative. If there is a real division to be made, it is perhaps this: that Descartes, Spinoza and Leibniz were much more optimistic than were the others about the possibility of a genuine science of nature. That difference is partly a difference in time (the 'Rationalists' were writing for the most part earlier, and were more concerned to advocate the boundless possibilities of the new view), and also partly a political, social and religious difference (Locke, Berkeley and Hume were writing for the educated bourgeoisie of a post-Civil War Protestant country). But it is also true that the Empiricists in general were much more suspicious of theories than were their counterparts across the Channel – though in each case for very strongly theoretical reasons.[1] Locke wanted to insist that science could never overthrow the good sense of practical men of the world; Berkeley held that every sensation was a message from God and therefore that too much theorising was impious, and Hume held that the only alternative to the prejudices of the ignorant were the no less irrational (but infinitely more sophisticated and therefore infinitely more ridiculous) prejudices of the learned.

After the sweeping philosophical vision of a Spinoza or the bizarre metaphysical calculations of a Leibniz, Locke's work reads as much more commonsensical, even dull. But that appearance of normality can be misleading, because Locke is a challenging thinker in at least two ways. Politically he was a revolutionary: when he fled the country with the manuscripts of his political writings in his luggage, he was in real danger, if he had been caught, of being hung, drawn and quartered for his views, something to which even the excommunicated Spinoza never came close. Second – and more important for our concerns – the obviousness and commonsensical nature of his ideas should not obscure from us the fact that the consequences of what he says are quite incompatible with some beliefs which we hold very dear. Locke's work therefore stands as a challenge to us: if we accept his common-sense account of the nature of man and the world, how can we avoid accepting his conclusions as to the impossibility of a genuine science of nature?

Writing on the paper, furnishing the mind

Locke, then, begins with the familiar facts of human experience, with the contents of the human mind. Where do all our thoughts come from? And what can we do with them? Those are the questions he sets out to answer in his attempt to explain what kind of creatures we are, what we can and can't do, and how we should live. His first move is one of those cases where his radical views are obscured to us by the familiarity which they have acquired since he wrote. He starts out by saying that everything we can understand, all the categories in terms of which we think and in terms of which our views of the world and of ourselves and each other are framed, are not things we are born with, but are picked up in the course of our lives. In Lockeian language, all our ideas come from experience.[2]

When a child first comes to exist, Locke says, it knows nothing.[3] It knows nothing, because it has no thoughts, and it has no thoughts, because it has nothing to think with. It has a mind, of course (and we will see later what Locke thinks that means), but that mind can't think, can't function, because it has no materials to think with – no concepts, no 'ideas'. In order to think even something as simple as 'The ball is red', for example, the child needs to know what a ball is, and what red is, and at this stage of its existence it has no such understanding. Locke compares it to a blank sheet of paper, waiting for life to write words on it; or an empty closet, waiting to be stocked up with useful concepts, to be 'furnished' with 'ideas'.

So how does the paper get words on it, how does the mind get furnished with all the vast and complicated clutter of thinking materials that the developed adult mind normally contains? By 'experience'. I learn what red is, for example, by seeing red things; I learn what warm is by being warm, learn what pain is by feeling it: simple, sensory concepts like these are acquired through the senses of sight, smell, taste, touch and hearing – what Locke calls 'sensation'. And as I get older, I develop another sense, to add to those five, another source of ideas. I learn, for example, what thinking is – or hoping, or remembering – in basically the same way I learn what red is: from doing it, from experience. From acts of thinking I learn what thinking is; from feelings of hope I learn what hope is, and so on. This gives me a kind of extra sense, an extra source of ideas which Locke calls 'reflexion' – the 'inner sense' of introspection, or my awareness of my own mental processes.

According to Locke, absolutely everything you can ever think, any thought you can ever have, no matter how original, creative or downright bizarre, can be traced back ultimately to concepts that you have acquired in one of these ways, through experience. Does that sound like a plausible story? Do you think there is any concept you possess that you think is *not* derived from experience?

There are two things we need to make clear about Locke's theory before you can really answer that question.

Simple and complex ideas

The first is that he is certainly *not* saying that all the ideas we have are simply imprinted on the mind by something we have directly encountered, in the way that it seems plausible to say that the idea of red is given to us by our having seen red things. An obvious example would be something like the idea of the Martian Three-Headed Snapper, terror of the outer reaches of the solar system, which lives by biting the heads off passing space explorers. That is an idea that I have, and which you now have, and yet it is something that none of us has experienced (yet). Is that a disproof of Locke's theory?

No. It is a central feature of Locke's theory that the mind, once it has been provided with the materials of thought, doesn't just retain them but can actually *do* things with them. In particular, it can:

- *Compare* ideas together – it can see, for example, that the idea of big and the idea of large are (at least almost) the same, whereas the idea of big and the idea of small are different. (And this, as we shall see later, he says is the basis of human reasoning.)

- It can also *abstract* from particular experiences and see what they have in common. It can produce the abstract idea of a person, for example, out of the ideas of all the particular people it meets, as well as producing abstract ideas like forgetfulness, science fiction and sport out of the ideas of particular instances of those things that it encounters. (And that, he says, is the basis of language.)
- And it can also *compound* ideas together – mix them up in new and sometimes bizarre ways so as to produce new discoveries and inventions, and also fantasies like that of the Three-Headed Snapper.

In Lockeian language the idea of the Snapper is a 'complex' idea, and it is very different from the kind of ideas we looked at earlier, such as warm, or red. The idea of the Snapper is compounded, or put together, out of other ideas, whereas the idea of red is not. As a consequence, I can give you a pretty good idea of what a Martian Snapper is like just by describing it to you, just as I can describe to you the Golden Temple in Kyōto, or the inside of my living room. But if you don't know what red is, what can I do?

If you have never seen a red thing, I can't give you any real idea of what red is like. I can use various kinds of analogy to give you some sort of conception of it (I once saw a film in which our hero explained red to a blind girl by putting a hot stone in her hand; Locke compares it to the sound of a trumpet), but really the only way I can explain it to you – the only way I can give you the idea – is to show you something that is red. Unlike the idea of the Martian Snapper, the idea of red is unanalysable and so inexplicable – what Locke calls a 'simple' idea.

A less silly example of the ability of the mind to make new compound ideas out of the materials it derives from experience is the idea of God. Locke is a committed Christian, and is quite happy to say that the idea of God is the idea of something that we never directly encounter (at least while we are alive). And indeed, since God is infinite in power, wisdom and knowledge the idea of God is perhaps the idea of something we never *could* encounter, and indeed in a sense something which no finite mind can ever understand. So where do we get it from? Locke has no time for people who claim (as we saw that Descartes did) that because the idea cannot be derived in any simple way from natural experience it must be implanted directly in the mind by God at creation. He observes that there are plenty of people in the world who appear not to have the idea at all (for example, he says, Native Americans), and he explains that it is simply something we create: we take perfectly natural, accessible ideas like power, knowledge and wisdom from our observations of people, and combine them with the idea of an increase without limit, and by that means we generate the idea of an all-powerful, all-knowing, all-wise, all-good God.[4]

(No) innate ideas

I hope those examples have made some sense of Locke's theory that all ideas derive from experience. Have you come up with any ideas which still seem to you not to fit the theory even as so amended? You need to be clear that what Locke is denying here is the existence of any *ideas* which are not derivable, either directly or indirectly, from experience; he is quite happy to say that the mind has certain natural *abilities*, or tendencies, which are just innate, and not derived from experience. The ability to compare, abstract and compound ideas once it has them, for example, is as we have seen something that is innate in the mind, something it is just born with – a kind of mental instinct. And that is how Locke would account also for what we sometimes (misleadingly, he would say) call innate knowledge, such as for example the baby's innate knowledge of how to suckle, or a weaver finch's innate knowledge of how to weave a nest. For Locke these are not exceptions to his theory, because they are really not *knowledge* at all, only abilities, or tendencies. The child is born with the ability to suckle, just as it is born with the ability to breathe; but its ability to do those things is not something intellectual, something mental; it is not really something it *knows* at all, just something it can *do*. So cases like that don't show that there are any ideas which are not derived from experience, do they?

The main point to grasp about this psychological theory of

Locke's is its political and social importance. It sits at the very beginning of his *Essay*, and was one of the most striking and influential aspects of the book. But it is much more than a contribution to epistemology or philosophical psychology.[5] The point is that if all our knowledge derives from our ideas, and if all our ideas are acquired from experience, then no-one has a monopoly on knowledge. If Locke is right, then no-one can argue that something is true because they say so, or because they have read it in Aristotle, or because it is part of the secret wisdom to which they alone have access. On the contrary, if he is right, then anything that is true can be shown to be true to any rational person who has the full use of their senses. His theory is therefore an attack, not on Cartesian epistemology, but on anyone who tries to pull the wool over your eyes and refuses to let you think for yourself. It is an attack on the corrupt and debased Aristotelianism of the universities, where people tried to pass off empty Latin slogans as deep wisdom (cf. Box 15.1); it is an attack on the magical tradition of occult knowledge which is available only to the magus, who understands the secret language and the hidden tradition of the ancients; it is an attack on the Catholic church, which Locke sees as holding that it is the job of the church to understand God and nature, and the job of the people to accept and obey. And indirectly, as we will see, it is an attack on any political system or theory which holds that some group or individual has a divine and inalienable right to rule.

Moving the furniture: Locke's three kinds of knowledge (or is it only two?)

It is a common oversimplification of Locke's position to say that he thinks that all knowledge comes from experience. He doesn't. All the paraphernalia of Lockeian psychology that we have just seen hasn't generated for him any knowledge at all; all it has done is to provide us with what he says are the *materials* of knowledge – the concepts, the categories in terms of which our knowledge of the world is framed. All of those materials, certainly, are derived from experience – from the senses or introspection – but a mind which had only those (if there could be such a thing) would in

Lockeian terms have no *knowledge* at all. It would be rather like someone who knew the meanings of all the words in the dictionary, but nothing else: such a person, if one could exist, would not in fact *know* anything about anything, because they would have no knowledge of how the meanings in their heads related to the world around them, or even one to another.

Of course, no such person exists, and Locke doesn't suggest they could. We all, automatically, derive knowledge from our ideas – but how? What else is needed, in addition to ideas derived from experience, to explain the knowledge that we have? What else would someone have to do, in addition to knowing the meanings of words, in order for us to say they have any real knowledge?

The answer is that they would have to be able to *think* about what they understood – to put two and two together, to see what all these ideas *mean*, as we might say, or what they tell us. Locke therefore defines knowledge not as the mere having of ideas, but as the ability to see the relations between them. Here is a Lockeian example. Merely having the simple, unanalysable ideas of black and of white, for example – having seen black things and white things, having learned to recognise them, and being able to call the ideas to mind when you choose to – does not in itself amount to knowing anything at all. But anyone who can do those things can in fact do a further thing: they can *see the difference* between the two ideas. Such a person therefore actually *knows* something – they know the trivial, obvious truth that black is not white.

Locke calls knowledge of this kind 'intuition', and he says it is the highest form of certainty there is. Anyone who has the two ideas in question can see immediately, intuitively, without any need to check or to work it out or to ask anyone else, that they are different.

Of course, not all knowledge is of this simple, intuitive kind. We can see intuitively that black is not white, that large is not small, and also that a triangle is a three-sided figure, and that 2 and 2 are 4. But just as we saw with Descartes, these rational intuitions don't take us very far. A second kind of knowledge is what he calls 'demonstration', or what we might call proof. That the interior angles of a triangle add up to 180 degrees, for example, is by no means intuitively obvious to anyone who possesses the ideas in question; but if you work through the proof (see Box 19.1) you *can* see intuitively that A = D, and also that B = E, and that C = 180 – (D + E). And once you've got that far you can if you think about it work out by means of those intervening steps that A + B + C = 180 degrees.[6]

Strictly speaking, according to Locke, intuitions and proofs like this are the only things we can *really* know. But of course, they make up only a tiny fraction of the things we normally say we know. I know there's a fly on the wall for example, because I can see it, right in front of me, very close up – much too close for it to turn out to be just a splodge on the paintwork or a small raisin someone has stuck to the wall for decorative effect. But no matter how obvious that fly on the wall may be, I don't know intuitively that it is there. There is no relation between the idea of a fly and the idea of the wall so that I can see there *must* be a fly on the wall; and there is no proof that anyone can come up with that will link the idea of a fly to the idea of the wall by any series of intermediate steps which *are* intuitively connected to it. I know the fly is there just because I can *see* it is.[7]

Does that mean I *know* the fly is on the wall? In typical style, Locke sometimes says yes and sometimes says no. He does say that strictly speaking it *isn't* knowledge, because it isn't a perception of the agreement or disagreement between ideas; but he also says that it does deserve the name of knowledge, because we would be crazy not to believe it, and he regularly refers to it by the name of 'sensitive knowledge'.[8]

Coming out of the closet: knowledge and the world

That then, is Lockeian psychology: his explanation of how the empty closet of the mind comes to be furnished with ideas, and of the different kinds of knowledge that they provide. Now that we have got that clear, we can begin to set out what things that apparatus reveals to us: what we can know of the world, and what that world is really like.

The first move is again very Cartesian. Just like Descartes, he says we know of our own existence by intuition: I can't doubt my own existence, because I can see intuitively that if I think, I must exist. But there is nothing else which I can intuitively know to exist. The existence of God is not intuitively obvious in the same way; but it is something we can prove.[9] Everything else, though, we can find out about only by sensitive 'knowledge'.

That structure has often been said to pose an enormous problem for Locke. If the only things we can know to exist by anything other than sensitive knowledge are ourselves and God, and if sensitive knowledge is at best the least certain of the three kinds of knowledge (and at worst not really any kind of knowledge at all), then it looks as if we can't really know of the existence of anything other than ourselves, and perhaps God. Locke seems to have put us back into the position that Descartes represented himself as being in at the end of Meditation 3 – we know ourselves and our own ideas and the existence of God, but everything else is problematic at best: perhaps all our experience of the world is just one long dream, or a fantasy imposed on us by some evil power beyond our control. It seems that Locke, for all his level-headed commonsensical descriptive approach and his insistence that our knowledge derives from experience, has failed to provide us with a clear, comprehensible, rational basis for a view of the nature of human beings and of our place in the world.

In fact, many people have thought that what Locke has done is the very opposite of what he intended: that he has actually made any such account impossible. By his repeated insistence that the mind must be furnished with ideas before it can know anything, and that all our knowledge is really knowledge of the relations between ideas, he seems to have trapped us for ever behind what later philosophers called the Veil of Ideas. We are cut off from any true knowledge of nature, trapped within our own minds and unable to make any direct contact with the world outside because of the intervening medium of our ideas. Those ideas, it seems, are the only things we can ever really know. They tell us that we ourselves exist, and perhaps that God does, but apart from that we can never know anything but what ideas we are having, and nothing of the world we normally take those ideas as informing us about. On this basis we can never give an account of human life which fits in with and makes sense of our pre-theoretical views; we take ourselves to be sensible, knowing, functioning parts of a greater world, but when we think about it, it seems that all such beliefs are at best groundless, and at worst mere fantasy. Scepticism rules (see Box 5.1).

This sceptical reading of the outcome to Locke's attempt to make clear the basis of our understanding of nature has been around since at least the time of Berkeley, as we shall see in Part 5. More recently there has been a lot of argument as to whether it is really the conclusion we should draw from Locke's position. Is he really making the depressing claim that all we can ever really have knowledge of is our own ideas, or is he merely making the much more reasonable point that all our understanding of the world is bounded by the sort of creatures we are and by the ways in which we interact with it through our sensory apparatus? Is he saying that apart from intuition and demonstration we have no knowledge, and so have no knowledge of nature? Or only making the much less startling point that our mathematical and logical knowledge are the only completely certain, provable, systematic areas of our understanding, and that all the other things we know are conclusions which we derive from our observations of the world around us?[10]

It is certainly very striking that Locke himself seems completely unworried by the Veil of Ideas problem which so many people have taken as the inevitable conclusion of the way he describes us. Is that because a more careful understanding of his work makes that problem disappear, or just because he was a bluff, crude Englishman who was incapable of seeing the obvious consequences of his own blind common sense? He occasionally provides something which looks like an argument for saying that the sceptical conclusion from what he writes is untenable, but most of the time he treats it as a position not worth considering, too obviously nonsensical to be discussed. If anyone is minded to question the existence of the world around them, he says, they are either joking or talking nonsense. Tell them to put their hand in the fire, and then let them ask whether there is really such a thing as an external world.[11]

Reading

Book 1 of the *Essay* contains Locke's attack on the belief in innate ideas, and the early chapters of Book 2 give his alternative 'empiricist' account of how we learn. The first part of Book 4 sets out his account of the kinds and range of our knowledge.

Questions to ask

(1) Is every concept you possess analysable into materials provided by experience? Or are there some concepts you make for yourself?

(2) Are any concepts simply imprinted onto the mind by experience? Take for example the concept of red. Do you have a concept of every possible shade of red, or only as many as you have words for? If your language had no separate words for red and orange, would you have a concept of red at all?

(3) Is there any real solution to the Veil of Ideas problem?

Chapter 14

Locke on nature (and our knowledge of it)

We have now seen what Locke has to say about the contents of our minds, and about what they can do, and what they can know. Now we need to look around us: given that starting point, what can we therefore say about the world that we find ourselves in, and the sort of creature that we are? As I said in the last chapter, whether he should have or not, in practice Locke has no hesitation in telling us what lies beyond the Veil of Ideas. So what is it?

Appearance and Reality: Locke on Primary and Secondary Qualities

The first move is to separate Primary and Secondary Qualities (see Box 14.1). In some of the most discussed (and worst presented) sections of the *Essay*, he divides all the properties of objects into three kinds:

(1) *Primary or Original Qualities*. He lists these to make the position clearer – but the lists vary. Usually they are size ('bulk'), shape ('figure'), and motion, but sometimes also number, texture and/or solidity. These, he says, are properties which a thing always has, no matter what you do to it. That doesn't mean you can't *change* those properties (although Locke often writes as if it did). Obviously you can change a thing's size, for example. The point is rather that if an object doesn't have *some size or other*, it isn't an object at all – things can be tasteless and colourless, but they can't be sizeless. He also says that our ideas of primary qualities correspond to ('resemble') something in the object itself: shape, size etc. are real, irreducible features of an object. Its Secondary and Tertiary Qualities, by contrast, are not further features, but only facts about how an object with those primary qualities interacts with its environment.

(2) *Secondary Qualities*. Examples are colours, tastes, smells, hardness and softness. These are not really properties of a thing at all, he says, so much as powers to cause ideas in our minds. This is particularly misleading, since he also says that all properties are powers to cause ideas in our minds. What he means is that it is in virtue of their Primary Qualities that objects have the power to cause ideas of Primary Qualities in our minds (it is because the book is square that in relevant circumstances it looks square); and it is *also* in virtue of their Primary Qualities (and those of our perceptual system) that they have the power to cause ideas of Secondary Qualities (it is because of the sizes, shapes and motions – not the bluenesss – of the particles on its surface that in relevant circumstances the book looks blue).

(3) *Tertiary Qualities*. He gives as examples such things as the power of heat to melt wax, or of magnets to attract iron. These too he says are not really properties but only powers; the only difference between these and secondary qualities is that this time they are powers not to cause sensations in us, but to cause changes in other objects.

As I've tried to show, Locke's presentation of this part of his story is particularly unclear. But his purpose is clear enough.

He is agreeing with Descartes, Spinoza, Leibniz and the rest of the 'new philosophers' that the best way to explain all natural phenomena is as the result of mechanical forces. In other words, he believes that we can account for everything that happens (in the material world, at least – see p. 166) by reference to the mechanical properties of the microscopic and submicroscopic parts of matter – what he calls the Primary Qualities of their Insensible Parts.

Box 14.1

Primary and Secondary Qualities

I started this book by saying that the most important fact about the people we now call the philosophers of the seventeenth century was their belief in a radical and systematic distinction to be made between the world as it seems and the world as it really is – between the world as it is experienced and the world as science reveals it to be. (See Introduction.) A central part of the task of explaining and justifying that separation was the job of drawing up a list of the properties which things could truly be said to possess, which could feature in an accurate, scientific description of how it really is, as opposed to those properties which we attribute to it in our ordinary lives, but which strictly speaking are features of how *we experience* the world, rather than facts about how it is *in itself*.

An obvious example that Descartes discusses is that of tickliness (*chatoüillement*).[1] In one sense, of course, it is an obvious, objective truth that some things are tickly and some things aren't. Silk isn't, wool usually is, and the plastic labels that manufacturers sometimes sew into the necks of garments often are as well. But none of us think that the reason for those differences is that wool and labels possess a special and mysterious property of tickliness which silk doesn't have; it's obviously just that the way the fibres of the wool are arranged means that, given the nature of human skin and its level of sensitivity, wool produces one kind of reaction in us and silk, because of its different structure, doesn't. That is just obvious common sense. The tickliness of the wool, you might say, isn't a separate property of the wool; indeed in a sense it isn't a real, inherent property of the wool at all, so much as a fact about how the wool behaves, and in particular how it interacts with the human sensory system. The real, inherent properties of the wool in this example are the way its fibres are arranged, and it is those properties, when combined with the inherent properties of our skin and nervous system, which result in the fact that wool can be described as being tickly.

The great breakthrough of seventeenth-century thought – the Appearance/Reality distinction – was to extend this kind of thinking much more widely than it had been taken before. Huge numbers of properties which had previously been taken to be unproblematic features of objects – colour, taste, hardness, beauty, and lots more – were now treated in the way that we have just said it is natural to treat the property of tickliness – as being not really facts about objects, so much as facts about how those objects interact with their surroundings, and in particular with human beings. And the writers who sought to popularise this new view duly spent a lot of time in drawing up lists of which properties survive this process of explaining away features of our experience, and which don't. Classic instances are found in Galileo, and in Descartes, and also very famously in Locke, where it is described as the distinction between Primary Qualities (the inherent properties of objects) and Secondary Qualities (things which in ordinary speech we say are properties of objects, but which are really just facts about how we perceive them).

Locke, like most of the advocates of the 'new learning' of the seventeenth century, was a mechanist – he thought that every natural event can in theory be explained as being the result of mechanical interactions between particles of matter, usually microscopic and/or submicroscopic. His list of primary qualities therefore included only mechanical properties – basically size, shape, motion and number – because his mechanism meant that all natural events are the outcome ultimately of collisions, and in order to understand the outcome of a collision between a number of objects, all you would need to know is how many there were, how big they were, what shape they were, and how they were travelling.[2]

Unfortunately Locke's presentation of this part of his picture is one of the most loosely written sections of the whole *Essay*, and it is very easy to miss the point of what he is trying to do. This is a shame, because it tends to obscure from us the extent to which we all now tend to take for granted a distinction of the kind he is making. Few people nowadays would claim to be mechanists, certainly – but that only means that our list of primary qualities would be different from Locke's. It is still true that most of us, if asked why the grass is green, would say – with varying levels of sophistication depending on our training – that it was something to do with the way the microscopic and/or submicroscopic particles of the grass are affected by light and the way that light affects our eyes. If asked to spell out what precise properties of the grass and the light and of our eyes were responsible for this effect many of us would struggle, but the list would certainly not include tickliness, or colour, or beauty, or softness, tastiness, or the tendency to dissolve in water. All of those properties, we think, can be explained in terms of the basic, inherent, *primary* qualities of the object and of its environment. If we were able to specify all the primary qualities of a thing and of its surroundings, we believe, we would have said all there was to say about it. The objective view, the scientific view, aims to do exactly that.

That attitude is something we have inherited from the work of people like Locke and Descartes. Berkeley and Hume both claimed that it made no sense at all. Which do you believe, and why?

Common sense and metaphysics: Locke on substance and mode

On the nature of knowledge, and in his mechanistic picture of how the world works, then, Locke, for all his alleged 'empiricism' (see Box 13.1), is very Cartesian. When it comes to metaphysics, though, it looks as if he is not.

Descartes, you will remember, insisted that the common-sense view that the world consists of a large number of individual things was wrong. We may *talk* as if trees, houses, wardrobes, mountains and hockey sticks are all individual objects, but in reality they are just conventionally individuated areas of a material continuum. In technical terms, Descartes rejected common-sense *pluralism* in favour of his own material *monism* – he denied the traditional, Aristotelian sense-based view that individual things are separate individual *substances*, and claimed instead that ultimately there is only a single material substance, of which each individual thing is only a *mode* (cf. pp. 12–17).

Locke will have none of this – but for reasons that are more political than metaphysical. He is much too respectful of the common-sense views of down-to-earth, practical men of affairs like himself to say that the things they take for granted in their day-to-day lives are just mistaken, so he simply takes for granted the kind of commonsensical pluralism that Descartes, Spinoza and Leibniz had, as we have seen, all rejected. For Locke, all the things we normally talk of as substances *are* substances. A tree, a house, a butterfly, a cloud, a hockey stick and a novel about a fish, all of these for Locke are not just groups or collections of properties, they are *things which have* properties – individual substances. There are also general substances – natural kinds, of the sort that we still call 'substances' today. Gold, for example, is a substance; lead, water and air are others.[3]

But obviously not everything we see around us is a substance. A line of trees, for example, is not a substance, not a separate thing, but only a mode, which in Locke's usage means an arrangement of things, a *consequence* of the way things are, or a way in which we talk about them. The trees themselves are substances, things in the world; the line they make is a mode – not an extra thing, just a way those things are.

Yet at the same time as he adopts this traditional way of speaking, Locke is quite insistent that it is, for scientific purposes, quite useless. To try to explain the world, as the Scholastic Aristotelians did, by reference to substance he thinks is absurd. He compares it to primitive, mythical ways of thinking, in which for example the question of what holds up the earth is answered by saying that it rests on the back of an elephant; and then the elephant is held up by a tortoise, and the tortoise by . . . something else.[4] At each stage, we cover up our ignorance by inventing another creature to support the last one, and no link in the chain goes any way at all towards answering our original question (cf. Box 15.1). This is how he regards traditional Aristotelian science: if you want to understand what underlies and explains the properties of a tree, for example, you are told by the learned doctor that the tree is a substance, in which the properties of leafiness and woodiness inhere. And what does that explanation amount to, when stripped of the obscurantism of bad Latin in which it is phrased? It says there is something that stands under the properties and under-props them. And what is that thing? A stander-under, an under-propper – a sub-stance. All of that is clearly nonsense, and must be swept away and replaced by a mechanical natural science which gives real explanations of the world by reference to the primary qualities of its invisible constituent parts. The tree is green, we hypothesise, because it is made up of tiny corpuscles which are arranged in such a way that when particles of light hit them they bounce off with a particular kind of speed and spin; and when light particles moving in that way hit us in the eye, they give us the kind of feeling we refer to as 'green'.

And what about the mental world? What about the minds in which those green ideas are to be found? Again, Locke (in this case like Descartes, but quite unlike Spinoza) is a pluralist: minds too are individual substances, individual things. Can they too be explained mechanically, by the primary qualities of material corpuscles? Where Descartes, Spinoza and Leibniz in their various ways said certainly not, Locke says perhaps: perhaps it will turn out in the long run that there are no separate mental substances, just physical ones. But typically, he also insists that the question of the ultimate constitution of the mind doesn't really matter much. We know well enough what people are, and how to treat them, without a deep understanding of what, in the final analysis, they may be.

We see this attitude most clearly in his discussion of Personal Identity.[5] What is it that makes you now the same person you were when you were a child, even though you are probably quite unrecognisable as that child, and even though there is probably not a single particle of your body now which was also part of your body then? Do you have an unchanging immaterial Cartesian soul which has been attached to the successive material collections that have made up 'your' body? If so, could that thinking substance have once been attached to a different person who is now dead? Could it in theory one day migrate from you to someone else, or move into a dog, a parrot, or a banana? Locke's answer to all these questions is a very definite 'maybe'. His point, though, is not to lament these important things we can't know, but to stress that they are simply irrelevant to what we need for our lives. The only identity that really matters, he says, is responsibility. What we need to know is not the answers to these recherché questions about the sameness of your underlying substance, but the practical question of whether we can reasonably hold you responsible for an action performed by someone in the past. And that question he claims we can and do have an answer to.

Quite simply, if you can remember performing the action in question, if it is part of your present consciousness, then you are the person who did it, you are responsible for it, and you deserve whatever praise or blame attaches to the act, regardless of whether you are or are not the same substance as before; and on the other hand, if you have no recollection of the action in question, and cannot be brought to a consciousness of it, then it was not your action, you are not the person who did it – and that would be true even if it could somehow be shown that the same material or immaterial substance inhabits your body now as inhabited the body of the person whose action it was.

There is a lot more that could be said about that story. (Do I get let off my crimes if I have a bad memory? How many people have I been in my life?) Its significance for us is the kind of practical, down-to-earth agnosticism about the reality behind the appearances which is central to Locke's whole project, and which many people find very appealing in contrast to the speculative reasonings of his predecessors. In other areas, as we shall see, that same attitude comes to look more problematic.

Knowledge and the world: real and nominal essences

Just as Locke attacks Aristotelian science for its obscurantist appeal to substance as an explanatory concept, so he also attacks it as being concerned only to explain the meanings of words, not the natures of things. Consider a general substance, like gold, for example. What is it? Locke says in effect that there are two ways you can answer that question. First, you can explain what gold is in the sense of explaining what the word 'gold' means – how we recognise it, the definition of the term. An explanation of this kind, Locke says, gives us only what he calls the 'nominal essence' of gold, or the meaning of the word, and would go something like 'gold is a soft, heavy metal which doesn't rust, has a distinctive colour and reacts in this way to these chemicals'. Definitions of that kind are helpful, and enable us to tell the difference between gold and less precious metals; but we must be clear that a nominal essence of that kind tells us nothing at all about gold, the stuff, but only about 'gold', the word. To ask what gold is in itself is to ask a quite different question. Here we are concerned, not with words, but with things, not with *nominal* essences, but with *real* essences.[6]

As we have seen, for Locke as for us the real essence of a substance like gold is given by its particular microscopic and submicroscopic structure, by the way the invisible particles are put together. It is this inner nature, this atomic structure as we would say, which constitutes the real essence of gold, and which is responsible for all those properties of gold which feature in the nominal essence by which we recognise it. It is because of its atomic structure – because of the primary qualities of its invisible parts – that gold is yellow, for example, just as we saw that it was because of its atomic structure (and those of our eyes and light) that the book is blue. In the same way it is because of its atomic structure that gold is heavy, and soft, and reacts as it does with other substances.

The position is quite different when we are dealing with a 'mode', rather than a substance. A mode, as we saw, is not a thing, but a way we talk about a thing. In the case of a mode, therefore, the definition we give to the word is all there is to it. What we mean by the word 'line' or 'triangle' is what those things really are; but what we mean by the world 'gold' is not. Gold is a thing, a substance, a part of the world, so it has a reality of its own which is quite independent of the ways we think and talk about it; a line is a mode, a category of our invention, so what we say about it is what it really is. In Lockeian language, therefore, in the case of a mode the real and nominal essences coincide, but in the case of a substance they are very different.

All this is, I hope, fairly straightforward and – like most things in Locke – commonsensical. But here we come to the big divergence of his theory from our contemporary assumptions. Which is right, Locke, or modern common sense?

The essence of knowledge and the knowledge of essence: the possibility of a science of nature

If we put together what we have seen here of Locke's account of real and nominal essences with what we saw earlier of his views on the nature of knowledge, the next step becomes clear. Knowledge in the strict sense, we saw, is the perception of the agreement or disagreement between two ideas (with or without the use of intermediate ideas to make those agreements and disagreements obvious through a demonstration). The properties of a thing (including the properties which make up its nominal essence) are all derived from, are all consequences of, its real essence. It follows that if we have ideas of a thing's real essence, we will be able to see the relation between those ideas and the thing's properties, and so we will have knowledge, in Locke's strict sense, of those properties.

Take the example of gold again. If you know how to recognise gold, you know its nominal essence, you are aware that it is a soft, heavy metal. That is sensitive knowledge, observational knowledge which you have acquired from your experience of gold and from what you have been told about it. But if you know its real essence, you will know what we might loosely call its atomic structure, or what Locke would call the primary qualities of its insensible parts. And if you know that, you can see *why* it is soft, for example: it is soft because the corpuscles of which it is composed are of such and such a shape and size, and are held together in such and such a way, so that when pressure is exerted on them they move relative to one another to some extent – and that is what we observe as the property of being 'soft'. If you have an idea of the real essence, therefore, you can see how it is related to the property of softness, and so have genuine *knowledge* of that property, in place of the mere observational familiarity – the sensitive knowledge – that you started out with.

This is the kind of knowledge we can have in the case of something like geometry, according to Locke. It is one thing to have observational, practical, sensitive knowledge of the way shapes behave, and another thing to have real *knowledge* of those facts. The ancient Egyptians, for example, had learned from experience – they had sensitive knowledge – that one of the angles of a triangle whose sides are three, four and five units in length is always a right angle (and modern-day builders still use the same principle in marking out land), but they didn't in Locke's terms 'know' that it was true, because they didn't understand the geometry that lies behind that fact. By contrast, the Greek geometers (most famously Euclid) knew the real essence of the shape, and so could by means of a proof see how the property of being right-angled depended on it, and so knew in a much stronger sense that such triangles must always be right-angled (cf. Box 19.1). They weren't merely familiar with it as a fact, they really *knew* it.

But the point Locke is making is that such knowledge is attainable *only in the case of modes*, where the real and nominal essences coincide. In the case of substances – real things in the world, as opposed to our inventions – the real and nominal essences are different. And because the real essence of a substance consists in the primary qualities of its *insensible* parts (i.e. those which are not detectable by our senses), and since all our ideas of things in the world come from our senses, it follows, he said, that we can never have ideas of the real essences of substances, and as a result that we can never have knowledge, in the strict sense, in what we now call natural science.

This is a huge change from anything we have seen so far, and is another one of the many things that some people mean by calling Locke an empiricist. For Descartes and Spinoza especially, a true science of nature was not only possible, but necessary. The only way to see things as they really are is by seeing how the phenomena we observe flow from the underlying facts of nature. For Descartes that is the only way to truth, the way we recapitulate in our small way the non-sensory, rational understanding of the God on whom we depend. For Spinoza it is the only way to achieve freedom from the enslavement of appearances, the way to achieve the intellectual love of God, our only possibility for lasting satisfaction, co-operation with other people and a kind of eternal understanding. And here is Locke saying it just can't be done.

Not surprisingly, what some have called Locke's empiricism, others have called a kind of desperate scepticism.[7]

For Locke himself, though, as in the case of Personal Identity, it is nothing like so limited and depressing. Just as in that case, he sees this very limitation of our faculties as a kind of liberation.

He compares himself to a sailor, whose lead line tells him how deep the water is. The fact that that lead line cannot reach to the bottom of the deepest oceans doesn't mean it is useless; provided we know how long it is, we can sail the seas in safety. In the same way, the fact that our faculties don't provide us with a genuine science of nature is no real problem to us; provided we know how far our understanding can reach, we can proceed about our business in the world with confidence, and without the danger of either wasting our energy in trying to find out what we can never know, or of having the wool pulled over our eyes by magicians who know some clever tricks and speak an arcane language of their own and who claim to understand what in fact they never can.

It seems to me that that challenge of Locke's to the obscurantist scholastics of his day would apply all the more forcefully to the pretensions of some natural scientists today. According to Locke, science in the strict sense is impossible, and we should not be misled by its wonderful creations into thinking it is in touch with the ultimate nature of reality: it isn't, and it never can be.

This pragmatic, practical challenge to the over-estimation of our scientific knowledge is beautifully summarised in a passage where he talks about a watch, and what we can and can't know about it. If we had 'microscopical eyes', he says, we would be able to see into the innermost structure of the spring of the watch, and see the way the particles of the metal are put together, and so we would understand why it is that the spring is springy. We would then have ideas of the real essence of the substance that is the metal, and we would have true scientific knowledge of its springiness. That would be a wonderful thing, and who knows what secrets we would thereby become party to? Unfortunately, of course, such an ability would be worse than useless to us. If our eyes were made in that way, we would perhaps know all sorts of wonderful truths about the watch – but the watch itself would be no good to us at all, because with eyes like that we wouldn't be able to see what time it was.[8] We are simply not made for knowledge, according to Locke. We are made for social life – for commerce, for politics, and for religion – and we should seek our satisfactions and our freedoms not in vain attempts to penetrate into the mind of God, but in making our way in the world, setting up just societies, and using our practical, empirical knowledge of the way the world around us behaves to help us do those practical things better.

I don't want to give the impression here that Locke was an opponent of the new science of the seventeenth century, because he was very far from that. He was a great friend of Boyle and knew Newton,[9] and he was an enthusiastic supporter of the Royal Society of London. Locke is a great supporter of science – but he says it must be kept in its place. Because our knowledge is limited by the kind of creature we are, we can never know science as we can know geometry or mathematics; but that doesn't stop us from improving our lives by our investigations of nature. The fact that our senses don't allow us to penetrate into the secrets of the spring's springiness doesn't mean we can't study mechanics and metallurgy. We can and we should – because it can do a lot to help with the practical lives of human beings. All he is pointing out is that the knowledge we can attain in such fields will always be *hypothetical*: we can have *theories* in science, but not knowledge. We can have no direct access to the real essences of substances – but we can make theories about them, and test those theories, and improve them, and develop them, and expand our practical, instrumental knowledge of nature without limit. But we should remember that such theories will only ever be that – useful hypotheses to enable us the better to conduct our lives on earth, not a true knowledge of the nature of nature.

How does this story strike you? It seems to me that in our current view of science most of us are partly Lockeian, and partly not. We are familiar with the idea that science is provisional, hypothetical – that tomorrow we may make a new discovery which will show that all we have thought so far is wrong, and that we have to reassess the whole basis of our understanding of the world. That is a truly Lockeian attitude. Yet somehow at the same time the practical impact of our investigations of nature is so enormous (and the politics of scientific knowledge so important) that many of the things we say and think about science and scientists are not easily reconcilable with that belief in its provisional nature. We seem sometimes more like Cartesians, convinced that the view of the scientist is the only true account, and that scientific theories are theories only in name, that they have reached the status of scientific *fact*. If Locke is right, that can never happen:

our common-sense view of the world is grounded in the kind of creatures we are, and can necessarily never be overthrown by anything we could ever discover. To think that it could would be to devalue our humanity without the possibility of ever putting anything in its place.

Reading

Locke sets out the basic distinction between primary and secondary qualities in *Essay* 2.8. His main discussion of substance is in 2.13 and 2.23, and of essence in 3.3. For the denial of the possibility of a natural science, see especially 4.3.

Questions to ask

(1) Why should we accept the distinction between Primary and Secondary Qualities?
(2) Can Locke's memory criterion of personal identity give an adequate account of moral responsibility?
(3) Does the history of science since Locke's day bear out his belief that a genuine science of nature is impossible?

Chapter 15

The life of man

Locke's political thought

Our obligations to God and to man

Unlike all our other philosophers, Locke was more influential as a political thinker than as a thinker of any other kind. I have tried already to bring out the political dimension of the topics we have looked at. He speaks throughout from the engaged perspective of the man of affairs, and his whole thought is organised around the demand for freedom of the individual – or at least for freedom of middle-class white European males such as himself. We saw this in his rejection of the doctrine of innate ideas – we are born as white paper, nothing is beyond question, and all knowledge is in principle available to anyone who has full use of his faculties. The same attitude lies behind his account of personal identity and his denial of the possibility of a true science: no-one has access to the hidden secrets of nature, but what we need to know for practical purposes we can know. Even the most arcane scientific discoveries yield only provisional hypotheses which are testable by experience and which are valuable to the extent that they provide useful practical results for practical people of the world. The ideal life for man is not the contemplation of eternal verities or the recapitulation of the understanding of God, but the life of the free man who knows his obligations to his fellow men and to God. So what exactly are those obligations?

In religion, Locke is a convinced Christian of a fairly conventional kind. But it is his *reasons* for his religion that are important. As we have seen, he thinks that the idea of God is explained in the same way as other complex ideas of things we have not directly experienced: it is put together out of the ideas of things we *have* experienced (see pp. 152–3). We know that God exists, not because it is revealed to us in some blinding vision, not because we feel it in our hearts to be true, not by a leap of faith, and certainly not because we take it on trust from either political or religious authorities. We know of God's existence and nature because it is rational to conclude that God exists: anyone who considers the nature of creation and the way it is organised would come to the conclusion that there is an all-good and all-powerful creator. Locke is quite happy to concede authority to scripture and to the church – but only in so far as any reasonable person confronted with the evidence of scripture would come to the conclusion that it is the word of God, and so would give authority to it. In other words, we should submit to the authority of religion only if and to the extent that we *choose* to do so; and we choose to do so only if and to the extent that we see good reason for that choice.

In a sense, we could say, what Locke calls obedience to scripture is not obedience at all, since we obey only where we have *chosen* to obey. The same principle, as we will see, is central to his attitude to the state.

Original appropriation: Locke and the rights of man

As befits the practical, social nature of his work, Locke is the first of our philosophers to think carefully about society and government, and to ask not only how it came to be as it is, but also the much more dangerous question of how it *ought* to be.[1] What is the basis of the law? What right does the state have to tell us what to do? As we have seen, his basic story is that people must be free to

live their own lives and make their own choices; he therefore provides a theory of law and of government which represents them as
legitimate only if and to the extent that they permit and enhance
such freedoms. But before we can decide what law and the government should
be like, we need to get clear about what they are for. Why do we
have them in the first place? In order to answer that question,
Locke imagines what the world must have been like when there was
no government and there were no laws, and he tries to show how
they might have come about, and what purpose they are supposed
to serve. In his own language, he looks at what people would be
like in the State of Nature – he strips away all the trappings of
society and community life, and imagines people living alone or
in small family groups away from other people, and he then asks
what rights and what obligations, if any, they would have in that
situation.

Natural laws and natural rights

A good way to ask yourself this question is to look, not back in
time, as Locke does, to a time before society, but forward, to a time
when society has been destroyed. Imagine that the world as we
know it has been largely destroyed by nuclear war or massive
ecological disaster. As soon as the air is fit to breathe again, you
climb up out of the bunker which you had so thoughtfully built
for yourself, and you emerge into a silent, empty world, 98 per
cent of the population of which has been wiped out. There is no
electricity, there is no government, there are no policemen – just
you and a few other survivors scattered here and there through the
silent landscape. Ask yourself: what rights and what obligations do
you have in that situation?

In one sense, the answer is that you have none at all. If government and civil society have been wiped out, then all rights and
obligations have been wiped out with them. For example, there is
food and clothing lying around in the shattered remains of the
shops. You would surely be crazy just to leave it there and starve
and/or freeze to death on the grounds that it isn't yours and the
owner isn't around for you to buy it from. (As if all the money

hadn't melted anyway.) In a situation like that, surely, it's nonsense to say you can't take it because it isn't yours. It isn't *anybody's* any more, is it? It's just lying there, like the fruit on the trees in the empty world that Locke imagines. The whole notion of owner-ship, of rights, seems to have been destroyed, along with all the institutions that preserved it.

Well, perhaps not entirely. According to Locke, even in the State of Nature, when there is no government and no society, there are still laws of a kind. They are not legal laws, obviously, because there are no laws any more. And they are not moral laws, either, because Locke sees morality as a matter of social rules, and so with no society, there can be no morality in that sense. So what other kind of laws, and what other kind of rights, could there be?

Some people would say there are moral facts, moral obligations, in *any* situation – moral necessities which are independent of whether or not there is any society to recognise and enforce them, in the sense that some things just are, in their very nature and regardless of circumstances, just right, or just wrong. But that is *not* what Locke says. He does think there are still rules – rules as to what we can and cannot, should and should not, do – but they are not moral laws but purely *natural* laws: they are laws of *nature*, general facts about the world which tell us what it is and isn't reasonable, or sensible, for us to do. By thinking about what life would be like in the State of Nature, he thinks we can see what these natural laws are, and what natural rights they produce.

There are two ways you can bring out what Locke is getting at here. Ask yourself: leaving aside all moral and legal considera-tions, what sort of thing would it not be sensible (or prudent, or reasonable) for me to do as I wander through the ruins? Or to put the same question another way, what sort of thing would I object to, even in that situation, if one of the other survivors did it to me?

According to Locke, the first and most basic rule of living in such a situation is that you don't mess with other people. If you are attacked, you will fight back if you can. If anyone tries to kill or injure you, or to make you do anything that you don't want to do, you will resist – and you would expect other people to react in the same way if you did it to them. Locke puts this point in a way that is easily misunderstood: he says we have a 'natural right' to life, health and liberty – meaning by that simply that people will defend these things, and resist interference with them, even in a state of nature, and therefore that anyone living in a state of nature would do very well to realise that fact.

Importantly, these 'rights' extend not only to your person – to your body and your actions – but also to what you produce with them. If there is a lifetime's supply of cornflakes on the shelves of the burnt-out Safeway down the road, you are unlikely to object if someone else helps herself to a packet. But what if you go down to Safeway's and get yourself a box, and she then comes into your bunker and takes it away from you? The chances are that you will object. Why?

Well, because in a sense it was yours. Again, it wasn't legally yours, because there are no laws any more; and it wasn't morally yours, because there is no morality. But because you had *worked* to get it – even if only by walking down the road and taking it off the shelf – you had a 'natural right' to it, in the sense that if anyone tries to take it away from you, you will object. In Lockeian language, you had 'mixed your labour' with it – i.e. just as you have a 'right' to do what you want with your own body and will resist interference with your actions, so you have a 'right' to what you produce by those actions, and you – and other people similarly – will resist interference with such products.

The point of this consideration of the State of Nature is that Locke is trying to represent the whole of our moral and legal systems as conventional and institutionalised forms of these basic, irremovable rights of nature, given to us by the law of nature, i.e. by the basic facts of the kind of creatures we are, and the kind of attitude we naturally take. This story therefore has two purposes. It serves to *explain* our legal and moral institutions as deriving from some basic characteristics of human beings; and it also works to *legitimise* those institutions if and to the extent that they correspond to those basic facts of nature.[2]

The limits of appropriation: Locke's two conditions of ownership

So far, then, we have a theory which explains the institution of property as perfectly 'natural' – not something created by the legal and social systems which enshrine it, but something deriving from fundamental facts about the sort of creature we are. Many people have seen this as self-justifying. They allege that Locke has simply formed a notion of what is natural from an examination of people like himself – people who live under a certain kind of political system – and then used that notion to justify our all living in that way, living a life which takes acquisitiveness and selfishness as the defining characteristics of all human beings.[3] We can't go into that debate here; but one thing we do need to get clear about is that Locke is certainly *not* saying that since ownership is a natural right, greed is good, and we are perfectly justified in owning as much as we can possibly get our hands on. I do have natural rights over my own body, and I therefore have rights over whatever it enables me to produce; but for Locke these natural rights have natural limits. Specifically, there are two limitations which he sets to our acquisitiveness.

The first of these limitations is that I have no rights over what I can't use. Go back to our post-holocaust scenario again. It seems reasonable, as we have said, that anything I have rescued from the remains of the supermarket and stashed away in my closet is mine; but what if over a period of time I stash away more tubes of anchovy paste than I could possibly eat in several lifetimes, so that they all rot away in my bomb shelter when other people might have been enjoying them? That would seem crazy – quite apart from the fact that I ought to have better things to do with my time than to accumulate stuff I can't possibly use, it is also *unreasonable* of me to take it out of circulation, and you would be quite justified in breaking into my store and helping yourself to a few tubes if you could get there before they went off. There seems to be another natural law: that I can't reasonably keep to myself – I have no natural right over – what I can't possibly use.

There is a second constraint which Locke places on our right to appropriate which is more significant and more problematic, and depending on how hard we insist on it the whole interpretation of his political thought can alter. What happens if there are only two jars of chocolate spread left unbroken in the whole city, and you and I both want them? Assuming I eat the stuff at a reasonable rate, there is no danger that I won't eat them both before their sell-by date comes round, so the first restriction doesn't apply. Does that mean that if I get to the shop before you I am justified in running off with both jars and leaving you without a single delicious spoonful of the stuff? Think about it. How would you react if I did? Would you say 'Fair enough – you got here before me so I can't complain if you eat both jars'? Or would you say it was unfair, unreasonable on my part, to run off with both jars and leave you with none? Locke says the latter. I can sensibly be said to own what I have appropriated to myself only if (i) I can use it, *and* (ii) there is 'as much and as good' left behind for other people to enjoy.

A lot has been written about this second condition and how we should interpret it. Gloss over it, and Locke's theory seems to say it's OK for us to own as much as we can get our hands on; stress it and it begins to look as if he's saying that all goods should be divided equally among the people. The truth, I guess, lies somewhere in the middle: that he is advocating a kind of sensible and responsible ownership and due regard for the plight of others less fortunate than oneself.

Institutionalised ownership: the role of money

How does this State of Nature story strike you? Does Locke's attempt to explain and legitimise political, legal and moral systems by a consideration of how it would be sensible to behave if we didn't have them seem to you make sense of the world as we know it? Or do you think that all this talk of original appropriation, rights of nature, states of nature and post-holocaust survival is so far removed from the kind of complex international political and economic structures that we now inhabit as to be completely useless? Before you make your mind up on that, you need to take account of what Locke says about the use of money.

The introduction of money transforms the State of Nature into something rather more like the world as we know it. Some people say that therefore the conclusions Locke draws from his imaginary world are of no relevance.

The first thing that money does is to transform completely the first of Locke's restrictions on ownership. It is a real restriction on my wealth to say that I can only legitimately accumulate as many apples as I can eat before they go off; but if I can exchange those apples for gold coins or for numbers in the bank's computer, neither of which need ever go off, then the limitation seems to be completely removed. The theory therefore legitimises the vast differences in wealth in both Locke's day and our own; at most the restriction says that no-one should own more than he or she can use. But how much is that? Similarly also with the second restriction. Since the quantity of money in the world is not fixed, what seemed at first to be a sensible limit on the accumulation of wealth seems again to have evaporated, since however much I have, I can always claim there is enough left for other people.

Consent to be governed

We have talked so far about ownership and about rights. Where does the government come into the story? To answer that, Locke again goes back to the State of Nature. As long as there are not too many of us wandering around in the ruins of the city, there will be no need for a system of government at all. But on our own there is little we can do. If we want to restart the power station, reopen the hospital and the opera house, or stage a football match, then we will need to co-operate with other people. The rights of nature provide a framework for such co-operation, because the laws of nature are general truths which any sensible person can appreciate. But as numbers of people and the complexity of our dealings increase, disputes are bound to arise. When they do, of course, even sensible and level-headed Lockeians will tend to lose their objectivity when they are arguing about whose turn it is to clean out the sewers, or whatever, and this means that the only way we can enjoy the advantages of co-operation with other people without spending all our time squabbling is for us to appoint someone to settle our disputes for us – and that is the role of government.

There is lots more to say about this, but we have to stop at the bare bones. The vital point to see is that the government is therefore the *servant* of the people. No-one has a divine right to govern (as for example Charles I had claimed), and the powers of the government are not unlimited (as Hobbes had famously said they must be). On the contrary, just as we saw Locke say that the church has authority because we can rationally see that it should have authority, so he says that the government has power over us only because we decide to give it such power. All the people who participate in the society are by so doing giving their *consent* to be governed: we are tacitly agreeing to be bound by its rules in return for the advantages we derive from it. But if the government ceases to do the job for which we use it, then the people can and will withdraw that consent, and rebel. And that is precisely what Locke and his faction did in 1688, when James II was removed from the throne and William and Mary installed in his place.

Locke's *Essay* was published in 1689, two years after Newton's *Principia*. Between them the two works established something of an orthodoxy for educated thinkers at the beginning of the eighteenth century. But George Berkeley thought that new orthodoxy was completely wrong.

Box 15.1

Explanation and pseudo-explanation: Molière's dormitive virtue and the Scholastics

In the third interlude of Molière's play *Le Malade Imaginaire*, there is a little comic song in which the university student sings of his lessons at the hands of his master. 'The learned doctor has asked me the cause and reason why opium puts people to sleep. I reply that it contains a dormitive virtue, the nature of which is to deaden the senses.'

The point of this little joke is, of course, that the student, although he has got the 'right' answer, hasn't actually answered the question at all. What was he trying to explain? The fact that opium puts you to sleep. How does he explain it? By saying it has a *virtus dormitiva*. And what does it mean for something to have a *virtus dormitiva*? It means it deadens your senses, or puts you to sleep. The officially sanctioned 'explanation' has actually explained nothing at all: all the student has done is to translate the problem into Latin, and announce it as if it were an answer.

Molière's little joke sums up the attitude of most thinkers in the modern movement of the seventeenth and eighteenth centuries to the established learning of the day. It is very noticeable that none of our philosophers worked in a university.[4] The universities at the time were in a period of steep decline. They were standardly referred to as the 'Schools', and the people who taught there as 'Schoolmen', 'Scholastics', or sometimes (because the dominant tradition of learning there derived from Aristotle) as Aristotelians, or Peripatetics – and all our writers to different degrees and in different ways derided the work that was done there. Like Molière, the new philosophers claimed that Scholastic philosophy provided no real explanations of anything, and that all that the learned doctors of the Schools managed to achieve was at best an impressive display of useless information, and at worst, as in Molière, all they did was to cover up their ignorance with meaningless technical jargon.

I suggested in the Introduction that the great change that took place in the seventeenth century was the shift from a chiefly descriptive science, based on the classification of phenomena and the tracing out of their interrelations, to a more analytical approach centred on the idea that the world of experience is only the appearance of an underlying reality that science aims to reveal. Our philosophers, as part of that revolutionary movement, rejected not only their contemporary Scholastics, but the whole tradition they were working in, and the classical authorities (chiefly Aristotle, but also Plato) from whom it was derived.[5] The standard objections were that traditional learning:

• Doesn't provide explanations (because it classifies, instead of analysing)
• Invents a complex technical vocabulary which sounds impressive but has no meaning to anyone but the philosophers themselves. (In part this attack was a consequence of the abandonment of Latin as the language of science.)
• Talks only of the meanings of words, not of the nature of things (because their work took the form of definition by classification).
• Bases its views not on rational investigation of nature but on what past authorities – chiefly Aristotle – had said.

The later, 'empiricist' writers Locke, Berkeley and Hume in particular liked to challenge their opponents to cash out their technical language in clearly comprehensible, empirically definable terms. Locke especially (following Hobbes) insisted on translating Scholastic Latin terms into English to reveal their lack of any clear meaning or explanatory power. And that is the weapon that

Berkeley uses against the notion of material substance, and that Hume develops into his critique of ideas like causation and the self. Look at the following three sets of terms and ask yourself which ones you think are mere meaningless verbiage, incapable of being given a clear sense, and which are genuinely meaningful terms. And ask yourself also how you know the difference.

1 Substantial Form, Haecceity, Quiddity (Scholastics, as mocked by our philosophers)
2 Matter, Cause and the Self (seventeenth-century science and current common sense, as attacked by Berkeley – in part – and by Hume)
3 Black hole, non-individuality, strangeness (present-day scholasticism, or hard science?)

Reading

The material covered in this chapter is set out in Locke's Second *Treatise of Government*.

Questions to ask

(1) Do Locke's 'natural rights' provide a naturalistic grounding for moral and legal obligations, or are they just moral obligations by another name?
(2) Does the notion of a State of Nature have any relevance to contemporary moral and political life?
(3) Is it true that you tacitly consent to the rules of a society just because you happen to live in it?

PART 5

George Berkeley

Biography

George Berkeley was born in 1685, the same year as G.F. Handel, J.S. Bach and Domenico Scarlatti. Spinoza had died eight years earlier; Locke's *Essay* was published when he was five. He died in 1753, six years before Wolfe's capture of Quebec, when Hume was forty-one, Kant was thirty, and Mozart was minus-three. His chief works are the *Principles of Human Knowledge* (1710), and *Three Dialogues between Hylas and Philonous* (1713).

He was born near Kilkenny in Ireland, and became first student and then fellow at Trinity College, Dublin. He was ordained in 1709, and eventually rose to become a bishop in the English-imposed Protestant Church of Ireland. For a time he was a well-known figure on the London literary scene, friend or acquaintance of figures such as Swift, Pope, Steele and Addison. He was convinced that the fashionable ideas of people such as Locke showed the intellectual and moral decay of Europe, and in 1728 he set off with his new wife to found an ideal college in the uncorrupted new world of Bermuda. They got as far as

Newport, Rhode Island, but failed to raise the money for the project, and came home in 1731. The couple had seven children, only three of whom survived beyond childhood.

Berkeley's work is an attempt to save the world from secularism, and to use the weapons of the Enlightenment to argue us back to a knowledge of our total dependence on God. Although best known now for his immaterialist philosophy, in his day he was perhaps more famous as an educator and economist, and his most successful publication was *Siris: A Chain of Philosophical Reflections and Inquiries Concerning the Virtues of Tar-Water* (1744).

Chapter 16

Denying the obvious

Berkeley's radical reinterpretation of human experience

Overview

All through this book so far I have been trying to put over the idea that the most important single feature of seventeenth-century European thought, as articulated, legitimised and popularised by our six philosophers, was what I have called the invention of a new reality – the development of the idea that our day-to-day experience of the world is only the superficial appearance of things, and that reality is known if at all only to the expert. All the philosophers we have looked at so far have been participating in or responding to the establishing of that view, and Berkeley is no exception. What is different about Berkeley's work, though, is that he thought that this new metaphysics and epistemology in general – and those of Locke in particular – were leading us in exactly the wrong direction. His whole philosophical effort was therefore devoted to the attempt to destroy them, and to replace them with radically different versions of his own. Unfortunately for him he failed to persuade his contemporaries that they were wrong. And what we have inherited from that time and now take for granted is something very like the views that he fought against as being harmful, irreligious, false and absurd.

Berkeley's rejection of modernity

Berkeley wrote 'in opposition to sceptics and atheists'.[1] As he saw it, the metaphysical and epistemological views of the new philosophers such as Descartes and Locke – which I have tried to show we share in many ways – were socially, politically, theologically, morally and psychologically dangerous, because they lead to scepticism and atheism. And if you think about it, I think you can see what he means.

Modernity and atheism

Modernity tends to promote atheism. Berkeley saw clearly how the new reality as proclaimed by the new science can come to replace God in people's thoughts. The reality which science discovers, like God, is infinite – at least in the sense of boundless. Like God also, it is eternal, in the sense that it will last until the end of time. More and more it comes to replace God as the stopping-point of explanation: where in other times people tended to refer to strange or unexplained events as the will of God, now they saw them as simply the deterministic outcome of the way the world really is. It is nature – matter, the scientist's reality – and not God, which is the cause of all we see around us. Of course, except in the case of Spinoza this was not the intention of the people we have looked at. God was the ultimate cause which lies behind nature in a way which is often at least closely analogous to the way in which nature underlies the world of experience. But for Berkeley the belief in that underlying nature meant that the move to God became a *further* step, an *extra* set of explanations, and he thought that it was a step which people would soon not bother to make at all, or if they did, the God they would believe in would be a remote, theoretical figure, not a living presence in their lives.

But it is not only as the cause and explanation of what goes on around us that nature can tend to usurp the place of God. A Christian sees herself and all around her in relation to God. God is her standard of truth, her ultimate, unchanging reality. It is in relation to God that she understands herself and the world around her, and it is by reference to God that she decides her values and judges what is important and what unimportant, what is good and what is bad. What Berkeley feared is that all those roles would also come to be taken over by the alleged hidden reality which science reveals. And again, he seems to have been right.

Most of us now tend to see ourselves in relation, not to God, but to the material world. It is science that provides our conception of truth, and the world it reveals gives us our notion of ultimate, unchanging reality. Our idea of what a person is, of what we can be, is set not by religion, but by biology. Our idea of how we should live is informed by a study of evolution. The object of our understanding is the material world as revealed by science, the standard in terms of which we measure the world and all around us is the standard of the facts which science reveals. We may not actually pray to the natural world, but it is that natural world to which we are answerable, which inspires our feelings of awe and of our personal insignificance, and which is the fixed point of our transitory existence. All of that has come about since Berkeley's day, and is exactly what he predicted, and what he tried to avoid.

Modernity and scepticism

His second fear was the rise of scepticism, which we can read in a number of different ways. On one level it is the simple point that if Locke's view of the world is taken at face value, then – as Berkeley read him, at least – we are for ever trapped behind the Veil of Ideas, cut off from any knowledge of the only reality we now allow. Even if we read Locke more sympathetically, there is no doubt that scepticism of some kind remains: as we saw, a true knowledge of science is beyond us (the real essences of substances can only be hypothesised about, not known); the only things we can know for sure are the appearances (the nominal essences) – we know what things do, but we can only develop theories as to why they do it.

But there is I think another sense in which the rise of the new metaphysic leads to scepticism. If all that is real, all that is lasting – the truth, the arbiter of our lives – is something that doesn't feature in our lived experience but is only accessible to the expert, then the condition of human beings is in many ways an unattractive one. Later philosophers have made this point by saying that we are *alienated* from the world around us, and suffer feelings of *anomie*: the world of our experience, the world in which we actually live and operate, is the rich, colourful, living world of emotion, of values, of interests, a dynamic world of constantly changing perspectives. Yet we have come to believe that reality is wholly different from that: it is unchanging, value-free, lacking in all the qualities which make our lived world what it is. The result is a kind of dissatisfaction, a loss of self-esteem. Our lives seem pointless, our concerns seem trivial; we are strangers in our own world. That estrangement, that sense of not belonging, is also perhaps part of what Berkeley foresaw and tried in vain to prevent.

Berkeley's work, then, was aimed at turning back the tide of scepticism and atheism that he saw the modern world as necessarily involved in. He was no Aristotelian, looking to take us back to a pre-Cartesian world without the radical distinction between appearance and reality; instead he offered us a different account of what that reality is. Quite simply, having seen what he held to be the danger of the Cartesian/Lockeian view of nature as something which as it were comes between God and mankind, he set out to show that there is no such thing. According to Berkeley, there simply *is* no natural world as we usually understand it – there is no matter, no material substance, no world-as-it-is-in-itself, no mind-independent reality. Despite everything you might think of as the obvious appearances to the contrary, what we call the real world does not, and could not, exist. All there really is in existence, in all the whole universe, is only God, and our minds.

The idea strikes most people as completely crazy – and so it did when Berkeley first presented it. He was mocked and derided as a lover of paradoxes and as a sceptic in disguise, and people reportedly closed the door in his face when he came to call, on the grounds that if there is no material world he should be able to get in anyway. But Berkeley was quite sincere in his belief. He holds, quite literally, that the only things that exist are minds, and that everything else you see around you (or you *think* you see around you) is in fact just a message from God to you, an idea in your mind, put there by the infinite mind that is God. What we call nature or the real world is in reality a kind of giant picture show, designed, produced and presented by God. All the order, complexity, richness and stability that we see around us is evidence, not, as we tend to think, of the independent existence of a world outside our minds, but of the subtlety and invention of the divine agent who keeps the show on the road. The belief in a mind-independent material world is not the obvious, basic truth that most of us take it to be, but a mistake foisted on us by the new philosophers – and one which can only lead us away from God and towards the desolate and estranged life of the sceptic. Fortunately, Berkeley thinks, it is not too late: the belief in matter can be shown to be not only false, but absurd; all we have to do is to think about it carefully, and attend to the obvious evidence of our common experience.

The plausibility of immaterialism

As I have said, hardly anyone has ever been a convinced Berkeleian.[2] Most people find his position incredible, outrageous, obviously unacceptable – a curiosity at best. So why bother to talk about him? There are two reasons why I think it is important to read what he says. The first is that, as most people find when they discover Berkeley, although his position seems so obviously wrong – to the point of complete lunacy, many feel – it is in fact extremely and frustratingly difficult to disprove.[3] We'll come on to this shortly. The second reason lies not so much with his positive account of how the world really is, but with his negative account of how it isn't, and indeed how it *cannot* be – namely, the way we all think it is. Berkeley's arguments against the existence of a material world I think turn out to be much more powerful than you might expect. To my mind, what they show is that our contemporary common-sense views are not the obvious bedrock of truth we have always taken them to be, but are in fact an indefensible mishmash of incompatible and ill-conceived opinions which have been foisted on us by our historical situation, but which are

completely unjustifiable once you take them out and look at them.
(But then, I do tend to have rather extreme views.)

So, the challenge that Berkeley's work poses to all of us is
twofold:

(1) Are you prepared to accept his positive claim that all that
really exists is only God and finite minds? If not, do you have
any *reason* for rejecting it, or is it just that you won't accept
what you're not used to? And second:
(2) Can you find any way of resisting his negative claim – i.e. his
denial of the existence of the mind-independent material
world in which we all believe?

The two questions are quite separate. Your answer to the first will
depend to a great extent on your attitude to his theism. Berkeley's
positive view is all about God, and is quite inconceivable without
it.[4] But the second is very different. Berkeley presents a whole
barrage of reasons as to why there can be no material world, and
as far as I can see only one minor one of those arguments takes
for granted the existence of God. All the rest work equally well
for the atheist as for the theist. Whatever your theological beliefs,
therefore, you have to decide whether you think those arguments
work, and whether you can successfully defend our common-sense
views.

I shall present those two questions in reverse order. In the next
chapter I will look at Berkeley's negative claim – his arguments
against matter – and give you a chance to think about whether or
not you accept them. The following chapter will then set out in
more detail his own alternative, positive position, so that you can
see how his own view hangs together. But before we go into all that
we need to be clear about what exactly is at issue between Berkeley
and us.

Johnson's attempted rebuttal

How would you set about trying to disprove Berkeley's claim that
there is no such thing as a material world, that all that exists are
minds and their ideas? A famous contemporary of Berkeley's was

Samuel Johnson, the English lexicographer and man of letters.[5] Boswell reports that on hearing of Berkeley's theory he kicked a stone and said 'I refute him . . . *thus!*'[6] Is that an effective disproof of what Berkeley says?

The Johnson manoeuvre nicely catches our natural response to Berkeley's position. If someone suggests that the dagger you see before you is not a real dagger, but like Macbeth's is really only an hallucination, a vision, a hologram or a trick of the light, your first reaction is to reach out and try to touch it to prove that it is really there. If you can feel it, cut yourself with it, slip it into your pocket and ruin your nice new trousers with it, then the suggestion is wrong – there's obviously more to it than just something in your head or some kind of image. If you can touch it, move it about, do things with it, then surely it's a real, solid, material, mind-independent dagger. Quite naturally, then, when Berkeley tries to tell us that everything we ever see is really just a system of visual impressions, we tend, like Johnson, to react in the same way – we kick the stone, feel the edge of the knife, bang our hands against the table: obviously there's a real world!

How Berkeley can reply to Johnson

But actually this is a completely hopeless attempt to refute Berkeley's position, and misses his point entirely, because what Berkeley is claiming is not that what we think are material objects are really just a set of visual images or impressions, but that they are just a set of *sensory* impressions of various kinds – including impressions of touch. Think about it a moment. According to us, what is going on when Johnson kicks the stone? Well, light from the sun hits the stone, bounces off and hits big Sam in the eye. This produces a whole series of events in his nervous system, the upshot of which is that he has certain visual impressions which he has learned to associate with stones. And when his foot hits the stone, the story is similar: interruption of foot movement by stone causes compression of foot by boot, causes various events in Sam's nervous system resulting in the kind of pain or pressure sensations he has learned to associate with foot coming into contact with a solid object like a stone.

And what is Berkeley's analysis of the same process?

Well, it's much simpler, but in some important respects it is exactly the same. The visual impressions Johnson gets when he looks at the stone are exactly the same as in our account; all that is different is the *cause* of those impressions: where we have the complicated paraphernalia of light and stone and eye and nervous system, Berkeley simply has God, who gives Johnson the visual impressions direct. And exactly the same is true with the pressure sensations that Johnson feels in his foot. Both accounts are in complete agreement that the lexicographer has some nasty pain-in-the-toe sensations; where they differ is only that where our story has all the complicated business of legs and boots moving through space, and impulses carried along the nerves of Johnson's material body to his material brain, Berkeley again just has God, giving the lexicographer the crushed toe sensations direct, without the need for any intermediary.

Get the idea? There aren't any stones as we normally think of them; what we call stones are in reality only consistent and regular sets of stone-impressions – visual, tactile and all the rest – in our minds. And that's what toes and boots turn out to be as well – nothing but a perfectly regular and consistent system of toe-impressions and boot-impressions which is perfectly co-ordinated in all our minds.

Think of it this way. As Locke has shown us, all our knowledge of the world is derived, either directly or indirectly, from the ideas we get from our senses. Every thought we can ever think is either a sensory impression, an impression derived from introspection, or something made up of or derived from such 'ideas of sense', as Berkeley calls them. So what do we need the material world for? Everything that we can do with our idea of a natural, material world, Berkeley can do directly with his God, planting ideas of sense straight into our minds, with no material world in between. Johnson's gesture of frustration is no more than that – Berkeley knows full well what it feels like to kick a stone; and he also knows from experience that when God gives us the kind of visual impressions we call 'seeing a stone', then anyone who is unwise enough to swing their foot in that direction will receive from God the kind of tactile impression we call 'banging your foot against a solid object'. Berkeley's account of the nature of our *experience* is exactly the same as Johnson's, or ours, or anyone else's; what he disagrees with us about is not the *content* of that experience – what kind of experiences we can expect to get in what kind of situation – but the *cause* of those experiences. And Johnson's attempted refutation tells us nothing at all about that.

If this story is making any sense to you at all, then by this stage you may be thinking of two objections to what I have said so far.

(1) But the intermediaries do exist! All I have said is that we can't tell the difference between a visual impression of a stone which is caused by light affecting my eyes and setting up a response in my nervous system on the one hand, and an exactly similar visual impression directly implanted into my mind by an all-powerful God on the other. That may perhaps be true.[7] But the fact remains that I do have eyes, and they are sensitive to light; we know that light really does bounce off stones, and if you cut me open you could detect the response in my visual system and in my brain. Perhaps it's true that a God-implanted feeling would feel the same as a naturally produced one, but as a matter of observable fact sensations *are* naturally produced!

Ask yourself: what would Berkeley say in response to that?

The answer is that he would say exactly the same about the inter-mediaries as he said about the stone. Of course I have eyes and a brain, for example. But what does it mean to say I have these things? Well, take the example of my eyes. To say I have eyes is to say, among other things, that whenever I look in a mirror in an appropriate way I see my eyes – i.e., says Berkeley, whenever God gives me visual impressions of looking in a mirror in that way, he gives me visual impressions of my eyes. 'Yes, but there is more to my eyes than the visual impression I get when I look in the mirror. I can feel them for example.' Well, yes, of course. God often gives me the sensation of blinking, for example. (And every time he does, he interrupts my visual impressions.) And if while looking in the mirror I am foolish enough to poke myself in the eye to see if it is real, he will give me the visual impression of the reflection of my finger moving towards the reflection of the eye, followed by the interruption of those impressions, an impression of pain in the eye, and a squidgy feeling in the fingertip. In general, *everything* that we want to say exists, Berkeley will agree with us; but where we want to say that these eyes, fingers, stones or whatever are independently-existing material objects which *produce* various sensations in us, Berkeley will insist that they *are* just systematic sets of impressions, produced in our minds in a law-like way by an omnipotent God communicating directly with our minds.

(2) A second objection that may have occurred to you is this: if all there is is minds and ideas, and all the other things that exist in the world, including our own bodies, are just sets of interconnected impressions produced in our minds by God, then what can it possibly mean for Berkeley to talk about deliberate physical actions such as swinging my foot to kick the stone, or moving my hand to poke myself in the eye? Think about it: what is his answer going to be?

His answer here is simply the same answer all over again. To talk about my foot is to talk about ideas: the feel of my shoe against it, the visual impressions I get when I look at it, the pain I get from my bunions, etc. etc. All these ideas come directly and in a systematic way from God. If I decide to put my foot on the table, I am asking God to give me the sensation of the table under my foot, to have the visual impression of my foot on the table, the sensation of a twinge in my knee when I move it, etc. etc. etc.: and providing everything is working normally, God duly gives me those ideas when I ask for them.[8] Sometimes, of course, things don't work normally; if the table I want to put my foot on is in Botswana and I'm in a little village in Manitoba, for example, then God will not oblige me with the appropriate ideas – I obviously haven't learned the kind of thing the human body is and isn't capable of (i.e. the kinds of idea sequences God is and is not willing to give me). Or if unbeknown to me my leg has secretly been tied to the chair with one of my mother's hairnets, then again God will not give me the idea sequences I had hoped for, but a rather different set involving a pinched feeling round the ankle, shouts of an enraged mother, and so on.

By now I hope you are beginning to see the frustrating unassailability of the Berkeleian account. There is simply NO test that you can carry out to disprove his hypothesis, because *everything* that nature can do for us, God can do for Berkeley. Johnson's kicking of the stone is in the same position as Locke's injunction to put your hand in the fire if you doubt the world around you (see p. 158): all that any such test can tell us is that our experience is or is not consistent with the expectations we have formed on the basis of past experience; it can tell us *nothing at all* about whether the underlying cause of those experiences is a mind-independent material universe, an infinite divine mind, or something different again.

If you're still puzzled about why I say Johnson's rebuttal doesn't work, look at Box 16.1, and go on to the next chapter, especially (pp. 202–5), which covers some of the same ground. In the next chapter but one we will look in more detail at Berkeley's positive account, and some of its strengths and weaknesses. But first we must turn to his negative critique of the natural world we all believe in. Given that, as we have just seen, there is no test we can devise which will enable us to decide which is the correct theory – that the two are, as we might say, functionally equivalent – what other kinds of reason might we have for preferring one to the other? Berkeley is going to try to show us that his is the only theory any sensible person can adopt.

Box 16.1

Ideas of sense: interpreting the data of experience

What do you see when you look around you?

Look around you now, and list three things you can see.

The chances are that your list consists mostly of medium-sized material objects, like chairs, tables, walls, toilet paper, oranges and people. The question I want to ask is: are those really things you literally *see*? Or are they things you *say* you see, but which really you work out, infer, interpret, *on the basis* of what you see?

In my case, the list includes a couple of rather large and tasteless apples, lying in a dish. Do I actually *see* that they are tasteless?

Well, not really – they look to be of the large and watery kind, and the one I ate yesterday had less flavour than the average lettuce; but strictly speaking, you might say, their tastelessness isn't something

I *see*, so much as something I *remember*, something I have learned to *associate* with apples that look like that. Tastelessness, we might say, isn't itself a visual property, but we can detect tasteless things by sight because we have learned which visual properties it is associated with.

So what *is* a visual property? What can I *really* see? How about the property of being an apple? Is that a visual property? Is it something I literally see, or is it too something I work out on the basis of what I see?

Two reasons for saying I don't really see that they are apples:

1 First, someone could (if they had the time and resources and nothing better to do with their lives) make something that looked exactly like an apple out of wax, or paper, or plastic, or even old newspapers, for all I know. These things could, if they were well enough made, look exactly the same as the things I can see in front of me now. But they wouldn't be apples (at least, not real apples). Doesn't that show that there's more to being an apple than looking a certain way, and therefore that the fact that these things in front of me *are* apples isn't something I can just see, but something I have to work out on the basis of what I see?

2 Second, a person with perfect eyesight but absolutely no knowledge of fruit or of fruit bowls and who sat where I am sitting would not know that those things there were apples. Yet she would surely *see* exactly what I can see (if she looked). So being an apple isn't something you can see, is it?

Try the same arguments with examples from your own list.

It starts to look as if the number of things you can actually see is much smaller than we normally say it is. The things I see, it would appear – really see, as opposed to inferring on the basis of what I see – must be only the basic, uninterpreted visual data which my eyes receive. Everything else that I say I see is really an *interpretation* which I put on to what I see, on the basis of things I have seen in the past. And what are those basic uninterpreted visual data like? What are you left with if you strip away from your visual experience everything you yourself bring to it, and leave only the basic visual information which your eyes themselves provide?

Berkeley's way of focusing on this question is to say you only really see those things you would see if you had been blind all your life and suddenly gained your sight. Can you imagine what that would be like? A confusing mass of visual data, with no clues as to what any of it meant. You certainly wouldn't be able to see how tasteless the apples were. It's not even obvious that you would be able to see what was apple and what was dish, because the difference between, say, a round apple sitting on a table and a circle drawn on a flat background is actually a very subtle one which it takes years of practice to see, but which we now do so quickly and easily that we tend to overlook what a complex feat it really is, and to talk as if it were something just given to us in the act of looking. But it isn't. It seems as if the most your eyes themselves can ever provide you with is a two-dimensional world of shapes and colours. Yellow circles with red blotches and shiny areas, darker areas (shadow), a black circle with a line coming from it (the apple stalk), and so on. Everything else I see, everything that can't be described in those basic colour-and-shape terms, is not what I see, but how I *interpret* what I see.

And what goes for sight, of course, goes for all the other senses too. You don't hear voices, you hear sound-impressions which make you think of voices; you don't taste strawberries, you taste taste-impressions which you have learned to call strawberry tastes. You don't feel how comfortable the chair is, you just feel touch-impressions of the kind you have learned to associate with other kinds of impression, and so on. The only things we really – or immediately, or directly – experience through any of our senses are, it would seem, these bare sense-impressions – what Berkeley called 'ideas of sense' and Hume 'impressions of sensation', and for which later philosophers invented the term 'sense-data' (singular 'sense-datum').

Is that true?

If it is, then the problems that Berkeley raises and the anxieties that Hume expresses as to the nature and existence of the world around us become much more difficult to deny. Would it be possible instead to deny that perception is this kind of two-stage process of the reception of data and its interpretation by the mind in the light of past experience?

There seem to be two main reasons why people find that hard to do:

1 First, it seems to deny what many hold to be the obvious fact that we do have basic, uninterpreted data of sensation – the feel of the table under my hand, for example, prior to my conceptualising it and describing it in that way is surely a fact of my inner

experience which no theory can take away? The baby's experience of seeing a red ball, long before it knows what red is or what a ball is, is surely an experience it undergoes, even though it couldn't tell you it was undergoing it?

2 And second, the denial of such uninterpreted data can seem to make our access to the world around us even more problematic than Berkeley and Hume said it was. If there are no uninterpreted sensory data, then it would seem that there are no sensory *facts*. My *interpretations* of my experience are as we have seen soaked through with my personal experience, my education, the language I speak and all the other political, economic, cultural and historical factors that are involved in my seeing the world the way I do. If there were no basic data of experience, no Berkeleian 'ideas of sense' or Humeian 'impressions', then we would have no knowledge of the world that wasn't in these ways culturally or personally relativised – there would be no objective facts, only subjective interpretations, wouldn't there?

Reading

The best place to see Berkeley's basic position is the *Treatise Concerning the Principles of Human Knowledge*, Part 1. (He lost the manuscript of Part 2 on holiday, and never rewrote it.) The *Three Dialogues Between Hylas and Philonous* cover the same ground in dialogue form.

Questions to ask

(1) Is it true that the belief in a material world is socially and psychologically harmful, as Berkeley suggests?

(2) Is there any test you can invent to establish whether or not the material world exists? If not, does that mean there is no real difference between Berkeley's position and our own?

(3) Assume that it is true that there is no empirical test to establish whether Berkeley is right or wrong. What other kind(s) of argument could you give in defence of the belief in a material world?

Chapter 17

Berkeley's disproof of the existence of matter

Overview

In this chapter I shall try to explain what I think are Berkeley's reasons for thinking that his theistic immaterialism, crazy though it may seem to many people, is preferable to our common-sense view. I shall do my best for Berkeley here, and will try to bring out the force of his position as strongly as I can; it is up to you to decide whether or not you find the arguments convincing. I have made no attempt to follow Berkeley's order of presentation, but have grouped what I think are genuine Berkeleian arguments under headings of my own.

Before we start, let's get clear exactly what we are arguing about, and what the arguments are supposed to show.

Berkeley's arguments against matter: what he is trying to prove

Berkeley is trying to show that there is no such thing as matter, or what we might call the physical world, or what he calls material substance. He holds that all there is in existence is minds and their ideas, and that everything we normally think of as being a material object is actually just a set of ideas in our minds. Those ideas are of two kinds: sensations or 'ideas of sense', which are put into our minds directly by God; and 'imagination': copies of those ideas which our minds can conjure up, divide and mix together at will. In what follows I shall be contrasting this view of Berkeley's with what I shall call for convenience our common-sense realism, which is simply the claim that there is such a thing as a mind-independent physical reality. For the purposes of this chapter it doesn't matter whether you think that physical reality is all there is (a materialist position), or whether you think – as for example Descartes did – that although physical reality exists in some form or other, there are also other, non-physical things in existence as well.[1]

Argument number one: the facts of experience don't support it

We have no experience of matter

You have been wandering in the desert for days without water. You scramble over another sand dune, and see in front of you a pool of water. But you are not stupid, and you have not been wandering for so long that you have forgotten all the bad films and cartoons you have ever seen about people in this kind of situation, so you are aware that perhaps what you see is not a real oasis, but a mirage. What do you do?

Well, in one way or another, you check. You might look more closely to see if you can see the kind of detail that oases have but mirages don't. Or you could just try to drink it, or swim in it. Or perhaps just ask your faithful travelling companion, Trevor, if he can see it too. But what are you actually doing when you carry out these tests? What you are doing, surely, is just having *more experiences*, getting more 'ideas of sense', to check whether the new impressions are consistent with what your eyes are telling you. What else could you possibly do?

Perhaps you happen to have with you a satellite link to a remote sensor which shows anything larger than a small puddle as a blue blob on the map, or something; or perhaps you are carrying your patent Acme Oasisometer in your pocket. But all you can actually do with those remarkable instruments is once again to *look* at them, *feel* them, sniff them, show them to Trevor, etc. – i.e. see what sense-impressions you get of them, as further evidence as to whether there is water there or not. The one thing you can *never* do is in some way to make direct contact with the material substance of the water which you believe to be there in the case of an oasis, but not in the case of the mirage. Because that material substance, matter itself, is not something you can *ever* be in direct contact with – all you can ever immediately sense is *more sense-impressions*, more ideas. It is on the basis of those sense-impressions that you make your *judgements* as to whether this is a real lake or an imaginary one (see Box 16.1).

Now, if all that is true, then Berkeley has a point. He says that a lake just *is* a consistent set of sense-impressions, whereas a mirage is an inconsistent set; we say an oasis is a material object which *gives us* a consistent set of sense-impressions, and a mirage is *just* a set of impressions. But whatever we may *say* about it, we *act* as if Berkeley were right. If we find we have a consistent set of sense-impressions – we can smell it and taste it and swim in it and sail on it and Trevor confirms it is real and the Oasisometer reads positive – then we say it is a real lake, and if we have an inconsistent set of sense-impressions we say it must be a mirage. In neither case do we make contact with any material substance, or matter itself.

The nature of sight

If you're not convinced by that, take it in conjunction with Argument 2 and see if it works any better. But before we go on to that, I will add another argument that Berkeley uses which can fit under the same general heading. Berkeley's first publication was *An Essay towards a New Theory of Vision*, and in it he goes to great lengths to explain that we don't actually see objects as being at any distance away from us; what we actually do is to *work out* that an object is at a distance from us, *on the basis* of the things we actually see.

It reads as rather a strange book, because in it he doesn't make clear his ulterior motive of denying the existence of matter, but presents it as simply a contribution to the geometry and physiology of sight. In the context of his later writings, though, the point becomes clear. One obvious objection to his theory is that of course there are mind-independent objects in the world because we can see that there are. There is a water buffalo, for example, out there in my front garden. Again Berkeley's point is that if we concentrate on the facts of what we *actually see*, as opposed to the judgements we immediately and unthinkingly make *on the basis* of what we see, we find that the situation fits his theory better than it fits our own.

When I say that I see the water buffalo in the garden, what I really see, says Berkeley, is some visual images of the kind that I have learned to call 'water buffalo'. Those images aren't in the garden; they are in my mind. The only reason I say the buffalo is in the garden is that because of the way my brain resolves the separate images from my two eyes, and because of all I have learned about how to interpret my visual images, I can tell immediately that if I want God to give me ideas of the smell of a buffalo, or of the feel of a buffalo's hide under my hand, or whatever, then I will have to will him to give me the sequence of sense-impressions we call 'going down the stairs and into the garden' first. Objects are never seen at a distance; what we see – *really*, immediately or directly see – is two-dimensional visual impressions of shapes and colours; and as the result of lots and lots of practice we have learned to *judge* what we call distance on the basis of that.

But in reality there are no distances, because there is no space; all there is, Berkeley tells us, is *temporal* distance, in the sense that I can tell from the impressions I am having that I will have to have some other impressions before I can have the ones I want. Surely, says Berkeley, these are the physiological facts about vision; and they fit more obviously with his metaphysic than with our own (see Box 16.1).

Argument number two: matter is unnecessary

Ockham's Razor

This argument is very simple, and combines naturally with the previous one. Argument one says that Berkeley's theory fits the facts of our experience better than ours does. Even if you don't accept that, and insist that both theories fit the facts equally well, we should *still* prefer his theory to ours. Why? Because his is so much *simpler*.

This argument works best against someone like Locke, who agrees with Berkeley on the facts of experience, and agrees with him on the existence of God, but wants to say that in addition to God and minds there exists also a material world. Berkeley's point is simply that if we can account for the facts just as well without matter, then it is obviously more rational to do so.

The underlying principle here is often known as Ockham's Razor: don't multiply existents unnecessarily.[2] We can explain the rainfall, for example, by reference to the known behaviour of water in different temperature conditions; we can also explain it by reference to a mighty rain goddess named Christine. But we don't. Why not? Well, at least part of the reason is that if we can do the job without postulating the existence of Christine, then it surely makes more sense to do it that way. The simpler explanation, the one which requires fewer existents for it to work, is always the one to be preferred, all other things being equal. So if Berkeley can do the job without matter, isn't the belief in it as ill-founded as the belief in the goddess Christine?

God does nothing in vain

We can add here another version of this argument that Berkeley uses, which is that because matter is in this way superfluous, God could have no reason to create it.[3] The significance of this argument is that it is the only time in Berkeley's attack on matter –

as opposed to his alternative theory of what there is – that his argument presupposes the existence of God, and so it is the only argument he uses which an atheist believer in a material world need not be troubled by. God does nothing without a reason, and created the universe for man's benefit. What possible reason could he have for creating a material world which would be necessarily undetectable to human beings? Berkeley has shown that everything that matter can do, God can do directly; so why create matter?

Argument number three: matter is unknowable

The Veil of Ideas

As we have just been seeing, there is nothing in our experience that could ever give us reason to think that matter existed. The hypothesis that there is such a thing as a material world is one which is at best just one possible explanation of our experience, among many. Berkeley's theory that it is God that is the cause of our ideas of sense is one alternative, but so is the suggestion that they are caused by fairies, or by a mad scientist who has implanted electrodes in my brain, and also the suggestion that Berkeley is right, except that there is not one God, but seventeen of them, all named Roger. Any such theory, it seems, is as good as any other in the sense that there is nothing in our experience that ever could tell us which is the correct picture to adopt.

If we are to make a choice between them, therefore, we will need some kind of *argument* to tell us which is correct. Berkeley uses a fairly standard Design Argument to support his theory that it is a Christian God doing the work: the order and interconnection of our experience proves there is an all-good, all-powerful intelligence controlling it. What argument can you think of to support the alternative theory of a material world?

Descartes, as we saw, tried to prove that matter existed on the grounds that we can't help but believe in it, and God wouldn't have made us that way if it didn't exist. Locke seemed to have no solution to the problem. Can you do any better?[4]

If you can't, then you seem to be left in an uncomfortable position, because:

(1) There seem to be no rational grounds for you to believe your theory, rather than one of the others, in that by your own admission no-one could ever have any evidence for it. The very best you can claim for it seems to be that it is no worse than the rest (assuming you can resist some of the stronger arguments that come later). But also:

(2) Not only can you not know that yours is the correct theory, but it seems to have the serious disadvantage that according to your theory material reality is for ever unknowable. As we saw earlier, it is matter, the world that science reveals, that is the unchanging reality of our lives, which provides us with our notions of truth and by which we judge what we should believe. But it begins to look as if we can never know that such a thing exists, or if it does exist, as if we can never know anything at all about it. We seem to be for ever stuck behind the Veil of Ideas, which means that reality, the object of our knowledge, the cause of all natural phenomena, the truth about our world, is forever cut off from us, and all we can ever actually know is its effects, the world as it appears, but not the world as it is in itself.

This takes us back to the point we made earlier, that Berkeley's theory avoids scepticism, atheism and alienation. If there is no way we can *test* which theory is correct, and if you don't think there is any knock-down *argument* one way or the other, then factors like this are surely relevant: if we have no way of deciding which is the *true* theory, perhaps we should consider which is the *best* theory – socially, politically, psychologically – for us to believe. Berkeley would say that his theory avoids the hopelessness and despair that are the inevitable consequences of believing in a reality from which we are necessarily always cut off. And from the point of view of a Christian, of course, he can add that it serves the ends of religion: it brings home to us both our complete dependence on God, who is involved in our lives at every moment, and also the greatness of God, who designs and maintains this fantastic picture show from moment to moment.

The problem of interaction

We can add in here a further argument Berkeley uses which is closely related to the unknowability of matter. Ever since Descartes' separation of mind and matter philosophers had wondered about how the two are related. How can an immaterial mind affect and be affected by a material world? Leibniz's Pre-established Harmony, Malebranche's Occasionalism and Spinoza's parallel attributes can all be read as attempts in one way or another to solve or to avoid that problem. The unknowability of matter is one particular instance of this general problem. But for Berkeley, of course, the problem simply doesn't exist.[5]

Argument number four: matter is impossible

So far, the effect of Berkeley's arguments, if you think they work, is to make the belief in matter a good deal less attractive than it seemed at first sight. The burden of proof seems to have shifted: it is now up to *us* to find some reason for our belief, or accept that it is groundless, whereas when we started it was up to Berkeley to show that we were wrong. But nothing we have said so far actually *disproves* the existence of matter. We have seen at most that it doesn't feature in our experience, that we have no good reason to believe in it, that if it did exist we could never know about it, and that there may be some advantages to a theory which denies it – but none of those amounts to a *disproof* of its existence. But that isn't enough for our George. He wants to go the whole hog and show that matter doesn't exist, and it is a mistake to believe in it.

The way he does that is by attempting to show that matter – for various reasons and in various ways – is impossible. It doesn't exist, because it *couldn't* exist. In his own ontology there exist only minds and ideas – and we all know what those are. We are ourselves minds, and as Descartes argued, we cannot doubt the existence of our own minds, and of our own ideas we are immediately conscious of.[6] Matter, by contrast, turns out to be much more difficult to get a handle on, and he attempts to show, in what I think are essentially four interrelated ways, that matter is impossible, because it is inconceivable.

If he is right, then he seems to be in a very strong position. If matter is inconceivable, if the idea of it makes no sense at all, then Berkeley can argue that it is not the sort of thing that *could* exist – believing in matter turns out to be as silly as believing in square circles or white things that are completely black. And even if you can find a way of denying that, it seems at the very least to follow that, since we don't know what matter could be, no-one could ever have any good reason for thinking it exists. The conceivability or otherwise of matter is therefore the point on which Berkeley's case will turn. It is complicated by the fact that it isn't at all clear what will count as conceiving of it. Berkeley is aware of that problem, and sets his own criteria of intelligibility (see Box 17.1).

Box 17.1

Berkeley on abstract ideas

A large part of Berkeley's denial of the existence of matter depends on his claim that matter is not *possible*: we know that it *doesn't* exist, because it *couldn't* exist. And the way we know it isn't possible is that it isn't *conceivable*. Berkeley's reasoning here is a lot more subtle and more persuasive than some people give him credit for, and thinking through what he's saying casts some interesting light, not only on Berkeley's case against matter, but also on our own metaphysical, epistemological and political attitudes.

Berkeley takes it for granted, and often explicitly asserts, that if something is inconceivable, it can't exist. Do you agree?

Well, consider. Are there any round squares in the universe? Are there any four-sided triangles?

I assume you said not. Yet you didn't feel the need before you answered to go outside and look in the garage to see if there were any lying around, and you said it despite the fact that no-one knows what might be waiting to be discovered on unexplored moons of Jupiter. So why are you so confident that if you look you won't find such things? Because there *couldn't* be any. Because they're impossible. And how do you know they're impossible? Because they're inconceivable – they make no sense. So Berkeley's principle seems to work, doesn't it?

I can't see any other way of explaining the confidence we have in cases like those. The trouble with the principle, though, is that other

---

cases are not so clear-cut. What if, for example, I were to tell you that
I had an unmarried uncle, named Wilfred, who was an only child
and lived all his life with his parents, who were circus artists? In fact,
of course, you ought not to believe me, because again it is
inconceivable – there can no more be an unmarried only child who is
an uncle than there can be a circle that is a square. But is it *obvious*
that it is impossible? To some people it is, but to others it isn't. I could
write a whole biography of this fictional uncle of mine, and many
people could read it and understand it and feel they got to know him
really quite well – when all the time a central feature of the whole
story is unthinkable. How is that possible?

What it shows, surely, is that understanding something, 'conceiving' it, isn't an all-or-nothing affair. You can understand the story
about my uncle Wilfred on one level, but as soon as you start to think
about it in detail, you find that it doesn't make sense.

There are lots of cases like that. In fictions very often we can follow
a story, understand what's happening, even when we know full
well that the events or objects described are impossible (think of
Lewis Carroll's Cheshire cat, which disappeared entirely apart from
its smile), or when we strongly suspect that if we thought about it
at all carefully we would see that they were in fact incomprehensible
(the Invisible Man; time travel). In fiction this ability to suspend
disbelief, to think something without thinking it through, as it were, is
harmless – indeed beneficial; in other contexts it is less innocent.

Berkeley, following on from Locke, was much exercised about the
dangers of this ability of ours to overlook incoherence: not in the case
of fiction, but in that of philosophy and science. As a modern
example – mine, not Berkeley's – of the kind of point he is making,
consider the question as to whether there might be a disembodied
mind somewhere in the room with you. That seems to me an example
of something which seems to make sense, which you think you
understand, but which is something that when you try to think it
through, you find is nonsense. After all, if this thing is disembodied, it
can't be *anywhere*, can it? So it can't be in the room. Things which
are immaterial don't have spatial co-ordinates at all.

Many people nowadays take this attitude towards Christianity:
they say that talk of the existence of God is either false – it asserts the
existence of an old man with a beard somewhere up in the sky – or it
is meaningless; again, the suggestion is that religious language
seems to make sense when you hear it, but when you try to pin it

down and think it through, it turns out to be nonsensical. We saw earlier that Locke, like many people at the time, took the same attitude towards the corrupt Aristotelianism of the universities. People were making comfortable livings 'explaining' the world by means of intelligible species, substantial forms and haecceities – all of which sound very impressive when pronounced by the learned doctors in their arcane languages, but none of which makes any sense at all once you spell out exactly what it is supposed to mean (see Box 15.1). The significant thing about Berkeley is that he used exactly the same weapons against the new science of his day, and would if he were now alive take the same attitude not only towards large parts of contemporary science, but also towards the science-based common-sense view of the world which we all live with. And he produced a clear and carefully worked-out theory in support of his position.

The main work of this is done in the Introduction to the *Principles*, where he makes what looks like an uninteresting attack on Locke's theory of concept formation, although its relevance to his real interests is not easy to see. The point he is making is that what Locke calls 'abstract general ideas' are examples of the kind of concealed nonsense we have been talking about. Locke says that we can have an idea of a person, for example, which is not the idea of any particular person, but is a sort of unspecific compound of all the people you have ever met; or you can have an idea of a triangle, which is not the idea of any particular triangle, but some composite notion of a triangle which is formed out of the ideas of all the triangles you have ever encountered. Berkeley says that such ideas are all of them inconceivable: yes, we can use the word 'person' or 'triangle' without having any specific triangle or person in mind, but that doesn't mean that when we do so we have a *general* idea of them, any more than the fact that I can understand a story about an unmarried only child uncle means I have an idea of one of those. There are *no* general ideas, only particular ones; if I want to think clearly about people in general, says Berkeley, I don't form a general idea of some vague, unspecific person, I form a particular idea of one specific person, and I *use* that idea to stand for all similar things – i.e. all people – just as when I draw a picture of a triangle I don't draw a picture of something which is no particular kind of triangle, but I draw a picture of some specific, arbitrarily chosen triangle, and let it stand for all others which are like it in relevant respects.

For Berkeley, the way we tell the difference between a real idea – something we have thought through – and a mere word, with no idea attaching to it, is that real ideas can be thought through, worked out in detail. Thinking a clear thought, for Berkeley, is a matter of envisaging in detail what it is you mean, having something in your mind which is as close as you can get to what it would be like to experience such a thing. So visualising in your mind a person, in as much detail as you can manage, is what it is like to have an idea of a person, and thinking vaguely of something with some legs and a head is the kind of dangerous nonsense that opens the door to charlatans and obscurantists.

Now, the point of all this stuff in the Introduction to the *Principles* is that Berkeley thinks that when we talk of matter we are again thinking vaguely and carelessly; we *think* we understand what we mean by the word, but as soon as you try to spell out what it is, you find that it is nonsense. He uses reasoning of this kind in three ways to back up the arguments set out in this chapter.

1 We think that we can give a complete description of an object specifying only its primary qualities; its secondary qualities aren't extra qualities in addition to the primary ones, they are merely ways in which those primary qualities react with their environment. Berkeley says that makes no sense: there couldn't, for example, be an object with shape and size, but no colour (see pp. 216–18). To think there could be is to engage in abstraction – we feel as if it makes sense to say that colour is a function of atomic structure, but that the atoms in themselves have none (even though they have shape and size) – but when you think clearly about it, try to envisage such a thing, you see that it is nonsense.

2 The so-called Master Argument (see pp. 218–19) says you can't really make sense of the idea of a tree which no-one is thinking about – because in trying to make sense of it you are yourself thinking about it. Many people reply to that by saying that Berkeley is muddling up what is true – that we can't envisage a tree that no-one is envisaging – with what is false, namely the suggestion that we can't *understand the proposition* that there exists an unperceived tree. But that reply seems to me to miss his whole point. We *can* understand the proposition – but then, in some sense we can understand the story about my Uncle Wilfred. But can we *really* understand the idea of an unperceived tree? Can we think it through in detail in the way Berkeley says we

have to if we are to count as really understanding it? Or are we just thinking the words without any clear ideas attached?

3 His argument against matter as 'Naked Substance' (see below) again relies on the doctrine of anti-abstraction. Can you really understand what matter is? Is it really conceivable? Try it: try to think clearly about matter itself, as opposed to thinking of some of its detectable properties, which of course Berkeley will say are just ideas in our minds. So leave aside shape, size, hardness, colour, etc. etc. etc., and think clearly – don't just think the word to yourself – about matter itself, the alleged cause of all those ideas. Can you do it?

Nowadays people tend to respond to arguments like these by deferring to higher authority. The Primary/Secondary argument is particularly good for this. *I* can't imagine what it means to say that an atom has shape and size but no colour, or that it has no properties that are expressible in sensory terms. *I* can't understand what it means to say that a particle can also be a wave. I know the theory, I can understand it on a certain level – just like the story of my Uncle Wilfred – but I can't think it through, as Berkeley says I should be able to if it is not to be nonsense. Yet we don't regard these things as nonsense, but as fact – even though they are inconceivable to us. We take it on trust that some people can understand them – just as many people in Berkeley's day took it on trust that some people had a clear understanding of Substantial Forms, Intelligible Species and Haecceity. Philosophers like Locke were concerned to liberate us from the intellectual and political powers of such obscurantism. They thought it was psychologically and politically dangerous to give power and authority to people who were unable to make their ideas intelligible to the people who give them that power and authority. Nowadays we seem not to agree.

Matter is a 'Naked Substance'

We have seen this already when we looked at the unknowability of matter. It seems very easy to understand what matter is. There stands a rubbish bin in the street. It's hard, metallic, dirty, dented, round. What more do you want? Well, says Berkeley, I want to know what the matter in itself is, as distinct from the ideas I have in my mind and which – according to your theory – are caused by

GEORGE BERKELEY

the bin. I have the visual impressions of shape, and shine, and colour; I have the feel of the hardness and sharp edges; I have the nasty smell. Subtract all those from the bin, and what are you left with? What is the object *itself* like? The problem is that whatever you say in response, Berkeley has his answer ready. If what you say has any clear meaning, then it is an idea, and so not what we are looking for – not matter itself, but another idea we get from it. And if what you say has no clear meaning, then he has proved his point, hasn't he? Can you see any way out of that trap? Matter is solid – yes, but solidity is an idea. Matter is made up of atoms – but atoms are either ideas (if you can clearly explain them), or they are nonsense (if you can't). So what are you talking about when you talk about matter?

Matter is contradictory

This is a classic Berkeleian argument: it strikes us as outrageous, absurd, obviously fallacious; but it isn't easy to refute.

(1) Matter is, by definition, not itself mental, not a mind (or what Berkeley calls a 'spirit').[7]
(2) Yet material objects have sensory properties, such as red, square, hot, or whatever (what he calls 'sensible qualities').
(3) But sensory properties are ideas.
(4) Therefore matter is a non-thinking thing which has ideas – which is a 'manifest contradiction'.

What are you going to say to that argument?
The obvious response is to try to deny step 3: properties aren't ideas, they are the *causes* of ideas. The problem is that if you say that you fall straight back into the Naked Substance argument above, because Berkeley simply asks you to explain what the properties in the object which cause my ideas, as opposed to the ideas themselves, are like. And again, whatever your answer, he will claim it is either an idea, and so again matter becomes contradictory, or it is unintelligible – in which case matter is saved from being contradictory only at the cost of being completely incomprehensible.

214

And if it's incomprehensible, then like a round square it can't exist, can it?

Are you happy with that? Do you have some other way to resist the contradiction argument?

The arguments against Primary Qualities

We have encountered the Primary/Secondary distinction already (see especially Box 14.1). It is a distinction between the way things are in themselves, and the way they appear to us; between the primary qualities (which are inherent properties of things, which any complete account of the thing in question must include), and the secondary qualities (which are facts about how a thing's primary qualities affect us and things around us). I have argued that a distinction of this kind is essential to the Appearance/Reality distinction which began in the seventeenth century and which is still dominant in our way of understanding the world today. Berkeley said it was nonsense. You need to decide whether he is right or whether we are.

As usual, he has a whole set of arguments for his point of view. Here are two of them.

All qualities are observer-relative

In explaining the distinction, Locke in particular talks of the fact that secondary qualities vary from observer to observer, and from moment to moment. He talks at length, for example, about the fact that the same water can feel hot to a hand that has been in cold water, and cold to a hand that has been in hot water, whereas the primary qualities of an object are not in the same way observer-relative: subjective qualities like hot/cold or hard/soft will vary for different observers, but the objective qualities which underlie them – the shapes, sizes, motions and numbers of their constituent parts – are what they are, regardless of who may look at them or think about them.

Berkeley seizes on this, and points out that primary qualities like size and shape vary with different observers in just the same way as secondary ones – a round coin seen from an angle looks elliptical; a tall tree seen from a distance looks small, and so on. Isn't that true?

Well, yes, it is. But Locke knows that, and Berkeley is often accused, here and elsewhere, of taking advantage of Locke's rather sloppy presentation of his ideas and not paying enough attention to what he *means*. Of course people's *perceptions* of primary qualities vary, but the primary qualities themselves don't.

The point is that regardless of how a thing may *look* to someone, there is a *fact* of the matter as to primary qualities like its shape and size, whereas there is no comparable fact of the matter about secondary qualities like colour or taste – the only fact of the matter there is the fact of the atomic structure of the object and of its environment – facts which are again describable in terms of primary qualities.

But Berkeley is perhaps not as stupid as he can seem. If we are going now to separate perceived primary qualities from actual primary qualities, then the door is open to him to ask what these actual, but unperceivable, qualities are like. We are no longer, it seems, talking about size and shape – which *are* perceivable – but about something else. What? We are back to the Naked Substance argument above: if you can give any account of what these primary qualities are, then they are perceivables, and so not primary after all; and if you can't, then they are unintelligible.[8]

Things without secondary qualities are inconceivable

If you can get around that, here is another argument. The primary qualities of an object are *all* the properties that really belong to the object, as opposed to facts about how it consequently behaves. Therefore it is in theory possible to give a complete description of a thing specifying only its primary qualities. But Berkeley argues that a thing which possesses only primary qualities is inconceivable, and therefore impossible.

Think about it. What colour is an atom? I tend to envisage them as being pink, because models of atomic structure made of balls and wire tend to use pink balls for some reason – but I don't think they are really pink. Really, atoms aren't any colour. And yet they're not transparent, either. Colour is what people now call an 'emergent' property of matter: it's the way atoms are arranged that determines what a thing's colour is, so a single atom, by itself, is neither coloured nor not coloured – it isn't the sort of thing that could be coloured.

At least, that's the theory. Berkeley thinks it doesn't make any sense. What is an atom like, then? It has shape, and it has size – but it is neither coloured nor not coloured. Is that really a coherent story?

I can, of course, think of a thing's shape and size without thinking of its colour. For example, if I imagine a football, I think of it as round and football-sized but I don't necessarily *have* to think of what colour it is. I may do, or I may not. But it's one thing to say I can think of a thing without thinking of its colour, and quite a different thing to say I can form a clear understanding of the suggestion that there might be an object which *does* have a determinate size and shape (however small it may be) but which *does not* have any colour properties at all. What sense does that really make?

To Berkeley this is a classic example of an 'abstract idea' (see Box 17.1) – something which seems to make sense if you say it quickly enough, but which when you try to think it through clearly – to imagine what it would be like to encounter such a thing – you realise is quite unimaginable, and cannot exist. There just *can't be* an extended object with no colour properties, can there? How can it be extended – fill space – without being either coloured or transparent?

Perhaps you will respond that this objection of Berkeley's works against a crude, mechanistic picture like Locke's, where atoms are envisaged as something like very small billiard balls, but not against the sort of more sophisticated picture we use today. After all, quantum objects in contemporary physical theory don't have shape and size in anything like the sense in which a billiard ball does, either, so the problem doesn't arise, does it?

In a sense that is true: but I suspect a Berkeleian would say that you have avoided the problem of saying that objects have an inconceivable mixture of properties (shape and size without colour, etc.), only at the cost of saying that none of their properties are conceivable *at all*. Do you really have a clear understanding of what it means for something to be a non-individual wave-particle duality which is smeared out across the universe? And if you don't, how do you respond to Berkeley's claim that the matter in which you believe so confidently is something that could not possibly exist?[9]

The 'Master Argument'

This argument has recently been given the name 'the Master Argument' simply because Berkeley says that he is prepared to let his whole case stand or fall by it. If you can even think of a single mind-independent object, he says, then he will give up the game and accept that you have proved that matter exists.[10] But can you?

The problem, he says, is that as soon as you try to think of something that is mind-independent, you form an idea of it, and that means you bring it into relation to your own mind. But then it ceases to be mind-independent, so you fail, don't you?

The example that Berkeley takes is to challenge his opponent to think of an unperceived tree, a tree somewhere deep in the forest that exists in itself, independently, out of all relation to any mind. Can you do it?

Berkeley says no: that as soon as you try to do it, you necessarily bring that tree into relation to a mind – namely, your own – and so must always fail in the attempt.

Again we seem to be back to the Naked Substance argument, above: if you succeed in thinking about matter, it isn't matter that you're thinking of, but some idea you're having; and if you can never succeed in thinking about it, doesn't that mean it's unthinkable?

Again, there is an obvious way out of the problem; again, it seems to me to miss the point. Can I think about a tree I'm not thinking about? Well, in one sense I can, and in another sense I can't. There can't be a tree such that I am simultaneously both thinking about it and not thinking about it, that's for sure; but that doesn't mean I can't understand the proposition 'There exists a tree I'm not thinking about', does it?

Well, it depends what you mean by 'understanding'. You can use the sentence appropriately, no doubt; but can you really form a clear understanding – a genuine 'idea' in Berkeley's sense – of its meaning? Or do you have only what he would call an 'abstract' idea of this tree? (See Box 17.1.) Again and again we hit the same problem: we feel as if we know very well what we mean by talking about the material world; but as soon as we start to spell it out in detail, it seems to evaporate into something we can make no sense of.

Perhaps Berkeley's position has more going for it than at first appears. Or perhaps he is just pulling the wool over our eyes, and if you think it through carefully enough you can show where he goes wrong. I leave that for you to decide. In the meantime, we need to look in more detail at his positive account of what the world really consists in.

Reading

The arguments against matter are scattered throughout the *Principles* and *Dialogues*. His most systematic presentation of them is in *Principles* 1–24.

Questions to ask

(1) Are there really any uninterpreted data of experience? If so, what exactly are they like? (If you answer, does that mean you have interpreted them?)

(2) Does Berkeley succeed in showing that there is no real distinction between primary and secondary qualities?

(3) In what sense(s), if any, is it true to say that matter is inconceivable? Is it inconceivable in any sense that means it is impossible?

Chapter 18

On what there is
Berkeley's virtual reality

This chapter will be almost purely expository. Having explained in the last chapter why Berkeley thinks we are wrong to believe in a material world, I want in this one to set out in a little more detail his positive account of what the world *is* like, now that we've seen what it *isn't*.

The world as divine simulation

The short story, as we have seen already, is that the world consists of minds. There is the infinite and eternal mind of God on the one hand, and the finite minds of God's creations on the other. A finite mind is an independently existing immaterial individual, dependent only on God's conserving power for its continued being – just as Descartes had described. Finite minds are the *only* things that God has created, and to which he has given independent existence. They include primarily human beings, but also angels, and whatever other higher intelligences there may be.[1] And apart from minds, the only other things that exist are the ideas in them.

It all sounds very implausible, but it makes much more sense than might at first appear. God gives you your sensations – the patterns of shape and colour that you see, the sounds you hear, the sensations of smell and taste, and the feel of things against your skin. Those sensations are pure, uninterpreted, and are fed into your mind by God at every waking moment. The sensations are not random – though children find them so at first – but come in identifiable sequences which we can learn.

Take for example the visual sensations involved in seeing a cup of coffee in front of you. That set of visual sensations remains roughly constant for as long as you want to look that way – they are never suddenly replaced by the set of visual experiences we call seeing a banana, for instance. If you perform the act of willing that we call moving your head to the left, the images God feeds you will alter slightly – different parts of the cup come into view, as we say, and others go out of sight. Move your head back again, and you get another new set of sensations just like those you had to start with. And just as these visual sensations are predictable, so are the others: the sight of the coffee is accompanied by the smell sensations we call the smell of coffee, and not by those we call the smell of burning rubber; stretch out your hand and you get the kind of pressure in the fingertips that we call touching a hard, hot object, not those we associate with touching a jelly. In general, there is order and regularity in the sensations we receive, and because of that we can learn to predict them.

Notice that all these sensations are fleeting, temporary feelings, not unchanging objects. The only unchanging things are minds, or perceivers (see below, pp. 228–31); the perceptions themselves are in constant flux. The only features in experience that *don't* change are the sequences or patterns the perceptions fall into, and it is those patterns that we learn to recognise and identify as objects: as soon as I get the shape and colour sensations of the coffee, I immediately know how it will look from different positions, what it will smell, feel and taste like, and so on. What we are doing in perception, in other words, is not so much observing, as *predicting*: we are interpreting the messages from God that are our sensations, and predicting on the basis of past experience what other sensations are coming our way. If we are sufficiently experienced, we generally get it right without even thinking about it – we just see the coffee, reach out a hand, and drink it. Sometimes, though, we get it wrong – it turns out that someone has put ink in the cup, and the smell is coming from next door. Correct predictions we call true beliefs, the way things are, reality; mistaken ones we call falsehood, illusion, error.

The regularities in our experience are what Berkeley calls the Laws of Nature, and those are what science seeks to discover. Science is therefore concerned, just as we always thought, with finding out what the world is really like – which of course doesn't mean telling us about a material world beyond the Veil of Ideas, but discovering what sensation sequences we can and can't have. Thus when Copernicus says the Earth moves and the sun stands still, he means that if you were up in the sky you would have this kind of sequence of sensations and not that one; and when Locke and his friends say that objects are made up of invisible particles, he means that if you could construct a suitably powerful microscope you would have this kind of sensation, not that one. What science certainly does not do, according to Berkeley, is explain the *causes* of the events we see around us. The stone I throw is in reality just a sequence of sensations, and so is not the sort of thing that can cause the breaking of the window – which is itself another sequence of sensations. The only causes are minds – the will of God, which causes all our sensations, and the decisions of people, as a result of which God gives us one set of sensations rather than another. What we call causes in the natural world – things like the stone which breaks the window – are in reality just regularities in perceptions: there are laws of nature to the effect that stone-throwing experiences are regularly followed by window-breaking experiences.

The role of God

I hope you are beginning to see the sense in which Berkeley says that it is in God that we live and move and have our being.[2] Our lives are like one great computer game (see Box 18.1), but instead of a programme created and left to run by a designer,

God does the work immediately by putting the sensations directly into our minds. And since every conscious moment is one in which we are receiving some sensory stimulus or other, then at every moment we are in direct communication with God.

Box 18.1
Berkeley's virtual reality: the world as divine simulation

One way of making sense of Berkeley's account of human experience is to think of the whole world as a kind of giant computer game. Consider the similarities between the imaginary computer game Mega-Death Monster Slayer 3, and the world as Berkeley describes it.

MEGA-DEATH	BERKELEY WORLD
I sit at my screen, and see images created there by the programme designer.	My mind receives sensory impressions – 'ideas of sense' – from God.
The images on the screen are just constantly changing patches of colour on a flat screen, accompanied by noises on the sound track.	Ideas of sense are constantly changing two-dimensional visual images, and also sound impressions, taste impressions, smells and feels.
The screen images are not random and haphazard, but follow a strict order corresponding to the programme of the designer.	Ideas of sense are given to me by God in accordance with his design.
Because the images are regular and not random, I know they are not occurring by accident, but that the programme is running in accordance with its design. I don't know what that design is, and if I saw it I wouldn't understand it.	Because my ideas of sense are not random I know there is a God who controls them in accordance with an overall design which I don't know and can't understand.

The objects in the game – such as Thoth, the triple-headed ferret of Mogadon, for example – are never actually there on the screen. All that we actually see on the screen is a sequence of transitory images, whereas Thoth itself I regard as an enduring entity which comes and goes at different points in the game. Thoth itself, therefore, is strictly speaking not an object I actually see on the screen, but a kind of shorthand way of talking about many different sets of similar images which I see at different times.

To say that Thoth exists, therefore, is not a literal report of what I see on the screen, but an *interpretation* of what I see. Whether I'm right that there exists a triple-headed ferret named Thoth will depend in part on what happens later in the game: if when I smite it with my elf-sword it isn't harmed, for example, it may turn out that there is really no such thing as Thoth, and that what I call Thoth is really the wicked wizard G.E. Frog-Bottle in one of his many disguises.

Although none of the objects in the game has any existence outside of it, there is still a clear difference between reality and illusion, true and false. Either the gold is in the cave, or it isn't; either the laser hammer does crush these beetles, or it doesn't.

The objects of experience – mountains, rivers, trees etc. – are complex sets of interrelated ideas that I learn to refer to as a single object on the basis of regularities in my experience.

To say that a certain object exists is not a report of any of my ideas of sense, but an *interpretation* of them. To say that there is a fly in the ointment is to say something about the ideas of sense which God gave me in the past, and something about the ones I expect him to give me in the future.

Although none of the objects in the world has any existence outside of a mind, Berkeley makes the distinction between reality and illusion in exactly the same place as we do.

Because the objects in the game are not screen images but interpretations of what is on the screen, or constructs out of screen images, it is not true to say that they don't exist when they aren't visible; the Bog of Birmingham continues to exist when I can't see it, in the sense that it is written into the programme, and if I make a wrong move I will fall into it.

In the game, of course, there is really no causation at all. All there is, is image-sequences, and the sequence I call hitting-the-giant-beetle-with-the-laser hammer doesn't actually *cause* the sequence I call the-giant-beetle-going-all-flat-and-squishy; what really happens is that when I initiate the first sequence the programme carries it out, and then follows it up with the second. We say the one causes the other, but it would be more accurate to say that sequences like the first are regularly followed by sequences like the second; the only real causation that is going on here is that the programme causes the images on the screen, and I cause it to present one sequence rather than another.

I can only really come to understand the game because I can *interact* with it. The pattern of images on the screen isn't fixed in advance, because which

The objects of experience don't go out of existence when they are not perceived; the room behind me still exists because it is part of God's grand design, and if I turn around I will see it again.[3]

There is no causation in nature. The only causes are minds. What I call the stone's causing the window to break is really just God's giving me stone-throwing images followed by window-breaking images. The only true causes here are God's causation of the ideas, and my choice that he should give me one sequence rather than the other.

I can only understand the world because I have some control over which ideas of sense God gives me. I can't have whatever experiences I fancy, because images are shown depends on which moves I make. Nevertheless, there are only some moves I can make, and some moves I can't, because the designer of the game thought it would be less interesting otherwise. And it is still a deterministic system, in the sense that the outcomes of my actions are fixed and unchanging – if I turn right, I will always fall into the Bog of Birmingham, and if I turn left, I will inevitably have to tackle the Giant Spider.

there are rules – called Laws of Nature – governing which ones I can have in what sequences. But Nature is still deterministic, in the sense that the outcome of my choices is inevitable.

At this point you may be wondering why. Why does God put on this great show, this non-stop infinite arcade game, complete in every detail?

If the question means 'Why does God make it look as if there were a material world when there isn't?', then Berkeley's answer is that he *doesn't* make it look that way. As we have seen, there is absolutely *nothing* in all our experience that would lead us to believe we are in a material world rather than in direct communication with God. The belief that we are in such a world, according to Berkeley, is simply a *mistake* which people have got into the habit of making, a misinterpretation of the divine language of sensations. That misinterpretation is encouraged and legitimised by philosophers like Locke, who are therefore leading us further astray, further from a true understanding of the facts of experience. In fact, Berkeley often talks as if it is *only* philosophers who make and propagate this mistake: he says that ordinary people, uncorrupted by philosophical theories, have no belief in the dualism of an inner world of thoughts representing an outer world of matter, but simply take things as they find them. They know, he says, that everything they experience is fleeting, and that things are real only if and to the extent that they are actual or possible objects of experience, and sadly the deluded philosophers, who could lead them from that knowledge to an understanding of their intimate relation to God, have misled and betrayed them by inventing the story of an invisible, untouchable, unknowable material world instead.[4]

If, on the other hand, our question about why God bothers to give us all these ideas of sense means why does he bother to give us these sensations at all, then we and Berkeley are on much firmer ground. The question is exactly the same as a non-Berkeleian Christian's question as to why God created the universe – because in Berkeley-world the sensations he gives us *are* the universe. And all the standard Christian answers are available. God created (or more accurately, as Descartes said he is constantly creating: see pp. 31–2) the universe to express his glory, to enter into communication with his thinking creatures, and to provide them with an opportunity to know him and his works, and to make choices between good and evil, and so on. Again, the story is the same: whatever we common-sense realists can say, Berkeley can say with only minor alterations; and whatever a common-sense Christian can say, Berkeley can say while claiming like Leibniz that on his story the centrality and glory of God are all the more prominent.

There is one area in which this immediate involvement of God in everything that happens is particularly striking for Berkeley, and for some people particularly worrying, and that is the Problem of Evil. If the difference between my having good eyesight and my being short-sighted, for example, consists only in the clarity of the visual ideas God gives me, then given that he could give me clear ideas as easily as he could give me foggy ones, it seems rather unfair of him to victimise me in this way; if the difference between the crippled child and the healthy one is just that when they decide to run through the meadow he gives one of them running-through-the-meadow-in-the-sunshine ideas and the other one pain-in-the-knees-and-falling-on-the-floor ideas, then God seems to be guilty of playing a particularly nasty practical joke.

What do you think? Can Berkeley respond to that charge?

The answer I think is again that he can do every bit as well or as badly with it as any more orthodox Christian metaphysician. No orthodox Christian, after all, can let God off the hook in these matters by saying that my dodgy eyesight or the little girl's deformed legs are inescapable consequences of physical laws and beyond God's power to do anything about; God, after all, is omniscient and omnipotent, so he deliberately chose to make a world in which those things would happen, in the full and immediate knowledge of what that choice entailed, and he was able to do otherwise with literally no effort at all.[5] So although Berkeley's system highlights the problem by making God's involvement in the world so prominent, it doesn't actually make the problem any harder (or any easier) to solve. And Berkeley duly replies to it in the traditional way: human evil is an inevitable consequence (God can't change the laws of logic) of the gift of free will, and natural evils are a result of the fact that (as Leibniz said in more detail) God wanted the universe (i.e. the system of ideas) to be vastly rich and diverse, but also to have regular rules which were simple enough for us to grasp.

The mind, knowledge, and knowledge of the mind

The place of mind in nature

The only thing we have left to do to complete our sketch of Berkeley's positive account of what there is is to show how the human mind and human knowledge fit into the story. The basic answer is that a Lockeian story, reinterpreted to fit a Berkeleian metaphysics, is right on everything except the nature of the mind.

All our ideas come from experience, and complex ones are put together out of simples (see above, pp. 151–3). All knowledge is derived from ideas, and is either intuitive, rational or observational.[6] We have intuitive knowledge of our own existence, but of nothing else; the existence of God we can work out rationally, because we know there must be a cause of our ideas of sense, and given the coherence and convenience of the world it can only be created by an omnipotent and all-good designer. The existence of other people is also known rationally: regularities in my experience – the fact that you move and speak and act in the same ways that I do – lead me to conclude that you are a finite mind of the same kind as I am. (But note that your existence is much less certain than that of God: some of the things I experience – your actions, your words, etc. – are evidence for your existence, and I rightly conclude that there is a mind behind them; but *everything* that I experience is evidence for the existence of God.) Everything else in the world is only regularities in the experiences given to me by God. These regularities are what make the world intelligible. I notice that if I plant in the spring I can harvest in the autumn, but not vice-versa; I notice that if I put my hand in the fire it will get burnt, but not if I put it in my pocket, etc.

The nature of mind itself

But what of the nature of the mind itself, or what Berkeley calls 'spirit'? Locke, as we mentioned, was a tentative Cartesian who was prepared to contemplate the materialist option that the mind is ultimately material. That of course is not an option for Berkeley, so what does he say about the nature of the mind?

The most interesting thing he says about it, is that we don't know what it is. Like Descartes, he says that it is immaterial, and that it wills and perceives. As such, it is a small-scale, finite image or copy of the infinity of God. The will is free, and will – the action of a spirit – is the only true cause. But what is striking is that once you have said that, you have said just about all there is to say about it, because according to Berkeley you can have no *idea* of what it is.

The problem here is very close to that which we saw with matter. All we can ever perceive is ideas; but the mind is not an idea, the mind is something which perceives and/or creates ideas. Ideas are events in minds, passive images or representations; but minds are active thinkers, and as such cannot be represented by one of their own perceptions. Just as matter is supposed to be not an idea, but something else, which lies behind ideas and causes them, so mind is not an idea, but something else which causes and perceives them. The result is the same in both cases: anything you can understand is an idea, so anything you may care to mention – be it matter or mind – is either an idea, and so not what you are looking for, or it is not, in which case it is necessarily unintelligible. Mind, it turns out, is just as inaccessible as matter.

But hang on: can he really say this? Surely his whole point has been to argue that the Lockeian view is impossible because matter in itself is unintelligible, and he has replaced the Lockeian world with a universe of spirits and ideas for just that reason. Yet here he is saying that spirits are in no better case than the very matter he has dismissed!

Well, yes and no. Look back at the arguments against matter, and ask yourself how many of them work equally successfully against mind as Berkeley describes it.

Your answer I think will turn on how convinced you are by the Cartesian argument that you can't doubt your own existence – that the fact that there is thought means there must be a thinker. If that is true, then the facts of experience *do* point to the existence of a self, even if they don't point towards the existence of matter (Argument Number 1); and spirit is not unnecessary in the way that matter is, because there has to be mind to support ideas, but there doesn't have to be matter to cause them (Argument Number 2). Mind or spirit will be unknowable (Argument Number 3) in the sense that we can never know *what* it is, but not in the sense that we cannot know *that* it is. In Berkeley's language, we have some 'notion' of it – we know it is there, and we know what it does, but we have no idea of it – we can't know what it is in itself.

But Berkeley's strongest weapons against the existence of matter were his arguments to show that matter *cannot* exist, because it is inconceivable (Argument Number 4). How does the notion of mind stand up against those?

The Primary/Secondary arguments obviously have no bearing; and there is no parallel to the contradiction argument, since there is nothing contradictory in thinking that a mind should have ideas. Similarly, the Master Argument gets no grip on the conceivability of mind, since there is no obvious requirement that we be able to think of an unconceived mind in the way that there is a need to envisage a material object existing without relation to any mind. All that remains, then, is the Naked Substance argument, which seems to work just as much against mind as against matter. Does that mean Berkeley's position turns out to be nonsensical in the end?

Berkeley himself considers the charge,[7] and says not. Mind is unthinkable, but not, he says, impossible: we know that we have one, and the fact that we can't attain a clear understanding of it isn't because there is anything contradictory in the concept of it, but just because of the kind of thing it is. To put it another way, mind may not be comprehensible, but at least it isn't downright absurd, the way matter is.

Are you convinced?

One person who certainly wasn't was David Hume.

Reading

Berkeley's account of 'spirits' is primarily in the last sections of the *Principles*, after 1.85. (But see also 1.28.)

Questions to ask

(1) Does Berkeley have a satisfactory answer to the Problem of Evil?
(2) Does Berkeley's theory of Abstract Ideas set the criteria for intelligibility too high?
(3) Are minds any more or less inconceivable than bodies?

PART 6
David Hume

Biography

David Hume was born in 1711, seven years after the death of Locke, when Leibniz was fifty-four and Berkeley twenty-six. He was two years old when the Treaty of Utrecht was signed, twenty-eight when Dick Turpin was hanged, and forty-four when Samuel Johnson published his *Dictionary of the English Language*. He died in 1776, the year of the American Declaration of Independence.

He was born in Edinburgh, in a family of landed gentry. He worked as a secretary, tutor and librarian, but was refused professorships at both Edinburgh and Glasgow because of his sceptical and atheistic views. He eventually made a successful career as an historian and man of letters.

His work casts doubt on the possibility of any stable and defensible understanding of ourselves and the world around us, and raises the suggestion that all the knowledge that we are so proud of is in fact nothing but a kind of innate instinct or prejudice which we can neither defend nor avoid. His views were always controversial, even outrageous, and much of his early influence was negative. Kant claimed to have invented his Transcendental Idealism as a defence against Hume's work. In the twentieth century Hume became very popular among positivistic philosophers for his iconoclasm, his empiricism and his love of argument.

Chapter 19

Hume's project for a new science

What it is, how it works, and an example

Overview

I have tried to show all of our six philosophers as involved in their different ways with the development of science in the seventeenth and eighteenth centuries. Hume's involvement is twofold: on the one hand, he is the great advocate of the Enlightenment view, seeking to develop a truly scientific account of human beings. At the same time, though, he seems to be the only one who comes to the conclusion that any kind of rational investigation is impossible, and that no defensible understanding can ever be achieved.

Of all our six philosophers, then, Hume is by far the most problematic. With all the others, you always know where you are: they have a message, a view which they are trying to promote, and your task is just to find out what that view is, and to decide what you think about it. Sometimes they may disguise it (Descartes' pretended doubt); sometimes it may be hard to grasp, either because it strikes us as intrinsically odd (Leibniz's striving compossibles), or because the author himself is a bit muddled as to what it is (Locke on substance), but at least you always feel that there is a view there which the author at least is happy with and which he is trying to put across to us over the chasm of time, accident and lost opportunities that separates the present from the past. But all of that changes when you get to Hume. Hume doesn't really have a view at all. More accurately, his view is that no view can be defended – including that one. He is the great champion of rational understanding, and the enemy of superstition; but he thinks that rational inquiry is itself only a particularly pompous and self-important form of prejudice. He mocks and derides the complacent self-satisfaction of his age as being insufficiently rigorous and scientific; but he sees only too clearly that the only conclusion to an appropriately rigorous and scientific inquiry is that no-one in their right mind ever would or could believe such a thing. He sets up a great project for the reform of philosophy; but he shows that such a project is self-defeating.

Reading Hume is therefore something of a challenge. He writes beautiful, sharp, witty prose, and is constantly challenging his reader with a succession of sometimes good, sometimes crazy and sometimes brilliant arguments which come tumbling over one another on the page. And as an author he is never still: he contradicts himself frequently, shifting his ground and his attitudes not only between different books and between different sections of the same book, but even within a single chapter, or on a single page. There is almost nothing he says that he doesn't elsewhere undermine – not because he is muddled or hasn't thought it through, but because he is a human being trying to think clearly about the way human beings try to think clearly, and he is constantly switching between the roles of subject and observer of his own experiments – at one moment asking himself what he thinks, and at the next asking what he thinks about people who hold opinions like that.

I shall present the story here in three stages. First we will look at the task Hume claims to set himself and at the way he thinks we should go about it, and we will examine how his inquiry works in one ground-breaking and relatively unproblematic case, that of moral philosophy. In the next chapter we will look at some more examples of his investigation, and at the kind of problems he says it runs into, and then finally we will try to consider his position overall, and where it leaves us at the end of this book.

The Science of Man

At the beginning of the *Treatise*, Hume adopts the posture of the great reformer of philosophy. His work, he tells us, will be the first to be written on the most central and most important of all the sciences, the Science of Man. By the systematic and objective study of human nature, he says, we will discover the true foundations of everything that can be known. After all, all our knowledge, in whatever field, is precisely that – it is *our* knowledge. It is arrived at by human beings, using human faculties. It follows that if we know clearly what human beings are – how they live, how they feel, and most especially how they think – then we will be able to unite all the different branches of learning under this one study.[1] We will be able to see what we can't know and what we can know, and how we can know it. We will know which branches of learning are reliable and to be developed, and which are spurious and to be abandoned; we will know whom we can trust, who is a charlatan, and who is a fool.

He compares himself in this investigation to no less a figure than Newton, whose gravitational theory was then the wonder of the age. Just as Newton had brought together such diverse phenomena as falling apples and the date of Easter into a single system based on a few simple laws, so he, Hume, at the time an unknown 25-year-old with big ideas, would bring together all the diverse subjects of human thought and action under the single set of laws of the new science of human nature.

Hume's method

The way to go about this investigation is therefore modelled on what Hume took to be the Newtonian method: we simply observe in an objective and dispassionate manner the facts of human nature, and seek to discover the laws of its operation. In this way we will base our theories not on accepted wisdom, not on what we

DAVID HUME

have been brought up to believe, not on what we find written in the books of Aristotle or the books of the Bible, but on the concrete data of experience. Now, since it is human beings we are dealing with, and since this is the very beginning of our new science, we won't need any complex and esoteric experiments to base our study on; all we need is an objective and scientific presentation of the common facts of human life – of how we feel, how we act, and first of how we think.

Impressions and ideas: the atoms of the mind

The first move is to establish the basic elements of human thought. What are the atoms of the mental world, the irreducible particles of thought? This is a development of something we have seen already in both Locke and Berkeley. Like both of them, Hume takes as his starting point the position that everything we can understand – every mental object – is derived either directly or indirectly from experience; and also that what is given in the content of one of those experiences, if you strip away from it everything that we add to it on the basis of past experience, is a bare, uninterpreted sensation (cf. Box 16.1).

Unlike either Locke or Berkeley, Hume invents some new terminology to talk about our mental contents. He separates out the actual sensations we experience – what he calls 'impressions' – from the concepts we form from them – our 'ideas'. As I sit here, for example, I see trees and houses and sky. But what I actually see, the 'impressions' I receive, are – like Berkeley's 'ideas of sense' – just patterns of shape and colour. All the rest – my knowledge that things that look like that are houses and trees, of who lives in the houses, when they were built, and what kind of trees they are, etc. – all of that is not *given* in the content of what I see as I sit here, but is supplied by my own mind on the basis of what I have experienced in the past. Those concepts which I bring to bear on my 'impressions' are 'ideas', and all of them are formed from preceding impressions. Complex ideas can be broken down into simpler ones, but simple ideas – like the idea of red, or of pain, or of warmth – cannot be analysed, and can only be acquired if you have had the relevant impression.[2] Even with simples, though, there is an important difference between impressions and ideas: the idea of pain that I form in my mind now is very different from the impression of pain I get when someone puts my head in a vice: it is much less vivid, is tied in less closely with other impressions I am having (sitting looking aimlessly out of the window isn't always accompanied by head-squeezing sensations), and is more or less under my control (whereas the real thing unfortunately isn't).

All that is familiar from what we have seen in Locke and Berkeley. What is striking about it in Hume, apart from the slightly more refined terminology he employs, is the aggressive *use* he makes of it. What it amounts to in effect in Hume's hands is a test of meaningfulness. For any idea you can come up with, Hume will ask you for an analysis of it: he will ask what impressions you have derived it from. If you can answer him, then we will have a clear explanation of what the idea is, or what the word means; if you can't, then he will proceed either to offer you his own explanation of its true meaning, or he will declare that it is meaningless.

A lot of the investigations we are going to examine in the next chapter take exactly this form. What is a person? What is a material object? What – most famously of all – is a cause? In each case, and others, he analyses the idea in question by tracing it back to the impression from which it is derived. And he comes to some surprising conclusions.

The association of ideas: mental gravity

Having established the basic elements of thought, the next thing we need is to discover the laws which govern those elements. Building again on something in Locke, Hume observes that thoughts don't simply wander through our minds in a random manner, but follow one another in regular sequences. I hear a certain sound, for example, and immediately identify it as someone saying 'wombat'. There is absolutely nothing about that particular sound that tells me it is produced by a human voice, except that I have heard similar sounds before, and learned to *associate* them with experiences like seeing people open their mouths, feeling the vibrations in my own throat, etc., so that now when I hear that kind of sound, ideas of human agency immediately come in to my mind, for no other reason than that I have learned to *associate* them together. Similarly, with this particular noise I have learned to associate the idea of a particular kind of furry creature. There is nothing about the sound that resembles the animal, and no kind of necessary relation between the two; but by a complex process of training I have come to associate that sound with that animal. According to Hume that simple process of conditioning is the whole basis of how we think: ideas are linked together in our minds by chains of *association*.

Armed with these basic elements of his new science – the atoms of thought held together by the force of association – we can proceed to the Science of Man.

The method in action: the principles of morals

The best example, to give us a flavour of Hume's project in action, is his account of morality. Moral terms are important: people use them to attempt to control their own behaviour, and that of other people, when they say this is right, that is noble, this is wrong, that is wicked. In a time of social change, moral authority is claimed by competing sets of people with competing aims and ideals, and the figure of the well-intentioned but woolly minded bishop pontificating on the evil times we live in, or of the equally well-intentioned but muddle-headed social reformer insisting that hers is the only path to virtue, are exactly the kind of self-important targets that Hume delights in embarrassing. If the new Science of Man can reveal to us the true basis of moral judgements, we will be able to dispense with all the confused and self-serving rhetoric of moral condemnation, and to make sense at last of the true Principles of Morals.

Reason and the passions

A common way to think about moral issues – then perhaps more than now – is to see them as essentially a struggle between reason and appetite. On the one hand there is what we know with our civilised, sophisticated, rational minds to be right, and on the other what we feel with our primitive, instinctive, animal appetites to be desirable.[3] Rationally you think that theft is a bad thing and likely to lead to punishment – but you want the book and can't afford to buy it; your educated mind sees that you should give money to charity – but what you want to do is spend it on yourself; intellectually you know that sleeping with your best friend's goat would be a bad idea – but your appetites and desires pull you in the opposite direction.

Hume's first move is to deny this perhaps natural-seeming account of the matter, and in so doing to deny the whole basis of accepted moral thinking in his day. Reason, he says, our rational understanding, can only ever tell us how things are in the world – it tells us what is true, and what isn't. But on their own, these facts about the world can tell you nothing at all about what you should *do*, because what you should do depends on what you *want*.

Take an example. Suppose you find out by the careful application of your scientific reason that a particular volcano is about to explode. Does that mean you shouldn't have a picnic on its slopes?

Well, not really. It means that if you do you're likely to get ash in the cups of tea and lava in the sandwiches – oh, and also to get burned to a crisp. But those things are only reasons for not going on the picnic *if* you want to have uncontaminated food on your picnic and to come back from it alive. But where do those wants, those *desires*, come from? Not from reason, but from our instinctive, appetitive, animal nature. 'Reason', Hume says, 'is, and ought only to be, the slave of the passions'.[4] It is our *desires* that tell us what to do: the job of reason, of science, of knowledge, is to tell us how things are in the world, in order that we can know *how to get* whatever it is that we (non-rationally) want.

Box 19.1

Reason and experience

Here is an example of a proof taken from Euclid's *Elements*. In Proposition 32 of Book 1 he tries to show that the interior angles of a triangle must add up to 180°: for example, in this diagram angle *a* plus angle *b* plus angle *c* must = 180°.

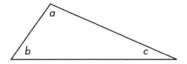

The way he does it is to extend the line which runs from *b* to *c*, and to draw a new line, parallel to *a-b*, and passing through *c*:

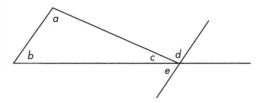

Figure 21.1 A Euclidean proof

He then gets to work on the proof.

(1) The first step is to show that angle *d* must equal angle *a*, because the *a-b* line and the new line are parallel, and he has already proved (in Proposition 29) that where two lines are parallel, the angles positioned as *a* and *d* are must be equal.

(2) The next move is to show that angle *e* must be equal to angle *b* for the same reason – again something he has proved in Proposition 29. We also know from Proposition 13 that because *c*, *d* and *e* all lie on the one straight line, the three angles added together must equal 180°.

(3) But if *c* + *d* + *e* = 180, and if *a* = *d* and *b* = *e*, then *a* + *b* + *c* must equal 180° as well – because it is an axiom of the system, which needs no proof, that if you add equal things together, the totals you get must be equal. Therefore the angles in our triangle – *a*, *b* and *c* – add up to 180°, which is what we were trying to prove (*quod erat demonstrandum*, or QED).

This proof is a simple example of what is now called a deductive proof in an axiomatic system, and what our authors most often called Demonstration.[5] What is striking about it is that from a few simple undeniable axioms, proceeding by obvious, undeniable steps, you work your way to a conclusion which is not obvious at first sight.

Four points to notice about such proofs:

- The knowledge you derive from this proof is a priori – you don't need to go out and measure triangles to know it. In fact we could know it was true even if no-one had seen a triangle before, and even if no triangles existed. (Contrast that with a posteriori knowledge like 'metals expand on heating': to know that, some-one needs to have actually looked at metals and observed their behaviour when heated. You can't *demonstrate* such a truth, only show it observationally, empirically.)
- The conclusion you reach is a *necessary* truth. It doesn't just happen to be a fact about triangles that their interior angles add up to 180 degrees, it *has* to be true. It wouldn't be a triangle if they didn't. By contrast, the generalisation about metals given above is a *contingent* truth – it is true, but it didn't *have* to be. (Indeed we may yet find a new metal which behaves differently.) There would be a contradiction in saying that something was a triangle but that its interior angles didn't add up to 180 degrees; there would be no contradiction in saying something is a metal but doesn't expand on heating.
- This fact about triangles is therefore often said to be *indubitable*. As we've just seen, it couldn't not be true – so there is no way you could possibly doubt it. By contrast, any contingent truth, because it is something that *could* be false, seems to be something you could doubt.
- By the same token, a priori truths are often thought to be *uninformative*, in the sense that they tell us nothing about the actual world. Precisely because they couldn't be false, they are compatible with any possible state of affairs. What we know for certain is that *if* something is a triangle, *then* its interior angles equal two right angles – but we have no a priori knowledge that something is or is not a triangle, or indeed that there are any triangles in existence at all.

See especially Descartes (pp. 51–3), Leibniz (pp. 108–9), Locke (pp. 154–6) and Hume (pp. 260–2).

Is and ought

This takes us to one the most important moves of modern
philosophy. Reason, we have just said, tells us *how* to do things, but
can never tell us *what* to do. But morality *does* tell us what to do.
Therefore, Hume claims, morality is not a matter of reason.

This shocking, deliberately provocative assertion by Hume
expresses a view which has been enormously influential. No
matter how much you may find out about how things are, Hume
says, no matter how well you might come to understand the way
the world is, you will never by such reasoning discover anything at
all about morality. Any such investigation can only ever tell you
what is and is not the case; but morality is concerned, not with how
things *are*, but with how they *ought* to be.

What Hume has done here, as in much of what he writes, is to
develop the work of Descartes and Locke to its logical conclusion.
As we have seen so often, the thinkers of the seventeenth century
were all concerned in one way or another with the creation of the
division between appearance and reality – between the way things
seem to us and the way they really are in themselves – which most
of us today take for granted in the way we live our lives. Hume here
is merely drawing the inevitable conclusion from that separation:
that given such a distinction, morality and values of every
kind must, like colours and tastes and feelings, be relegated to the
realm of appearance. Goodness and badness, vice and virtue, are
not things we find in the world, but things we put into it; they are
not parts of nature, but parts of our reaction to it.

Hume's projectivism, or feeling good

What, then, does it mean, according to Hume, to say that something is morally good or bad? If I see someone going out of her way
to help a friend, I say she has done a good thing, or that she is a
good person. But what does that goodness consist in? If we follow
Hume's method and trace back the idea of good to the impressions
from which it is derived, what do we find?

Well, no matter how closely you examine the action this person
has performed, you won't find anything in it which gives you an

impression of goodness. You may see that she acted quickly or slowly, elegantly or clumsily; you may say her action was kind, or was thoughtful, or was compassionate: any of those may be qualities of her action, provided we specify clearly enough what they mean. But where is the *goodness* of these qualities, or of this act? The answer, says Hume, is that it is nowhere to be found, because you are looking in the wrong place. The goodness resides not in the action, or in her character, but in *our feelings* about them; it is not an objective feature of the act or of the person, but a subjective feature of the feelings it inspires in the people who observe it.[6] 'That was good' means something like 'the idea of things like that is associated in my mind with feelings of pleasure'. It is misleading, therefore, to say that actions or people are either good or bad, because considered in themselves they are all morally neutral. Morality is, as beauty is often said to be, only in the eye of the beholder. We describe actions as good or bad because 'the mind has a great propensity to spread itself on external objects': the emotions which we associate with what we see colour our perception of the action for us.[7] We *project* our subjective feelings onto the objective world, and instead of saying 'that action was of this kind, and I like actions like that', we say, misleadingly, 'that was a good action'.

There is a whole world of philosophy in this move, and a great deal could be and has been written about it. For our purposes what matters is to see how it exemplifies Hume's method of cutting through the pretensions of the learned to the underlying facts of experience, which he seeks to explain in terms of the atoms of thought, governed as they are by the iron laws of association.

He goes on to produce a complex and subtle account of the way in which these associations work. The idea of cruelty, for example, is associated in our minds so strongly with the idea of suffering that it automatically brings to mind a feeling of distaste or disquiet, which we express by saying that cruelty is wrong; and the idea of kindness or generosity in the same way brings with it a feeling of pleasure or appreciation which we express by saying that kindness is good. There is absolutely nothing rational or considered about these judgements at all. The suggestion is not that we like kindness and dislike cruelty because we are concerned for other people's welfare, but simply that, regardless of whether we care about the people involved or not, we simply *can't help* but feel pleasant or painful emotions when we consider actions of certain kinds.[8]

In the case of other vices and virtues the story is less obvious, but essentially the same. It is easy to see why a 'natural' vice like cruelty should be associated in my mind with feelings of displeasure, and so tends to be condemned as wrong. All my experience of cruelty has involved suffering, and so the unpleasantness of the suffering has come to be associated in my mind with acts of that kind. But why should theft or dishonesty be regarded in the same way? Whatever people may like to think, it is simply not true, says Hume, that acts of this kind invariably lead to suffering in the way that cruelty does. We all know from experience that thieves and liars often do very well for themselves. So how does the idea of such actions come to be associated only with feelings of dislike? The answer is that 'artificial' vices like these involve thought, and education. We realise that the long-term consequences of acts of that kind are damaging to society and so are in all our worst interests, so the link to feelings of suffering is indirect, but is no less real. We then strengthen that link and intensify it by education and training, reinforcing the association by systems of punishment and reward and the careful training of children, so that they learn to react with displeasure to the kinds of action we see as socially harmful.

Hume was proud of this 'projectivist' theory of morality, and it is one of the few parts of his work that he doesn't elsewhere undercut or cast doubt on.[9] It remained for him as a shining example of what his new Science of Man could do for us, even after he had abandoned the whole idea of such a science, and of the foundational nature of philosophical investigations in general. In other areas, as he saw only too clearly, the results were a great deal less satisfactory.

Reading

The basis of Hume's new Science of Man is set out in the Introduction and in Part 1 of Book 1 of the *Treatise*. The basics of his moral theory are in Book 3, Part 1, and in the *Enquiry Concerning the Principles of Morals*, Section 1 and Appendix.

Questions to ask

(1) Is it true that all ideas are based on impressions, and that simple ideas are unanalysable? Give a clear example of a simple idea (without analysing it).

(2) Is it true that nothing you know about how things are in the world can in itself give you any reason for action?

(3) Is it true that moral values are not features of the world, but of our reactions to it? Does the theory depend on our being able to specify things that *are* features of the world, which can be described independently of our reactions to it?

Chapter 20

The failure of the project

In Book 1 of the *Treatise*, Hume proceeds to demonstrate the failure of his own project. He considers some of the most central and most fundamental concepts of human thought in the light of his new Science of Man, and asks what they amount to, how the knowledge of them is arrived at, and how they fit into a rational, objective understanding of human beings and of the world. And he concludes that they don't fit in at all. In this chapter I want to work through his treatment of some of those central concepts and examine the alarming conclusions he claims to come to about them; in the next chapter we will ask what we are supposed to learn from this analysis, and consider where his conclusions leave him – and where they leave us at the end of this book.

Causation

The importance of causal knowledge

When you think about it, says Hume, all our knowledge of the world around us depends on our knowledge of causation.

This is obvious in the case of practical knowledge of various kinds: you know to plant seeds at certain times and not at others, for example, because you know in what circumstances they grow and in what circumstances they don't – i.e. you know what actions lead to what outcomes, or what *causes* lead to what *effects*. Scientific knowledge of nature is a matter of explaining natural phenomena – i.e. of discovering their *causes*, and enabling us to predict their *effects*. Hume sees meaning in this way, too. The information you get from reading you get because you know what people do in order to convey certain ideas – i.e. you know the *cause* of the marks on the page or the screen, and you know what *causes* people to write those things – what they were trying to say. In general, he says, the only way we can ever discover anything about the world apart from the things we directly experience ourselves, is by working out the causes and effects of what we see around us. Isn't that right?

If it is, it follows that anyone who wants to understand the way human beings work and how the various branches of their knowledge are related – as Hume claims he does – needs to begin by getting an understanding of causation, or of what it means for one thing to be the cause of another. So, what *does* it mean?

The idea of necessary connection

Well, consider an example of a simple, mechanical cause: the white ball rolls along the table, hits the stationary red one, and the red ball starts to move. Obviously the impact of the white ball caused the motion of the red ball. We have seen this and similar cases a thousand times. But what, when you examine such a case closely, do you *actually see*? Well, you see the movement of the white ball, and the impact on the red ball, and the movement of the red ball. So you can safely say that the impact of the white ball preceded the motion of the red ball; and if you have the time and nothing better to do, you can repeat the experiment as many times as you like, and every time you will see the same sequence of events – impact followed by movement. Is that all it means to say that the impact *causes* the movement – that the one always follows the other?

Well, no. Surely, says Hume, to say that the impact immediately preceded the movement is only *part* of what we mean by saying the impact caused the movement – we also mean more than that.[1] We mean not only that the two events followed one another, and not only that they *always* follow one another, but also that the second event happened *because of* the first: the first event *brought about* the second one, or *made* it happen. In Hume's terms, part of our idea of a cause is the idea of a 'necessary connection' between the one event and the other.

Is that right? Does your idea of a cause involve the idea of a 'necessary connection' – that causes *make* their effects happen?

Most people think it does. Surely, it is just such a 'necessary connection' that makes the difference between a true cause, on the one hand, and a mere regularity, or correlation, on the other. The problem then is: it's obvious how we come by the idea that a cause precedes its effect; but where do we get this idea of a necessary connection from?

The origin of the idea of necessary connection

The first thing to point out is that there is no *logical* relation between cause and effect. Hume is very clear and very insistent on this point. There is no 'relation of ideas', as he calls it, between cause and effect, because if there were it would be contradictory to imagine that the red ball could *not* move when the white ball hit it. But it isn't contradictory, is it?

Certainly, I can imagine all kinds of strange causal sequences if I try. The white ball could simply bounce off when it hit the red one. It could fall to pieces, or even pass clean through it. The red ball could disappear, or melt, or even turn into a parrot and soar up into the sky singing highlights from Verdi's *Rigoletto*. Of course, we know that none of those things *does* happen; in fact, we are pretty sure that they *couldn't* happen. If any of them did, it would be extraordinary, amazing, fantastic – but it wouldn't be *contradictory*, would it?

By contrast, try to imagine that something *really* contradictory occurs. Imagine that when the white ball hits the red ball it turns into a spherical cube. Can you imagine that? Or imagine that the white ball both hits and does not hit the red one. Or that after the impact the red ball is both red all over and white all over at the same time. Can you do it?

I don't see how you could. None of those things could *possibly* happen. We can't even imagine their happening, because there is a logical absurdity about them. But in the case of the red ball's simply staying where it is when hit by the white one – or any of the other bizarre sequences I listed – there is no absurdity, no contradiction, involved. We know those things won't happen – but it isn't logic that tells us so. It's just our knowledge of what kind of thing we can reasonably expect, and what kind of thing we can't. The 'necessary connection' that's involved in the idea of a cause, in other words, isn't a *logical* necessity of any kind, so it must be some kind of 'matter of fact' – a contingent truth about the world that we have found out by experience.

We saw earlier (Box 16.1) that Berkeley held that all we really see is what a person who had been born blind would see when first given sight, and everything else we say we 'see' is really something the mind creates on the basis of what we see. Hume uses a very similar move to show that necessary connections are not given by the senses. He imagines that Adam, newly created and with no experience of the world, observes the collision of the two balls. Would he have any idea of what to expect? Would he be any more surprised if the red ball flew away than he would be if it simply rolled off into the pocket? No, says Hume. He has no idea of causal connections, because he has no past experience of causation to draw on.

The idea of necessary connection, then – of causal power, or agency – is something we learn by experience, not something we know from logic. The question is, *what* experience do we learn it from? Necessary connections aren't things you can see – or feel, or hear, or sense in any other way. All there is to experience in our causal case – or any other you can think of – is just the sequence of events. If a causal connection could be seen, then

Hume's imaginary Adam *would* be able to predict what would happen, because he would be able to see the necessity. But no matter how carefully you look, there is nothing to be detected by any of our senses but the sequence of events, with no connection between them. So how do we find out about causes? Where do we get the idea of a necessary connection from?

The difference between us and Adam, of course, is one of experience: we have seen cases like this, and collisions of other kinds, lots and lots of times in our lives, and that is why we know what will happen, and Adam doesn't.[2] But what kind of explanation is that? What have we seen that Adam hasn't? It doesn't matter how often you have seen billiard balls collide, there is nothing you see on the thousandth occasion that Adam doesn't see on the first day he is created. The difference between us isn't that he misses something that's there to see, only that he hasn't seen such things before, and so doesn't *expect* the red ball to move, whereas we do. Our past experience has not allowed us to detect something we missed on the first occasion; all it has done is to *condition* us to *associate* certain ideas together – to expect certain kinds of outcome from certain kinds of event, so that when they happen, we say things like 'I knew that would happen', 'It was bound to happen', or 'It had to happen'. And that Association of Ideas, according to Hume, is the origin of our idea of necessary connection.

Does that seem plausible? It makes sense, surely, as a piece of psychology. Because of things we have observed in the past, we come to associate the sight of the impact of the two billiard balls with the idea of the movement of one of them, so that when we see the first event, we automatically expect the movement of the second one to follow. The problem is that Hume didn't set out to give us a psychological theory. He set out to give us an analysis of causation. He was supposed to be telling us, not what happens in our heads, but what happens in the world – what the causal relation is, what ties together one event with another, what makes an effect follow when a cause occurs. And instead of that, all he has come up with is an account of how we come to form causal *expectations* on the basis of our past experience.

In the previous chapter we saw Hume's 'projectivist' account of morality – how he analysed away moral qualities as being not true features of the world around us, but feelings in us. Here we have a directly comparable projectivist account of causation: it seems that the world doesn't contain causal powers, any more than it contains moral values; all it contains is sequences of events, patterns, correlations; the causal connections between those events are entirely in our own heads.

But how can this be? Causation is what all our knowledge of the world beyond our own experience is based on. How can that be true if there is no such thing! It would mean that all our understanding of the world, all our science, all our reason, all that makes us different from mere unthinking animals, was just a sham: we talk as if we were finding out great secrets about nature, but in fact all we are doing is succumbing to the power of the Association of Ideas. When we calculate the motions of the planets or discover the circulation of the blood, we are not finding out how things are in the world, we are just being conditioned by our experience into forming certain expectations instead of others, like a dog that has been conditioned to salivate when the bell rings because the bell always rings at dinner time.

Could that be true? What would it mean for your view of human beings and their relation to the world? And what would it mean for Hume's new Science of Man which has led us to such pessimistic-looking conclusions?

Induction

The first conclusion Hume finds himself driven to contemplate, then, is that there is in reality no more to a cause than a well-established correlation. Search as you might, you will never find a cause in nature, because causes are not the kind of thing that nature could ever contain, any more than goodness is.

That conclusion is perhaps scary enough.[3] But it gets worse. If there is no such thing as a necessary connection in nature – nothing ever makes anything else happen, events merely follow one another in regular patterns – then how do we know that those patterns are going to continue into the future? If there is nothing about the impact of the white ball that *makes* the red ball move, what grounds do we have to think that next time it happens we will get the same result?

DAVID HUME

The problem of induction

This is the aspect of the problem that has come to be known since Hume's day as the Problem of Induction, and it is where the lack of necessary connections becomes a real worry.[4] Perhaps we don't need to bother about the surprising discovery that there are no real causes in nature, provided we can come up with some good reason to show that our natural conditioning by experience is not deceptive. After all, the problem for the dogs that have been conditioned to expect dinner when the bell rings is just that they have been conditioned artificially, and there is in fact no good reason to think that the connection between bell ringing and dinner will continue into the future. The fact that our expectations about the behaviour of billiard balls are produced by the same kind of psychological mechanism is no problem, we might say, because we can see that there *is* good reason to think that billiard balls aren't going to change their behaviour in the future.

Or, we think there is. But when you start to think about it, *what* reason do we have for thinking the next billiard ball impact will have the usual consequences? We are all of us – Hume included – absolutely confident that it will. But that is perhaps only a testimony to the power of our mental associations – we *can't help* but think the red ball will move, we *know* it will. But *how* do we know? What *good reason* can we give for our belief, over and above the fact that we just *feel convinced* that it will happen?

Well, the difference between the dogs' dinners and the billiard balls was that the billiard ball connection is a natural one, based on the way things are in the world, whereas the dogs' expectations are based only on the whim of the experimenter. So the question we have to ask is whether we have any good reason for thinking that the way things are in the world is going to stay the same – as Hume puts it, we need to be able to show that nature is uniform.

And how will we do that? How can we prove that there is a fixed way that things are in the world, and therefore that observed correlations in nature can reasonably be expected to continue?

THE FAILURE OF THE PROJECT

The impossibility of justification

Hume at this point tells us that there is no point in our trying to find a proof of this kind, because there is no way it can ever be done. There are, after all, only two ways in which we can try to prove the uniformity of nature:

(1) We can put together some kind of deductive proof, beginning with indubitable a priori premises and proceeding by necessary steps to the conclusion that nature is uniform (see Box 19.1); or
(2) We can argue not from pure logic, but from experience – we can reason probabalistically, beginning not from how things must be, but from what we know of how they actually are, and we can try to show that given what we know, it is reasonable to expect nature to continue in the same way as it has up to now.

Is there any other way we can proceed?

If not, then we are in trouble, because Hume claims that neither of these routes can possibly succeed.

(1) We can't prove a priori that nature must always be uniform, for reasons we have seen already. To try to argue it this way would be to say that nature *must* be uniform, that there would be some *contradiction* involved in assuming anything else. But there just isn't. We all know that billiard balls aren't about to sprout wings – but there is no *contradiction* in suggesting that they might. Things *could* all go completely haywire as from tomorrow; and that fact alone, says Hume, is enough to show that there is no a priori proof to the effect that they won't.
(2) So can we prove it from experience, from how we know the world to be? Well, no. The most our experience can teach us is that nature has been uniform *up to now*, but not that it will *always* be uniform. After all, the whole point of trying to prove the uniformity of nature is to enable us to show that when we work things out on the basis of past experience we are not just being conditioned by events, but are forming reasonable expectations. So obviously, any attempt to argue that nature is uniform on the basis of past experience is bound to

be circular – we will be arguing from past experience that arguing from past experience is a good way to go on. And that would be stupid, wouldn't it?

So where does *that* leave us? According to Hume it means that all of what we normally think of as our knowledge of the world, based as it is on cause and effect, is ungrounded. It doesn't mean we're *wrong* to believe the things we believe – that the sun will rise tomorrow, that if I jump out of the window I will fall to the ground, that this drug cures this disease, etc. – but it does mean that we have no *good reason* for any of those beliefs.

Hume compares us to animals, and the way they are conditioned by their experience to form certain beliefs rather than others, and also – more damningly perhaps – to the people we like to think of as irrational. A drunkard whose friend drinks himself to death swears off alcohol because the idea of drink comes to be associated in his mind with death and loss; but in time the association weakens, and he goes back to his old ways. That is thoughtless, irrational behaviour: the drunkard doesn't think through the situation and work out an appropriate course of action, he is completely at the mercy of his irrational fears and mental associations. And so are we, all the time – in ordinary life when we avoid putting our hands in the fire because we think it will burn us, and even in our most careful, scientific studies, when we persuade ourselves we are discovering the deep secrets of nature. Or take another case – of what we like to think of as irrational prejudice. Hume uses the example of people who think that all Irishmen are stupid, or all Frenchmen are fops; we might take the case of people who think women can't play football, or that black men have a natural sense of rhythm. What is going on in such cases, surely, is that people aren't being rational – they aren't thinking out or carefully investigating what's what, they are forming their beliefs haphazardly, by the association of ideas in their heads. But if Hume is right, that is all any of us ever does, in any example you might care to choose.

The great hope of the Enlightenment, which we have inherited, was that racists and bigots and superstitious people are not simply evil, and are not simply enemies who must be either controlled or defeated by those of us who take a more advanced, a more enlightened, attitude; the hope was that they are merely *mistaken* – that through lack of education they are thinking badly, and our responsibility to them is to bring them to a better understanding of how things really are. If Hume is right, those hopes seem to be entirely unfounded: our opponents are merely conditioned by their experience, yes – and we are similarly conditioned by our, different, experiences to different habits and ways of life. It is true, of course, that our opponents, if they had led our lives, would have had our opinions and our attitudes; but it is no less true that if we had lived their lives we would agree with them. And in those circumstances, how can we represent our dispute with them as anything other than a naked power struggle, a kind of tribal warfare between Us and Them?

The external world

Our beliefs about the world around us, then, seem to be based only on our own particular feelings. But can we at least establish that there is a world around us for us to have feelings about? Again Hume proceeds in his objective, scientific way to analyse the ideas we have – in this case the idea of a continuing, mind-independent world – and to investigate how we come by it. And again what he finds is that we have no good reason for believing in the existence of any such thing.

The idea of an external world

How do we think of the external world? What is our idea of it like? Well, it is the idea of an enduring, mind-independent thing. And where do we get the idea of such a world from?

The fact is that nothing in our experience can possibly give it to us. If you examine closely the contents of your own experience – i.e. the things you actually do experience, not the beliefs you form about them – all you ever really find, as we have already seen, are impressions and ideas. And every one of those is a *fleeting*, mind-*dependent* thing: they come and go, as our stream of consciousness flows on; and they would not exist at all if that stream of consciousness didn't exist. So how do we come to form the idea that there is such a thing as a permanent, unchanging, mind-*in*dependent reality?

This is, of course, exactly the problem we found in Berkeley. And as Berkeley showed, it is extremely hard to answer. Our experience cannot provide us with access to – or even understanding of – such a thing as a mind-independent world; yet there is no way we can reason our way to the idea either. So where does it come from? Hume's answer is once again that we get to it by means of the association of ideas: in fact, like the belief in moral values and the belief in causation, it turns out in the end to depend on a kind of mistake – mistaking features of our own, internal mental lives for features of a world around us.

The origin of the idea of an external world

The contents of your mind are in a continual state of flux – a constant stream of thoughts and feelings overlapping and inter-weaving as you jumble together your current sensations, your past experience, your memories and your feelings and your hopes and ideals. In all this flux there is, as we have said, nothing that is constant and unchanging; but there are recurring elements: if you look at the wall and then look out of the window and then look back at the wall again, what you experience the second time is usually very like what you experienced before you looked outside. The two experiences are quite plainly different, in the sense that the first one has now gone, and the second one has replaced it – but the content of the two experiences is very much the same. This kind of thing is happening all the time as we go about our lives in the world and the result, Hume says, is that without noticing it we come to regard some features of our experience as constant, even though in fact they are not. We rightly notice that there are some unchanging features of our experience – i.e. lots of different but similar experiences – and so we foolishly slip into thinking that we are experiencing some unchanging reality. And that, he suggests, is the origin of our idea of an external world – a vague and unexamined feeling of constancy projected outwards so as to produce the myth of a mind-independent reality.

As a piece of empirical psychology that story is perhaps rather crude and simplistic, and contemporary versions of the matter would be a great deal more sophisticated; but whether or not you accept his explanation for the origin of the idea, it is hard to find an alternative which will represent the belief in an unchanging external world as philosophically any more respectable.[5]

Hume's doubts about the external world don't go any further than Berkeley's, except in the matter of his perhaps questionable psychological theory of the origin of the mistaken belief. The big difference from Berkeley, of course, is that Berkeley has his own alternative theory as to where our sensations come from, given that they cannot come from an external world – they come from God. Hume has no such alternative to offer. Most of the time, at least, he is convinced, like the rest of us, that there is an external world, and he regards Berkeley's attempt to make us believe that there isn't as a waste of time. But the fact remains that if we look at the matter carefully we see that the belief is utterly groundless, founded on nothing more than the very kind of sloppy thinking and lack of careful observation that we like to deride in other people.

The self

The origin of the idea of the self

And once we are launched on this path, it is very difficult to stop. If we have no possible grounds for thinking that there is a continuing external world, what grounds do we have for thinking that there is such a thing as a mind, or self? (Compare Berkeley, pp. 229–31.) We speak as if there is such a thing as me – some continuing thing which is constant throughout all my life from (at least) my birth until my death, and perhaps beyond. But again, what experience can possibly give rise to such a belief? As we have seen, there is simply nothing unchanging in our experience – either mental or physical, internal or external. So why should we say that there is a continuing self? The case is the same, Hume says, as something like the famous ship of Theseus, which in the course of time had every plank and every rope and every nail replaced. We talk as if there were some continuous, unchanging boat, just because it is simpler than trying to state the reality of the situation. In the same way, we *talk* as if there were such a thing as me, as my self, just because the reality of my constantly changing stream of perceptions is too difficult to deal with. As with the external world, we slip from the awareness of constancy in our experiences, to the belief in the experience of constancy. All there really is is an ongoing stream, a mass, or a 'bundle' of interrelated experiences which come and go in a moment, and nothing at all corresponding to what we call our selves.

Reason

One more example of the way in which Hume's corrosive analysis seems to undermine our views of the world and of ourselves, before we move on to consider the difficult question of where all this is supposed to leave Hume, and where it leaves us. The subject this time is his analysis of reason itself.

So far we have been looking at our knowledge of the world around us, and asking how we come by it. The story throughout has been that pure reason – what Hume sometimes calls 'knowledge', and sometimes 'relations of ideas' (see Box 19.1) – is infallible, but tells us nothing about the actual world. All our knowledge of 'matters of fact and existence' depends on experience, and on the causal reasoning we engage in to take us beyond what we immediately sense. And it is the fundamental concepts of that empirical knowledge – causation, the world and the self – that Hume has examined and found to be wanting. But his pessimism (or is it his playfulness?) doesn't stop there, and he tries to call into question even our most certain knowledge, in mathematics and logic.[6]

How is that possible? How can he cast doubt on things like 1 + 1 = 2, or 'If A is bigger than B, then B is smaller than A'?

The way he does it is by conceding from the first that the laws of logic and mathematics are perfect and infallible – and then calling into question any and every *application* of those infallible rules by a fallible human being. If mathematical *judgements* (as opposed to the abstract – non-existent? – rules that we are so proud of) were infallible, why would we ever check a calculation? Even the most expert mathematician checks her workings, and has more confidence in her conclusions when other mathematicians whose judgement she respects have corroborated them. The more often you check, and the more corroboration you have, the more confident you are, of course. But look what that means: it means that your allegedly purely mathematical judgement depends on such things as your memory (of how many times you checked it, and what answer you got), and on such things as your beliefs about how good a mathematician you and other people are – beliefs which involve judgements about what schools people went to, what exams they have passed, what we have heard about their past performance etc. etc. – all of which are very far removed from the pristine certainty we associate with the dictates of pure reason. It looks as if all our mathematical and logical knowledge depends on reasoning of a very messy, practical, not-purely-rational kind, and so is open to all the doubts that we associate with that kind of practical judgement.

Is that true? Well, perhaps it is. But surely it casts no doubt on at least very simple and obvious rational judgements like $1 + 1 = 2$, does it? This is the kind of rational intuition that saved Descartes from his doubt, that Spinoza and Locke called the highest form of knowing; surely those things remain indubitable?

Hume says not, and to prove it he argues that if these simple judgements were infallible, then so would more complex ones be, since they are just combinations of simple ones. Try adding up a list of 100 single-digit numbers. Every step is of the form '$27 + 4 = 31$' – which seems like a good example of an indubitable mathematical truth. But at the end of the calculation, will you have infallible knowledge that the sum total is 879? Er, no – you will check and recheck, and get your friends to check it with you. How come, if each individual step is an infallible certainty? Where has the doubt managed to creep in? Surely, says, Hume, there can only be uncertainty over the total if there was a tiny element of doubt unnoticed in each of the constituent steps. And that means that even the most certain examples are not indubitable truths, but only very-very-very-very well confirmed practical judgements.[7]

But he is not content to show that all purely rational knowledge comes down in the end to practical judgements; he tries to go further, and to argue that *no* rational judgement offers us *any* grounds for belief. If the arguments above work, then they show that each rational judgement is actually a combination of judgements about the original question (e.g. the mathematical case), and about the likelihood of my getting it right, based on my skill as a mathematician, how much support I have from other people, how carefully I was attending to what I was doing, how tired I am, what I have been drinking recently, etc. etc. etc. We are not consciously thinking about these other questions, of course, but still the original judgement is made against a background of those other judgements, and my confidence in the likelihood of its being correct depends in part on those other beliefs. But where do those beliefs come from? Each of those ancillary judgements is *itself* made against a similar background of other beliefs, about the likelihood of my making *those* judgements correctly; and so on indefinitely. If we really wanted to be rational, and to be certain of our judgement in even a very simple mathematical case, therefore, we would have to carry out checks, and reassure ourselves that we have got it right; and then we would have to check those checks and reassure ourselves about those reassurances, and then ... There is no limit to the steps we would have to complete, and at every stage we are introducing new grounds for doubt, new factors which we could be mistaken about. That means that if we ever did try to give ourselves the kind of assurance we like to think we have in these areas, we would in fact end up with no belief at all, because the apparatus of rational judgements, if followed through to its ultimate conclusion, subverts itself, and removes all grounds for any belief whatsoever. Of course, we *don't* do that – if we check at all, we stop the process at some convenient point, depending on how easy the checks and how important the calculation. But that means that even our best and most 'rational' judgements turn out to be nothing more than rough and ready estimates based on practical convenience, doesn't it?

Reading

Hume's investigation of Causation and Induction occupies most of Part 3 of Book 1 of the *Treatise*, and sections 4–7 of the *Enquiry*

Concerning Human Understanding. His doubts about the external world, the self and reason are set out in *Treatise* Book 1 Part 4, especially sections 2, 1 and 6.

Questions to ask

(1) Is it true that causal necessities are not features of reality, but are projected by our minds onto a causally neutral world?

(2) If Hume's account of the understanding shows that there are no such things as causes, the external world, or selves, does that show it is wrong? If so, *how* is it wrong?

(3) Do Hume's arguments cast any doubt on the certainty of a priori reasoning?

Chapter 21

The lessons of Hume
Where do we go from here?

In the last chapter we saw how Hume tries to show that we have no rational grounds for our belief in causation or for our expectations about the future, that our basic beliefs in the world around us and in our own continued existence are just irrational prejudices, and that even our most secure rational knowledge is in reality just a complex kind of guesswork. Where are we supposed to go from there? Does Hume intend us to try to stop believing in anything at all? Is he just playing with his readers, revelling in his own cleverness and trying to do nothing more serious than to shock people out of their complacency and make them think?

Hume's conclusions

At the end of Book 1 of the *Treatise* he provides his own conclusion. He says that the attempt to understand ourselves and the world we live in is doomed to failure, because when you try it, you find there is no justification for even our most basic beliefs, and the only thing you can conclude from a careful study of philosophy is that you should never accept what a careful study of philosophy tells you. So we have a choice: either we try to understand, and drive ourselves to the conclusion that we can't do it; or we give up all attempt at understanding, and believe whatever takes our fancy – neither of which is a very attractive prospect.[1]

At this point, he says, he has reduced himself to the most deplorable condition imaginable, with no idea what to believe, or how to go on. Philosophy is impossible; understanding is impossible. We either have to accept that nothing makes any sense and everything we do is irrational, or just act irrationally anyway, because there is no alternative.

So what happens? Answer – he goes off down the boozer with his mates, has a few drinks, plays a game of backgammon – and lo and behold, he feels a lot better. All his doubts and confusion fall away, and he's back in the real world, the natural world, from which his dry, arid, self-defeating speculations seemed almost for a while to have removed him completely. He laughs at himself and at his own foolishness, and all the philosophical anxieties he felt when he was alone in his room seem strained, artificial, and ridiculous.

But that isn't quite the end of the story. On another occasion, when he's less excited and less cheerful – perhaps when he's taking a walk, or sitting and thinking by himself – he can't help but start to wonder about things again, to stand back from his day-to-day habits of thought and action, and to ask himself why he does what he does, and why he believes what he believes . . . and soon he is launched again on his enquiries, and because he can find nothing wrong with the line of reasoning he has followed, he is led step-by-step right back again onto the slippery slope that leads to despair and hopelessness.

Scepticism and Naturalism

What are we to make of this rather sad story? As I said earlier (pp. 162–3), pinning down Hume's meaning is never easy, and here he seems to be locked into a constant cycle of hope and despair, and it is hard to know on which side he wants us to come down. As a result readers of Hume have tended to fall into two broad camps, depending which phase of the cycle they have seen as more important. The traditional reading concentrates on the negative side, and sees Hume as a sceptic who mocks and derides us for believing in things for which we have no justification. It is a mistake, he says, to think the world contains independently existing moral values; and it is also a mistake, of exactly the same kind, to think that it contains causal necessities, or material objects, or selves, or that our reasoning is anything other than a kind of mechanical conditioning. Of course he finds these conclusions to be unacceptable, to be literally incredible; but typically enough he uses that very fact as proof that he is right. We don't believe these sceptical conclusions, he says, because our nature is far stronger than our reasoning can ever be. We are not built for truth, for understanding; we just believe what our mechanical thought-processes make us believe. And the final proof of that fact is that when he presents it to himself as carefully and objectively as he can, it has as much effect on his beliefs and his behaviour as it would if he explained it to a dog, a fruit fly, or a bicycle.

More recent, 'Naturalist' commentators have read Hume's rejection of his own sceptical conclusions in an altogether more positive light. Hume can't be a sceptic, they say, because he thinks scepticism is impossible: as he repeatedly shows, we can't *not* believe in the existence of these things, so it can be nothing but pretentious posturing for anyone to say that we should. As he puts it at the beginning of that difficult chapter on the external world, beliefs of this kind are not ones which nature has left it up to us to decide about: they are built in to us, hard-wired into the sort of creature that we are, and the only kind of lives we can lead. It is therefore true that we have no justification for them, but only because they are too basic, too certain, for any justification to be either possible or necessary. Beliefs of this kind – that there is a world, which has its laws, and that there is a me, who can think – are not things we could have evidence for or believe for a reason, because they are not the kind of thing we could learn, or could forget, remember, question or doubt. On the contrary, unless we took for granted beliefs of that kind, it would make no sense for us to doubt anything, or to claim any knowledge whatsoever.

What could we know, if those things were uncertain? What could it mean to doubt or to question anything, if our world picture didn't have this basic framework against which to measure truth or falsity?[2]

What do you think? We all of us, all the time, act as if Hume's negative conclusions were wrong. Is that because they *are* wrong? Can you see any way of denying the chain of reasoning that gets him into this mess? Or is it that we are just too set in our ways, too much the creatures of custom and habit, to do otherwise? Or alternatively, are you happy to say with the Naturalists that our most fundamental beliefs are just constitutive of the kind of creature that we are, and as such do not admit of, and stand in no need of, any kind of justification?

New directions?

My own view of Hume is that neither of the readings I have outlined above does justice to the depth of the problems that he raises, and that the only way we can make sense of both aspects of his work, both phases of his cycle, is to read him as coming down on neither one side nor the other, but as saying literally that there is *no* stable and defensible position that we can adopt. His sceptical conclusions are inescapable, but unbelievable; and his naturalist convictions are unavoidable, but totally indefensible.

In the Introduction to this book I said that what ties our six philosophers together and links them to us is the conception which is constitutive of the Modern era, the belief in a distinction between Appearance and Reality, and the possibility of a rational, objective science which can transcend the one and reveal the other. What Hume has shown, it seems to me, is that that way of thinking, which has dominated the world from then until now and which still structures the way most of us think and live, was an experiment which failed. If we accept, as we all do, that reality transcends appearance, that our subjective experience can never be part of the objective world, then we will never be able to reconcile the lives our natures oblige us to lead with the only kind of understanding we think can lead us to the truth – just as Hume said. The Modern View was a breakthrough which permitted the creation of a new world, and it legitimised a way of life in which we still participate, but was one which is every day showing more and more clearly its incoherence and hopelessness. It really is time we started doing something else.[3]

Notes

1 Introduction

1 This is a gross oversimplification. First, it isn't as if everyone
suddenly started thinking differently. It would be more accurate
to say that the people whose voices we now hear from that time –
the people whose books were read and talked about and which we
continue to read now – were in important ways different in their
attitudes, beliefs and interests from those who held a comparable
position in the years before. Not so much a change of heart, in
other words, more a takeover of the intellectual establishment by
a new group. And second, the ideas of that new group were not
entirely new, so much as a reformulation and reinterpretation of
ideas that had been out of fashion, or unorthodox. But the change
is no less real and no less important for that.
2 The distinction I am calling Appearance/Reality is sometimes
known (following Wilfrid Sellars) as that between the 'manifest
image' and the 'scientific image'. There is a long and fascinating
story to be told about its development out of the Platonic, magical
tradition in pre-seventeenth-century thought, and its eventual
triumph over the Aristotelian orthodoxy of the day.

3 Try it. Write a story about how they live. Could anything they say have any *meaning*?

4 Other illustrations of the same kind: rooms, bottles, pockets and the like are often said to be 'empty', when in reality we know that they are full – if only of air (an example which Descartes often used); water which is 'pure' we know *really* contains all kinds of different organisms and compounds. Think up some more examples of your own.

5 It is an interesting question to ask which. Literary criticism, for example, seems not to have it. (It makes no sense to ask 'What is *Hamlet* really like?') History is a disputed case, and psychology another. And where does philosophy fit in? (Can a philosopher tell you what life, the universe and everything are really like, as the physicist claims to with your table?)

2 Material Monism or the Great Soup of Being

1 **Introduction to PART I:** The small town he grew up in – La Haye, some 20 kilometres to the north-east – has since been renamed Descartes so as to honour the great man (and draw in the tourists).

2 Descartes calls this one physical object by a variety of names. It is 'material substance' or 'corporeal substance' or 'body'. He also refers to it as 'extension', because its universal and defining characteristic is the fact that it is three-dimensional, or spread out, as we might say, in space (it has the 'principal attribute' of 'extension').

3 Descartes' terminology here is actually quite inconsistent. At times he is quite willing to say that my arm, for example, is one substance and my body another; at other times he insists that each body is only accidentally or modally distinct from others. This willingness to play fast and loose with technical vocabulary is very typical of Descartes' attitude to traditional learning. The underlying story behind his various presentations is constant, and is what I present here.

4 Our word 'real' derives from the Latin *res*, meaning 'thing'. When Descartes talks of a 'real' distinction, therefore, he means more than just a *genuine* distinction: he means a thingly distinction, or a difference between *things*. Similarly, when he and other writers of his time talk of 'reality', they are talking of *thingliness*, and when they talk of 'realising' something's potential, they mean *making it into a thing*.

5 The microscope was one of the great tools of seventeenth-century science, developed in the early seventeenth century and enthusiastically adopted by Descartes. Indeed there is good reason to think that the whole success of the appearance/reality distinction in the seventeenth century was built around the differences between naked-eye observations and observations with a telescope/microscope.

6 Hence Descartes' denial of the existence of atoms, conceived of as irreducible objects. After all, even atoms must have right sides and left sides; and how thick is the line that you might draw to separate them?

7 In the same way, the wood burns because at the submicroscopic level its internal organisation – the way its parts move systematically together – can be smashed apart by the incredibly rapid and violent motions of the submicroscopic particles which make up the body of a flame. Setting fire to a piece of wood is in reality a matter of attacking it with millions of tiny darts, which smash it to pieces and destroy its internal organisation; but those same tiny darts, when applied to the loose, disorganised aggregation of parts which make up the air, have no effect other than to move them around more rapidly (i.e. to heat it up).

8 According to Descartes, there can't be a vacuum, because there can't be something which is nothing. To say there is a space is to say there is something spatial, something extended – i.e. matter; and to say that there is literally *nothing* between two planets, say, would be to say that they are in contact. How can a vacuum – nothing – have size, and shape?

9 A later term not used in this sense by Descartes himself.

10 *Principles* 2.37.

11 The 'quantity of motion' is calculated by multiplying an object's size by its speed.

12 *Il Saggiatore* (The Assayer), 1623. In Stillman Drake and C.D. O'Mallay (trans.) *The Controversy on the Comets of 1618* (University of Pennsylvania Press, Philadelphia, 1960).

13 It is interesting to bear in mind the extent to which the people we now see as the seventeenth century's Great Men of Science, such as Kepler and Galileo, were, like Descartes, part of the Neoplatonic tradition of number mysticism which we now tend to think of as anything but 'scientific'.

14 Nikolaus Kopernik, known as Copernicus, (1473–1543), suggested the Earth was not the centre of the universe but orbited around the sun. In the seventeenth century this became a much discussed

issue, and in 1633 Galileo was condemned by the church for expressing a belief in it.

15 See ch. 4 for detail on his account of human beings, and ch. 3 for a discussion of his relation to orthodox Christianity.

3 The possibility of atheism

1 'Letter to Dowager Grand Duchess Christina of Bavaria' (1615) in Stillman Drake (ed. and trans.) *Discoveries and Opinions of Galileo* (Doubleday Anchor Books, Garden City New York, 1957).
2 E.g. when in *Principles* 1.76 he says we should submit to divine authority even when it conflicts with our most evident beliefs.
3 *Principles* 1.51–2.
4 See e.g. Replies to Fifth Objections 3.9.
5 This line of thought was developed by followers of Descartes – most famously Nicolas Malebranche – into the doctrine known as 'Occasionalism': the fall of the leaf is 'caused' by the mechanical processes only in the sense that it is on the *occasion* of the matter's being disposed in a certain way that *God* causes it to fall. Thus God is the only 'true' cause of events in the world; mechanical processes are 'natural', 'secondary' or 'occasional' causes. (See Box 9.1.)
6 Note also the moral analogy: the free will naturally tends towards rectitude, but is turned aside from the straight path by the temptations and confusions produced by our physical embodiment.

4 Human beings in Descartes' world

1 If she did, it wouldn't be from her anatomical knowledge alone. If she *could* discover, by examining my brain, say, what it felt like to be me, it would not be *from that examination alone* that she knew it; it would be by analogy with *her own subjective experience* of what it is like to have a brain in such a state. Compare: you could perhaps find out by monitoring the condition of the nerves in my jaw that I had toothache; but you wouldn't know how that felt unless you had been in a similar condition yourself. An alien physiologist who had never felt pain could know all about the events in my nervous system; could it know I was feeling pain?

5 Doubt and Discovery

1 See R.H. Popkin, *A History of Scepticism from Erasmus to Spinoza* (University of California Press, Berkeley, Los Angeles, and London, 1979).

2 Note how Socratic this procedure is: like Socrates, Descartes believes the truth – in outline at least – is there within all of us, waiting to be discovered. All we have to do is clear our heads of the clutter of accumulated prejudices and look beyond the appearances of the bodily senses to the clear thinking of the soul.

3 As we shall see, neither of these analogies is exactly right. He is going to show that some of the things he believes are things he *can't* deny, and he uses those as the basis of his reformed view of the world. (Some parts of the house turn out to be so well built he can't knock them down; some of his apples are so sound they can't be tipped out of the barrel.)

4 There is great irony in this shift of focus: it is because Descartes and his like were so successful in selling their account of how things are that we lose sight of what he has to tell us. Precisely because so much of what he is saying is familiar, we tend to miss it, and see only what to us is striking, but to him was relatively incidental – the form in which he presented it.

5 *Meditations* 2.

6 It isn't easy to say exactly which of your thoughts come into this category. And some have seen that as a weakness in Descartes' position. It is clear, for example, that it varies from person to person, and from time to time. $2 + 3 = 5$ we can grasp as a single intuition; but what about $2 + 3 + 5 + 6 + 8 = 24$? If I break it up into separate steps, each one of them is intuitively certain, but the whole set of them is what Descartes calls a 'deduction', not an intuition – a string of intuitions linked together. But if I were a better and more practised mathematician, that sum might become as obvious and undeniable as $1 + 1 + 1 = 3$ is for me. See *Rules* 3.

7 *Replies to Objections*, 6. What this shows is that when Descartes and other seventeenth-century philosophers talk of 'reason' they are talking not about pure, a priori thought, but about rational investigation, most obviously what we would now call science.

8 Descartes would add that since death and destruction are processes of separating the parts of an object, the fact that the mind is immaterial means it is immortal – it doesn't exist in space, so it can't have its parts (spatially) separated. Hence his claim

in the dedication to the *Meditations* to prove the immortality of the soul.

9 I have done what I can to capture the thought behind this argument in Meditation 3. In the text it is even harder to follow because of the archaic and rather technical terminology in which it is expressed, particularly the terms 'formal reality' and 'objective reality' (also translated as 'intentional reality'). The formal reality of a thing is its level of *'realitas'*, i.e. thingliness, or substantiality (see ch. 2 footnote 4, p. 270). So a substance, such as matter, has more formal reality than a mode, such as a stone, which depends on it and can't exist without it; and that stone in turn has more formal reality than one of its own modes, such as its colour. Objective reality is nothing at all to do with what we would mean by those words. The objective reality of an idea is just the formal reality of the *object* of that idea, i.e. of the thing that the idea is an idea *of*. So because matter has more formal reality than a stone, the *idea* of matter has more *objective* reality than the idea of a stone. God has more formal reality than anything else; so the idea of God has more objective reality than any other idea. And the argument turns on the claim that you can't produce the idea of something that has more formal reality than you have yourself – i.e. you can't produce an idea with more objective reality than you yourself have formal reality.

10 This is known as the 'ontological argument' for God's existence. Descartes makes it out in the *Meditations* solely in terms of God's 'perfection'. But his notion of perfection is richer than ours, and contains not only the idea of being the best, but also that of being perfected, or completed, brought to be, actualised, realised (see pp. 71–2).

11 Does this look circular to you? Many people have thought that Descartes uses his reason to establish the existence of God, and God to establish the reliability of his reason – the 'Cartesian Circle'.

12 The classic example of the true nature of the material world as presented in the *Meditations* is the piece of wax of Meditation 2. It is hard and yellow and scented; yet when I warm it it becomes soft and colourless and has no smell. Yet it is the same thing, even though all its sensory properties have changed. So what is it really? It is an extended mass, describable only in terms of the sizes and motions of its constituent parts, and known not by my senses, but by my intellect.

6 God, or Nature?

1 Lens-grinding is sometimes portrayed by more Romantic-influenced commentators as a humble craft adopted in obedience to Talmudic injunctions; whether or not that is true, it was certainly at the cutting edge of scientific and technological advance at the time.

2 Remark by the German poet and novelist Novalis (Friedrich Leopold, Baron von Hardenberg, 1772–1801). See *Fragmente und Studien 1799–1800*, in *Schriften*, P. Kluckhohn and R. Samuel (eds) (Stuttgart: Kohlhammer, 1960–75) 3.562.

3 *Ethics* 4, Preface, and often.

4 As a citizen of the Dutch Republic it was much easier for him than for Catholic Descartes, of course. Even so, his books were banned and burned, and for fear of controversy the *Ethics* wasn't published until after his death.

5 *Ethics* 1, Proposition 17, note.

6 Letter 56.

7 See e.g. note to Proposition 15 of *Ethics* 1.

8 It is therefore wrong if you are a Cartesian to say that your mind is in your body. It is *united with* your body in a very intimate way (it can influence and be influenced by your body, but not that of anyone else), but it is not literally in your head, any more than it is in your pocket, your bathroom, or your car. It just isn't *anywhere*.

9 *Ethics* 2, Proposition 21, note.

10 *Ethics* 2, Proposition 2.

11 In fact, as we shall see, this is not true – but that didn't stop people thinking it.

12 See *Ethics* 2, Definition 6. We still have something like this usage in the verbal sense – to say something has been perfected can mean that it has been brought to completion, actualised.

13 In effect this means that the 'Ontological Argument' we saw in Descartes (p. 56) does in fact work for a God like Spinoza's (if it *is* a God). It really would be a contradiction to think that reality didn't exist: it would mean that nothing was true. But it can't be true that nothing is true, can it?

14 See below, pp. 93–8, for what this means about human action.

15 *Ethics* 5, Proposition 19.

7 The attribute of thought

1 *Principles* 1.53.
2 *Ethics* 1, Appendix.
3 He states this in *Ethics* 2, Proposition 13, note. For a modern attempt to explain panpsychism as a way of demystifying the mind, see T. Nagel, 'Panpsychism' in *Mortal Questions* (Cambridge University Press, London, 1979).
4 And in an infinite number of other ways, too. The categories of our understanding do not exhaust the whole of reality: whatever other ways there may be of something's being real, Spinoza says, it will be the same reality that is expressed.

8 Metaphysics and the life of man

1 This problem was one of the reasons which led to the theory of Occasionalism (see Box 9.1). See p. 41 for interaction in Descartes, and pp. 125–30 for Leibniz's view.
2 *Ethics* 5, Pref. (For Descartes' position, see p. 41.)
3 *Ethics* 3, Proposition 2 and note.
4 *Ethics* 3, Propositions 6–7.
5 Spinoza's definition of pleasure (also translated as 'joy') is 'passing to a state of greater perfection' (*Ethics* 3, Proposition 11 and note) – an odd-sounding expression. The idea is what we have seen: desire is the expression of conatus, the effort to be yourself. To achieve your desire, therefore, is to be more yourself – to realise your potential, to actualise your nature – to be completed, finished, or *perfected* (see note 12, p. 275).
6 When it comes to more complex, integrated and long-lasting parts of your mind, like conscious thoughts, the question of whether they are yours or someone else's is typically easier to resolve, as it is generally easier to say whether something of the scale of a leg is or is not part of your body. But we do talk about such things as the will of the meeting, or the committee's decision, and sometimes the opinion of such a body can be different from that of any individual member of it. Does that support the idea that what we call an individual mind is a matter of convention?
7 For example, *Ethics* 2, Proposition 48.
8 *Ethics* 3, Proposition 9, note.
9 There are of course lots of cases where people do *not* want to do what they think of as good, and *do* want to do what they think is

wrong. Do they disprove Spinoza's theory? I don't myself think so. They show (i) that people are extremely complicated, with many different desires deriving from many different sources in their natures and their experience, and often these desires can conflict, and (ii) that moral terms have come to have a derivative use, according to which 'good' means not 'desired by me now', but something like 'generally seen as desirable'.

10 Since this process of understanding and of growth is a source of pleasure derived from something outside of us – the world we are coming to understand – it is for Spinoza a kind of love; and since the object of this love is the world itself, reality, the whole of which we and everything else are parts, he calls it 'the intellectual love of God'. And since it fills our minds with truths, and truths are eternal, it provides the only kind of immortality of which we are capable. These facts of psychology and epistemology are for Spinoza the basic truths which religion has distorted and misconceived.

9 The principle of Sufficient Reason

1 Some people think that the mathematics of Chaos Theory casts doubt on this belief. More precisely, it suggests that a system can be fully deterministic but nevertheless unpredictable.

2 Many people nowadays take the Big Bang to be the first cause, as many people before have taken God to be. But the problem is the same in either case: if the Big Bang – or God – can be explained, then it isn't the first cause; and if it can't, then nothing is really explained by it, is it?

3 There is some uncertainty in Leibniz's writings over the precise scope to the term 'Principle of Sufficient Reason'. Sometimes he seems to use it for the general claim that every truth must have an adequate explanation. But as we shall see, that explanation can take either of two different forms, depending on the kind of truth we are dealing with. Sometimes he seems to use the expression to mean only the kind of explanation that is involved in the case of contingent truths. The point is the same whichever way you express it. For the sake of clarity I shall keep to the first way of speaking.

4 Though his theological reading of the laws of motion (see p. 32) is a gesture in this direction.

5 1638–1715. His *Recherche de la Vérité* was first published in 1674–5.

NOTES

10 The best of all possible worlds

1 The argument I give here – often referred to as the Argument from Contingency – is only one way in which Leibniz tries to show the unthinkability of a world without God, but it is the one which ties in most clearly with what I think are the key elements of his story.
2 See e.g. *Monadology* 36–8.
3 Leibniz criticises Descartes' argument from God's perfection to his existence on the grounds that Descartes doesn't include the requirement that a perfect being must be *possible*. See e.g. *Discourse on Metaphysics* 23; cf. *Monadology* 44.
4 Note that God's choice in these matters is not unconstrained. Unlike Descartes, who held that God could if he chose make 2 + 2 = 5 without changing the meanings of the symbols involved, Leibniz is happy to say that God can do only what is logically possible. So not even God can, for example, make a round square – or increase the plenitude of the world without decreasing its economy.
5 It is of course misleading to talk of God as performing calculations. Human beings perform calculations when they work out mathematical equivalences; to the omniscient mind of God there is nothing to work out – mathematical relations are simply transparent to such a mind, and in describing the 'calculations' which God performs we are really describing the *form of his understanding* of the question, not a process of reasoning that he goes through.
6 A similar diagram appears in Nicholas Rescher, *Leibniz, an Introduction to his Philosophy* (Oxford, Blackwell, 1979), p. 29.
7 The question of who invented calculus, Leibniz or Isaac Newton, was much disputed at the time between the two men and their supporters. Historians nowadays say it was a kind of draw: Newton got the idea first, Leibniz came up with the idea independently some years later. Leibniz was the first to publish it, and his notation was better than Newton's – a fact which held back the development of the subject in England, where staunch Newtonians refused to have anything to do with the work of the man who had 'stolen' the ideas of their hero. (Oh what sad creatures people are.)

11 The world as explicable

1 This aspect of Leibniz's thought was famously developed – and transformed – by Kant.

278

2 In his *New System of the Nature of Substances and their Communication* of 1695.
3 See Box 9.1. Leibniz often refers to Occasionalists as 'Cartesians', since the theory was developed as a way of maintaining and defending the views of Descartes.
4 B. Russell, *A Critical Exposition of the Philosophy of Leibniz* (Cambridge, Cambridge University Press, 1900), xiii.
5 Leibniz first set out his theory of substance some ten years before the publication of the *New System* in, for example, the *Discourse on Metaphysics*. He seems to have hit upon publishing the *New System* as a kind of back-door way of introducing his general theory, by publicising it through the particular application of what is now called the 'Mind/Body Problem'.
6 Therefore every property of every monad is contained in its essence. Every true statement therefore has an *a priori* proof, in the sense that if you had the complete concept of the monad, you could deduce all its properties. See pp. 140–2.

12 Matter, mind and human life

1 For a summary of the main lines of interpretation, see R.S. Woolhouse, Editor's Introduction 2, in R.S. Woolhouse and Richard Francks, *G.W. Leibniz, Philosophical Texts* (Oxford, Oxford University Press, 1998).
2 So is everything that exists a monad? Yes and no. What a tree is, ultimately, is a monad, an individual: and the same is true of all its leaves, and all their organic parts. But what about a pile of leaves blown by the wind into a puddle at the back of the newsagent's? According to Leibniz a thing like that is no thing at all: it is not a unity, it has no principle of organisation, it is only an aggregate. It is of course real, not imaginary – but it is real only because the things that make it up are real – i.e. real, individual monads.
3 Though there are of course possible worlds in which the statement 'triangles have five sides' is true. (Because it is not a necessary truth that the word 'triangle' means what we mean by it.)
4 I.e. it can be known a priori, or is an a priori truth. (See Box 19.1.)

13 The contents of the mind

1 This paradox is unavoidable, since it is not a fact of experience that we should restrict ourselves to the facts of experience.

2 *Essay* 2.1.2.

3 Locke says when a child is born – but this is typical Lockeian inaccuracy of language, because he does allow pre-birth experience. (See *Essay* 2.9.5.)

4 We will see later how Locke thinks we can know that such a thing exists.

5 Some people have seen it as basic to Locke's Empiricism, and as directed against the Rationalist Descartes, who had said that rational intuitions are innate in the mind. But by that Descartes meant that they are discovered by the mind's own power, and as we shall see, Locke's own account of such knowledge turns out in fact to be very Cartesian. (See Box 13.1.)

6 See *Essay* 4.1.1–2. This whole discussion is of course very Cartesian. (See pp. 51–4.)

7 This, of course, is what Leibniz both asserted and denied. He agreed with Locke that there is no proof we can find which will tell us that the fly is on the wall, and that the only way we can find out that the fly is on the wall is to look; but he claimed nevertheless that there is a sufficient reason for its being there, and that if we were in possession of the complete concept of the fly (or of the wall, or indeed of anything else) we would have an a priori proof of its being there.

8 See *Essay* 4.2.14, 4.11.3. What do *you* think about this? Is your knowledge of some blindingly obvious fact like your hand in front of your face more or less reliable than your knowledge of some relation between ideas, like black is not white? Can you imagine any conceivable circumstances in which you could turn out to be wrong about them? Which seems to you more certain?

9 He seems to think this can be done by some kind of argument from design: there must be a God as the only possible explanation of the existence of the world. But since the existence of the world can't be known intuitively or by proof but only by sensitive knowledge, that seems to mean that the knowledge of God rests ultimately on sensitive knowledge, too. See *Essay* 4.10.

10 Much of this turns on the question of what exactly Locke means by his notion of an 'idea'. If ideas are – as Locke often seems to describe them – something like mental images, pictures in the mind which the mind examines, then it is hard to see how he can avoid

the Veil of Ideas problem. Those who think he can avoid it tend to say that Lockeian ideas, for all his language of picturing, are not in fact lifeless images which we contemplate, but merely his picturesque way of talking about the mental act of thinking about something. If an idea is an image, it is very hard to see how we can say anything much about the alleged but unknowable things which those images represent; if ideas are acts of thinking, then the problem is at least less obvious.

11 *Essay* 4.11.8. For hints of a possible argument to this conclusion, see 4.11.3.

14 Locke on nature (and our knowledge of it)

1 See *The World* 1.
2 In fact mechanical processes proved to be a lot harder to explain than such a simple model suggests – as Leibniz was one of the first to insist. See e.g. R.S. Woolhouse, Editor's Introduction 3, in R.S. Woolhouse and Richard Francks, *G.W. Leibniz, Philosophical Texts* (Oxford, Oxford University Press, 1998).
3 See *Essay* 2.12. Typically enough, he also at times talks as if the only real material substances are not these macroscopic objects, but the individual atoms of which they are composed. See *Essay* 2.27.2.
4 *Essay* 2.23.2.
5 *Essay* 2.27.
6 This distinction between real and nominal essences is of course precisely the distinction between the two kinds of expert referred to in the Introduction.
7 Note how different is this kind of pessimism about the possibility of a science of nature from the kind of scepticism we saw Locke accused of earlier. This has nothing to do with the Veil of Ideas problem. Even assuming, as Locke does, that there is no Veil of Ideas and we have unmediated access to a real world, we *still* can have no knowledge of the real essences of substances, and so no science of nature.
8 *Essay* 2.23.12.
9 In one of the darker times to which he was prone (perhaps due to heavy metal poisoning as a result of his alchemical researches) Newton claimed Locke was trying to embroil him with women.

NOTES

15 The life of man

1 Spinoza's social thought is more explanatory than revolutionary. He argues passionately that people's beliefs should be their own affair provided that they live in accordance with the laws, but he doesn't try to tell us in any detail what the law should be, or who has the right to decide it.

2 Note how the theory also served to legitimise the appropriation of land by colonists, for example in North America in Locke's day and after. Quite apart from the fact that many didn't regard the theory as having any application to people of different races – who therefore had no natural rights of their own – it tended to encourage the idea that land which was used by nomadic tribes was 'empty', so that anyone who colonised it and built a fence around it was perfectly justified in claiming it for their own.

3 See e.g. Rousseau, who held that the day when the first person said 'this is mine' was the day when human society set out on the downward spiral of ever-increasing mutual enslavement (see *Discourse on the Origin of Inequality*, beginning of Part 2).

4 Spinoza turned down the chance to teach at Heidelberg; Hume would have worked in the Universities of Edinburgh or Glasgow if they had let him.

5 They typically made no attempt to separate the three different targets, and often showed very little understanding of what their opponents were trying to do. Leibniz is the only one of our authors who claims to find anything of value in traditional learning, but even he only in part. (And there are very few people with whom Leibniz does not claim to be in at least partial agreement.)

16 Denying the obvious

1 Subtitle of *Three Dialogues*.

2 But he wasn't the only one to think this way. His own contemporary, Arthur Collier, a country vicar in Wiltshire, seems to have arrived at views very similar to Berkeley's at around the same time. See his *Clavis Universalis; or, a New inquiry after truth. Being a demonstration of the non-existence, or impossibility of an external world* (London, Robert Gosling, 1713 and Chicago, IL, Open Court Publishing Co., 1909).

3 Different people interpret this fact in different ways. Hume, as we

will see, took it as evidence that human beings are not rational creatures: they see they should agree with him, but can't.

4 But this is not to say that you couldn't construct a kind of Godless Berkeleian position: that is exactly what twentieth-century positivists tried to do – see e.g. A.J. Ayer's *Language, Truth and Logic* (London, Victor Gollancz, 1936).

5 There is also another Samuel Johnson (1696–1752) who features in the life of Berkeley: the American whose *Elementa Philosophica* of 1752 is regarded as the first American philosophical textbook. He was very sympathetic to Berkeley's philosophical position, and their correspondence contains some useful clarifications.

6 See Boswell's *Life of Johnson*, 6 August 1763.

7 Note the similarity to Descartes' Dream doubt (see p. 49).

8 The account I have given here seems to make perfect sense (if anything in Berkeley does), and it fits with everything he says on the subject. The problem is that it sounds very like what Malebranche and the Occasionalists would say on the question (see Box 9.1) – which is a problem because Berkeley seems sometimes to be denying the Occasionalist account, and to be advocating something more direct than this 'I-take-the-decision-and-God-gives-me-the right-ideas' story. But what that can be which is consistent with the other things Berkeley says, I don't know.

17   Berkeley's disproof of the existence of matter

1 Berkeley confusingly refers to both of these positions as 'materialism'. This is a deliberate ploy on his part to try to get people to regard anyone who denies what he says as being as dangerous and as wicked as true materialists – such as Hobbes – were at the time generally held to be.

2 The principle seems to have been a mediaeval commonplace, and was much used by the English Franciscan William of Ockham (*c.* 1285–1347/49).

3 *Principles* 1.19.

4 As we saw earlier, it may be that Locke didn't actually ask this question. I suspect in fact the best way to solve the problem is to find some way not to ask the question in the first place. Philosophers like Thomas Reid tried this approach, as in a different way did Kant. But it is not easy to do.

5 The nearest you can get to it is to worry about how God can put ideas into finite minds; but then, we can put ideas into each other's

minds (if you're still awake, I'm doing it now) – and God, after all, is omnipotent.

6 But see the next chapter for the problem of understanding what a mind is.

7 This is not to deny that matter might be the basis of thought in some way. Berkeley of course would say it couldn't be, but he is not assuming that here.

8 It is interesting to note that in post-Einsteinian physical theory size and shape can no longer be thought of as primary qualities. What remains of the concept of matter if you take those away?

9 Perhaps your answer is that you don't understand it, but that like most of us you take it on trust from other people who say they do. Is there any *good* reason why you believe them?

10 See e.g. *Principles* 1.22. This is purely a rhetorical move on Berkeley's part, of course, expressing his confidence in this argument. It is certainly *not* true that just by defeating this argument you can defend realism against Berkeley's attacks.

18 On what there is

1 Berkeley doesn't commit himself on the question of whether animals have minds, but seems to think not. But that is a separate issue – you could be a Berkeleian and think either that they did or they didn't. If they do, they are in the same position as people – though presumably with lower (or at least different) levels of consciousness and of understanding. If they don't, they are in the same position as trees and mountains – i.e. collections of ideas in the minds of thinking things.

2 *Bible, Acts of the Apostles*, 17,28. Quoted by Berkeley in *Principles* 66 and 149.

3 People sometimes argue between realist and phenomenalist accounts of Berkeley – i.e. whether he says that unperceived objects continue to exist because God perceives them when no-one else does (a realist reading), or whether he means they exist only in the sense that if I look again I will see them again (phenomenalism). Both are true: God doesn't have ideas like ours, because our ideas are passive and sensory; but he has a fixed and unchanging will to give us certain patterns of ideas and not others.

4 It is very hard to say what 'ordinary people' in Berkeley's day thought about such questions, since they probably didn't ask them,

and being illiterate they certainly didn't write their answers down for us to read. The fact that most people today are probably more Lockeian than Berkeleian tells us nothing about what people then thought unless you think that common sense is unchanging and unaffected by such things as literacy and mass communication. The thought here, which is also found in Hume (*Treatise* 1.4.2), is perhaps not as crazy as it sounds, in that by Hume's and Berkeley's day the appearance/reality distinction may not have penetrated into most people's way of seeing the world the way it has into ours.

5 The alternative way of solving this problem – to say that bad things that happen are caused by some other agency and are beyond God's power to prevent – has not been popular among Christian theologians (the Manichaean Heresy). (Cf. pp. 121–2).

6 The problem of the Veil of Ideas, of course, cannot arise on Berkeley's view – we can never know anything beyond ideas and minds, but since the natural world *is* a system of ideas in minds, that is no limitation on our knowledge. (Berkeley's refutation of Scepticism.)

7 *Third Dialogue*, 232.

19 Hume's project for a new science

1 These three subjects – living, feeling and thinking – correspond to the three divisions ('books') of the *Treatise: Morals, The Passions*, and *The Understanding*, respectively books 3, 2 and 1.

2 Typically enough, Hume finds an exception to his own rule here in the 'missing shade of blue'. See *Treatise* 1.1.2.

3 This attitude, of course, is encapsulated in Descartes' theory of the immaterial mind confused and led astray by the demands of the material body.

4 *Treatise* 2.3.3.

5 Other terms used include deduction, synthesis, and also – confusingly – Knowledge, and Science.

6 In Hume's technical language, the impression from which the idea of value is derived is not an impression of sensation – a sensory feeling – but of reflexion – an inner experience, or a feeling which comes from my awareness of my own mental processes (cf. Locke, p. 151).

7 *Treatise* 1.3.14.

8 It is easy to be misled here by the fact that Hume uses the word

'sympathy' for the way that emotions get transferred to ideas that are associated with them. But he certainly does *not* mean that we feel sorry for other people in general. The only people we care about, he says, are ourselves and those near to us. He notes how when you are abroad you tend to be drawn to people of your own nationality, even if they are people you wouldn't much like if you met them at home, and he wryly suggests that the only way we could ever come to feel concern for human beings in general would be if we happened to be living on the moon.

9 People sometimes describe Hume's moral theory as a 'subjectivist' position. That is both true and false. He clearly, as we have seen, thinks that moral qualities are not objective features of the actions we ascribe them to but subjective features of the observer. But if subjectivism means that moral judgements are relative to the individual observer, then Hume is no subjectivist, because these moral judgements are grounded in human nature, not in the individual psyche. It is an objective fact for Hume that murder is wrong: an objective fact about how human beings (subjectively) react to it.

20 The failure of the project

1 In Hume's terms, two of the three ideas which make up the complex idea of a cause are those of 'priority' and 'contiguity', i.e. the two things or events are spatially and temporally adjacent (contiguous), and the cause is prior to the effect. He denies the possibility of simultaneous causes, or of remote causes (except where there is a chain of intervening causes). See *Treatise* 1.3.2.

2 In Hume's language, we have observed a 'constant conjunction' of events of these kinds – we have seen that they always go together.

3 'Positivist' philosophers don't think so. They say, often for very Humeian reasons, that the idea of a necessary connection is a childish mistake, and that in reality all causes *are* just correlations.

4 Hume treats the question just as part of the more general problem of causation – if there are no necessary connections, how do I know the next cause will have its usual effect? Later philosophers have generalised the problem to cover any case of expectations about unobserved cases based on observed instances: e.g., given that I've never seen a pink elephant, how do I know that the next

elephant I see won't be pink? Or more significantly, given that I have tested only a small number of genetically modified foods and found that they produce no ill-effects on people, how do I know that the next one I produce will be similarly harmless?

5 The chapter in which he sets this out (*Treatise* 1.4.2) is one of the most dense and puzzling in all of Hume's work. He begins it by saying that no-one can doubt the existence of the external world, all we can do is to look carefully at where the idea comes from. But by the time he has set out the story of its origin, he has done what he thought was impossible, and convinced himself that he would be mad to believe in any such thing.

6 Hume has a confusing tendency to use the word 'reason' in two different ways. Sometimes he means pure deductive reasoning, as in logic and mathematics. And that is what he tries to cast doubt on here. But at other times he uses it to mean inductive, scientific, or causal reasoning – which as we have seen he has already sought to undermine.

7 Are you convinced? You may feel that the example is a cheat, because in a long calculation additional factors – like tiredness, memory failure and lack of attention – begin to creep in, and the uncertainty derives from those additional factors rather than from the mathematical judgements themselves. But if so, that still seems to suggest that your confidence that you are right when dealing with the simple cases is not the pure rational intuition you think it is, but the outcome of a complex judgement about how many sums you have done recently, how tired you are, how well you are concentrating on the question at issue, and so on – in which case Hume's point still stands, doesn't it?

21 Where do we go from here?

1 He considers a third alternative, which is to pursue rational understanding up to a point, but not to go into the kind of depth that leads to these problems. But he rejects this as not only arbitrary and groundless, but as also self-contradictory: the only justification for giving up long trains of reasoning comes from the long chain of reasoning that got us to this point. In effect, though, this is what he does in his later writings.

2 This line of thinking is prominent in some of the later works of the twentieth-century philosopher Ludwig Wittgenstein. See his *On Certainty*.

3 In Hume's own day philosophers like Thomas Reid, and more importantly Immanuel Kant, perceived exactly this impasse in Hume's work, and offered alternatives – which have made little impact on contemporary common sense.

Bibliography

The purpose of this book is to encourage you to read, and to help you to understand, the works of our six authors. Those works have been published any number of times since they were first written, and for a beginner virtually any of those editions will do. For those who didn't write in English (Descartes, Spinoza and Leibniz), you may find more modern translations easier than some of the older ones you can still find. Here is a list of some good, modern editions which are readily available and not too expensive.

Descartes

You need to read the *Meditations*, but don't restrict yourself to that. The first entry contains all you're likely to need, the others are more basic.

- *Philosophical Writings of Descartes* (two volumes), ed. and trans. John Cottingham, Robert Stoothoff and Dugald Murdoch (Cambridge, Cambridge University Press, 1985)

- *Selected Philosophical Writings* (one volume), ed. and trans. John Cottingham, Robert Stoothoff and Dugald Murdoch (Cambridge, Cambridge University Press, 1988)
- *Philosophical Essays and Correspondence*, ed. and trans. Roger Ariew (Indianapolis, Hackett, 2000)
- *Meditations and Other Metaphysical Writings*, ed. and trans. Desmond M. Clarke (London, Penguin, 1998)

Spinoza

The *Ethics* is what you need; the *Treatise on the Improvement of the Understanding* (look out for different translations of the title) and *Correspondence* are helpful. The first is the standard scholarly edition; the others are smaller and cheaper.

- *Collected Works of Spinoza*, ed. and trans. Edwin Curley (Princeton, NJ, Princeton University Press, 1985)
- *A Spinoza Reader*, ed. and trans. Edwin Curley (Princeton, NJ and Chichester, Princeton University Press, 1994)
- *Ethics*, ed. Seymour Feldman, trans. Sam Shirley (Indianapolis and Cambridge, Hackett, 1992)
- *Ethics*, ed. and trans. G.H.R. Parkinson (Oxford and New York, Oxford University Press, 2000)

Leibniz

With Leibniz you are always dealing with selections, the contents of which vary quite a lot. Here are some recent ones.

- *Philosophical Essays*, ed. and trans. Daniel Garber and Roger Ariew (Indianapolis, Hackett, 1989)
- *Discourse on Metaphysics and Other Essays*, ed. and trans. Daniel Garber and Roger Ariew (Indianapolis, Hackett, 1992)
- *Philosophical Texts*, ed. and trans. R.S. Woolhouse and Richard Francks (Oxford, Oxford University Press, 1998)
- *G.W. Leibniz's* Monadology, ed. and trans. Nicholas Rescher (London, Routledge, 1991)

Locke

For Locke's epistemology and metaphysics you need to read the *Essay*, which is long and (by his own admission) rather rambling. You'll need to read it selectively, but beware of abridged editions, which sometimes leave out the best bits. The first is the classic edition. For his political thought, you need to read at least the second *Treatise of Government*.

- *An Essay Concerning Human Understanding*, ed. P.H. Nidditch (Oxford, Clarendon Press, 1975)
- *An Essay Concerning Human Understanding*, ed. R.S. Woolhouse (London, Penguin, 1997)
- *Two Treatises of Government*, ed. Peter Laslett (Cambridge, Cambridge University Press, 1998)

Berkeley

For Berkeley you need to read the *Principles*. The *Dialogues* are a useful back-up.

- *Principles of Human Knowledge, and Three Dialogues between Hylas and Philonous*, ed. R.S. Woolhouse (London, Penguin, 1988)
- *Principles of Human Knowledge, and Three Dialogues*, ed. Howard Robinson (Oxford, Oxford University Press, 1996)

Hume

Hume scholars divide into those who treat the early *Treatise* as primary, and those who base their accounts on the later *Enquiries*.

- *A Treatise of Human Nature*, ed. P.H. Nidditch (Oxford, Oxford University Press, 1978)
- *A Treatise of Human Nature* ed. D.F. Norton and M.J. Norton (Oxford, Oxford University Press, 2000)
- *Enquiries Concerning Human Understanding and Concerning the Principles of Morals*, ed. P.H. Nidditch and L.A. Selby-Bigge (Oxford, Oxford University Press, 1975)
- *Enquiry Concerning Human Understanding*, ed. Tom L. Beauchamp (Oxford, Oxford University Press, 1999)

Index

Big Bang 71, 112, 277
Boyle, Robert 149, 172

calculus 120–1, 124, 278
Cartesian Circle 274
causation 239, 249–53, 258, 266;
and creation 31–2, 110–11, 227;
mental 229; and necessary
connection 110–11, 249–53, 263;
occasional 111; and regularity
222, 225, 250; *see also* first cause
chaos theory 277
clear and distinct ideas 52–4; *see
also* intuition
cogito ergo sum 51–4, 156, 208, 228,
230
Collier, Arthur 282
colonialism 282
complete concepts 130–7, 144,
279, 280
complex ideas *see* simple and
complex ideas
conatus 90–1, 276
conceivability, and possibility/
necessity: in Berkeley 208–19;
in Hume 250–1, 255; in Leibniz
116; in occasionalism 109–10
consciousness *see* mind
consent 181–2, 184
contingency *see* necessary v.
contingent truths
Copernicus 22, 222, 271

demonstration (deduction) 155–6,
241–3, 273
dominant monads 136
doubt 46–51, 235, 261; *see also*
scepticism
'dualism' 41, 75–8, 84, 88–9, 226,
285

Economy, Principle of 118–21
Einstein, Albert 284
emanation 31–2, 76
emergent properties 216–17
empirical knowledge *see*
knowledge, empirical

empiricism *see* rationalism and
empiricism
entelechy 132
epoche (suspension of judgement)
44
essence 90; real and nominal
167–8; knowledge of 169–73, 189
Euclid 170, 241–3
evil, problem of 121–3, 227–8, 230,
285
explanation 3–6, 162–4, 182–4; in
Berkeley 188, 222; in
Descartes19–21; in Hume 249;
in Leibniz 102–9, 114–19, 123,
125–30; in Locke 147, 150, 162,
165–6, 167–8; in occasionalism
109–11; in Spinoza 66–9; *see also*
first cause
external world: existence of 56–7,
137, 157–8, 190–231, 257–9, 263,
266

first cause 27–8, 68–9, 105–6,
114–15, 277
freedom: of the individual 174–5;
Labyrinth of 125; and necessity
140–4; and reason 95–8, 175; of
the will 27, 38–40, 42, 93–5,
104–5, 142–4, 229

Galileo 9, 10, 21, 22, 24, 163, 271,
272
God, intellectual love of 277
God, nature of: in Descartes
27–33, 63–4, 278; in Leibniz 278;
in Locke 152–3; in Spinoza
63–74, 79–80
God, existence of 34, 58, 123; in
Berkeley 206, 223, 228; in
Descartes 54–6, 114–15, 274,
278; in Leibniz 114–15, 277,
278; in Locke 156–7, 175, 280;
in Spinoza 72–3, 114–15,
275

harmony, pre-established 125–30,
133, 208